SOMEBODY ELSE'S BUSINESS

Charlton James

Charlton Books

To people with vision,
continue to bring creative expressions from thought to action.

ACKNOWLEDGMENTS

I thank the following people for their loyalty and support in the development of this project.

To my lovely wife, Melbee, thank you for the inspiration and the Christmas gift of the laptop computer on which this manuscript was written. Thanks for your "in the trench support! And pre-promotion campaign. I got it done!

To Cheryl and Diana, my wife's friends, you guys were the adhesions of unity and the embodiments of luster that manifested and dazzled this project in the eyes of the awaiting public. A special thanks to the three of you [Melbee] for the influential reception and steadfast commitment in believing. [Hooray for the team! Yay!]

To James Ayetin, thank you for the technical support; "the go-to man," whenever there were issues within network operations. Didn't you get tired of me? Well, I'm no longer computer challenged. Thanks!

To Kenneth Robinson and Eric Sears, thanks for the therapeutic workout sessions at the park. The laughs and camaraderie prepared my mindset for the development of the manuscript's characters. Eric, when are you ever going to do a correct pushup? Ken, thanks for all the Pay-Per-View invites. How much do I owe? I may be able to start paying off that tab. Keep them crossed for me, buddy!

To Paula Charlton, my surviving parent, thank you for remaining here and allowing me to make you proud. Remember my promise, we have to sit next to each other in church again. Love you!

ABOUT THE AUTHOR

Living in California, Charlton James is a real estate investor and father of two. On a whim, he created and developed the manuscript *Somebody Else's Business*. Though this is the first written work from the aspiring author, the manuscript's creative genius caught the attention of a major motion picture production conglomerate, with an offer to bring the brand to the silver screen. Opting to forgo the life-changing opportunity, the author put the readers first and self-published the manuscript, with the purpose of revealing how good intent can be overplayed by the messenger. Readers are entertained with a savvy and methodical development of the manuscript's characters, with a straightforward lesson should they ever entertain the notion of becoming involved with "somebody else's business."

PROLOGUE

With the convenience of fallibility, people are quick to assume. Being much like termites, if unchecked, the smallest of assumptions eventually ruin the home of the host. Not properly handled, a festering assumption quickly compounds into a monumental circumstance. Should ever you encounter "somebody else's business," be thorough to eradicate the source or carriers that present assumption. No person walking under the sun is without fallibility. To a degree, we're all guilty when presented the opportunity to entertain the circumstance of another, whether to dabble discretely with a soft hand or be bold with a hard touch. Should ever you find yourself tempted, be prepared for the ruinous consequence when becoming involved with somebody else's business.

—Charlton James

Good morning, love. Should you wake up looking for me, no worries! I used my key to let myself out. You were in a world of your own when I left, so I didn't want to disturb you, especially after last night's intense release of neuromuscular tension. It was incredible! Well, for a guy my age, I guess I did my job, because you were still snoring as I left. [smile, ha ha.] Before leaving, I showered and had a cup of coffee with one of your vegan muffins. I enjoyed breakfast while watching you sleep. Can you believe it's been seven years already, and I'm still turned on by just watching you lie in bed? What sort of magic has been put over me? Well, I'm off to the office to make sure our itinerary's solid; you know me, the meticulous planner. I'm also making sure Ignacio and Marcus are well taken care of. Being as they're your special friends, I want them to be there with us for your birthday. As I mentioned earlier, please don't drive to the airport. Use a cab instead; let it work through the stress of traffic to get you on your way. The three of you will be flying to Rio together; use your positive energy to prepare for what's ahead. Since this is a business summit, I'm forced to fly with the partners in the firm. No worries! I'll be on the flight behind yours. Once your flight lands, I've arranged for the hotel to have transportation available to take you anywhere in Rio. We have three weeks together, birthday girl! Are you ready for this? I'm really looking forward for us being together, whatever it takes to make you happy. I've scheduled a consultation with one of the leading breast augmentation specialists there. You're coming back a new woman! We'll do this one step at a time. See you in Rio! I love you. Sincerely, Paul.

CHAPTER ONE

A couple walks hand in hand on the shopping galleria's main promenade. Regulars to the galleria's plaza, they make scheduled payments to the jeweler who has designed the wedding rings for their upcoming nuptials. Instinctively the pair stops at the creamery shop for ice cream. As the couple holds hands, the gentleman orders.

"Marla? Your favorite customers are back to punish themselves. Tiffany's having a double scoop of chocolate chip in a cup, and you already know how finicky Tiffany is. She wants hers pretty. I'm doing pistachio and butter pecan. I won't work you that hard today, Marla, just pack mine tall and plentiful."

Marla goes about with the orders,

"No worries; going out of my way for such a request will cost every bit of six dollars and forty cents."

"Marla, I saw it coming! I knew sooner or later that fee would catch up with me."

"Handsome, think nothing of it. I'm throwing in our new strawberry lemon tangerine jelly beans. You kids won't taste anything like them in this lifetime; that's for sure."

Tiffany declines the offer, "Marla, would you stop being so kind already? You've given us candy and treats since the Sunday John was on bended knee two months ago. Thanks for everything, but you know John doesn't feel right accepting things. Being a man in uniform, he feels he should be the one giving. Sorry, we're not accepting."

Marla tightens her apron strings to wink comically. "Honey, it isn't every day a sergeant major comes from church service with his sweetie to order from the creamery shop." She goes on with her recollection of the event. "It was just like in the movies. Tiffany's innocently spooning chocolate chip into her mouth, when out of nowhere, her tongue finds an engagement ring hidden between bits of chocolate. The way she panicked covering her mouth, my god, I'll never forget the look on her face, especially when she motioned for her man in uniform to help her. I thought for sure Tiffany had lost a tooth." Marla reminds, "Of course uniformed Johnny-on-the-spot provided a napkin for you to cough into. 'SURPRISE!' It seemed everyone in the galleria gathered to witness the event. I still hear the clapping when you put your arms around John's neck and kissed him. I'll tell you, since that *Officer and a Gentleman* scene, people still ask to this day what you two ordered from the menu before the big deal. From that enchanted moment forward, we've had a new selection on the creamery's menu. I named it personally, Chocolate Chips and Nut Surprise, on account of Tiffany's engagement ring in her chocolate chip, and John's usual pistachio and butter pecan.

"Can you believe it? Amazing is what it is. It just goes to show, timing and presentation mark the beauty of what we feel, especially when it's genuine and plays out from the unexpected."

Blushing from ear to ear, John downplays his chivalry with a smile as he explains how he set Tiffany up for the ruse. He reaches for Tiffany's hand, kissing her engagement ring. "Thanks, Marla! Tiffany had no clue of what was going on. The tricky part was to exaggerate as I explained the army's leave policy, just long enough for the ice cream to thaw a bit, before I hid the engagement ring inside. She had no idea!"

Tiffany puckers her lips to kiss John's cheek. In the same motion, she affectionately nibbles his earlobe. "From that day forward, believe it, you'll need an arsenal of tricks to get away from me, John Willoughby."

Tiffany offers John a spoon of her chocolate chip. Again he kisses the engagement ring before accepting the offer.

Witnessing the couple's happiness, Marla's eyes well with tears of joy. Overtaken with emotion, she offers peanut brittle and chocolate pretzels. "Kids, please accept my gestures of gratuity toward your wedding gift. I don't know what else to offer, with all the sugar and kisses going on between you two. Give me a break!"

Tiffany declines, giggling. "Marla, I can't accept any more treats of any kind. Remember, it's traditional to fit into your wedding gown. For the record we're looking forward to seeing you on our special day, and no, we won't accept any more gratuities, thank you."

Marla looks to John to intervene. He smiles, waving away the chocolate pretzels and peanut brittle. "Marla, we don't need to eat our way into marital bliss. We enjoy each other without any added ingredients. We're oddballs doing what oddballs do; we do other things to keep it exciting. During the week Tiffany tapes our favorite television shows. On the weekends, we position the sofa pillows on the carpet and catch up with what was taped. Believe me, everything works out really well. During commercial breaks I wax Tiffany's moustache. After dinner I lounge in my recliner, and from that point on, I pass gas for the rest of the evening to ask, 'Tiffany, honey, what's that smell?' Ha, ha, ha."

Tiffany's face dissolves into a grin. She elbows her fiancé in the ribs. "Honey, you're always being the joker. Don't joke like that; she's going to believe you." Dreamy eyed with the comfort of security, Tiffany turns to face John. She nuzzles her face into his uniformed chest to wrap her arms around him, giving his midsection a reassuring squeeze. John reacts affectionately, pecking the top of Tiffany's head with kisses before puffing intermittent puffs of air into her eyelashes.

Witnessing the love birds, Marla reacts. "What am I going to do with you two? All right already! I need an insulin shot just to level out the sugar between you. Gee whiz! Please, don't either of you get hot or start sweating; you'd have syrup coming out of your pores. Get a room, why don't you?"

John's dimpled cheeks break into a smile. "See I told you, Marla, its bliss naturally without the added sugar."

Coming up for air, Tiffany removes her face from within John's chest. Undoubtedly mesmerized, she looks into his eyes. "Baby, will you finish my ice cream?"

Marla throws up both hands. "Oh my god, you two, enough already! With all the twisting and dancing in each other's arms, you make Fred Astaire and Ginger Rogers appear dull. I'm sick of you two."

Breaking her gaze from John, Tiffany looks to Marla to playfully stick out her tongue.

Marla cackles. "Fine, I should be talking to real customers anyway. You're Barbie and Ken dolls posing with ice cream. The next time you're here, I'll make sure to have the yellow-striped taffy caramel pinwheel suckers." She sticks out her tongue to return Tiffany's gesture. "There! Turn that down. My taffy and caramel suckers; when was the last time either of you had those treats?"

Marla motions to the next customer. "Hi there. With today's purchase of ten dollars or more, The Creamery will donate complimentary passes for its customers to take a photo with Ken and Barbie. No worries about not being properly dressed. Simply ask for a raincheck to be rescheduled for another date at participating locations. M-m-m, h-m-m. Ken and Barbie! They're sure to make everything around them look pretty. Allow me to welcome you to The Creamery Shop. We offer famous pastries, blended yogurts, silk chocolates, and our world-renowned fruit dips. How can I help you to enjoy something wonderful today?" Marla's sarcasm concludes with a wink to Tiffany and John.

Having enjoyed the witty performance, the couple is all smiles. "Marla, we're gone. Thanks for everything. Come on Tiff; we need to get going, honey." Continuing their way enjoying their ice cream cups, the couple window shops through neon-lit storefronts. Without giving it any thought, they walk by an expensively clothed mannequin displayed in front of a men's clothing store.

The business owner solicits the couple. "Hello! I remember you both from the last time you were shopping in the galleria. Please come in and look around. I have a beautiful selection in his size, fifty regular. I can have a salesman lay out several styles and fabrics in colors that will complement his skin tone as well. I guarantee any suit you choose, he'll look just as good as he does in his officer's uniform."

Tiffany replies for the couple, "Wow, that's saying a lot, but I can't imagine John wearing a suit with a better fit than his officer's uniform. If there is such a suit, we'll have to set it aside for our big day, when we become Mr. and Mrs. John Willoughby."

"I agree with you, young lady. I have several designer suits in olive, in the same tone he's wearing. I'll even throw in a tie and pocket handkerchief. Don't worry about the cost; for you two there's a special price. You're the couple with the ice cream and the ring. Please allow me to make you happy on your special day."

Flattered by the public knowledge of his marriage proposal to Tiffany, John manages a concealed grin.

Without skipping a beat, the business owner goes on to

recall how he came about to notice the couple. "I remember the Sunday from two months ago. I was standing right here when people started clapping. I didn't know what the commotion was about at the time, until after you and your lady walked by my store. Several of my customers were excited because you had just proposed. They said you went down on your knee and asked your lady to marry you. She then kissed you before you picked her up in the air like a doll. Everyone said it was very romantic, just like in the movies. As you both walked by, I thought for sure you were movie stars. People were talking all through the galleria. I believe a few asked for your autographs. I'm very happy for you both. Congratulations!"

The recollection of events has held Tiffany and John captive with a sense of celebrity. John's handsome face radiates with pride to make the couple's introduction. "Nice meeting you. I'm John, and this is my fiancée, Tiffany. That was a nice compliment. You made it seem like the paparazzi are in the parking lot to ambush us. Should we be looking out for the unexpected?" John smiles with the fun.

Tiffany pokes him. "Stop being silly."

As the men extend their hands with a hand shake, the store owner smiles. "I like that; good jokes are good for business. "I'm Farouche. Nice meeting you both as well."

"Honestly, Farouche, we weren't expecting to buy anything, but once we get to the other side of our special day, we may come back to visit your store."

"I understand perfectly, believe me." Farouche presents Tiffany a merchandise bag with his store logo. "Please allow these dress socks as a gift to your man. This way, no matter what he's wearing—whether it's his uniform or merchandise from another store—he'll be sharp. Bring him back to see me after your big day, and I'll take care of him. I'll order something from our lady's boutique for you as well."

Placing her petite hand in John's enormous palm, Tiffany eyes her fiancé with admiration. "Well, it shouldn't be too hard to bring him back. Thank you, Farouche." Tiffany motions the merchandise bag to John. "Here handsome; they're the same color as your uniform. They're cute."

"Okay, leave it alone Tiff; they're men's socks not footsies." John nods to Farouche. "And to you sir, thank you. You're a true gentleman."

On cue, John guides Tiffany to where the couple turns together in an about-face. Continuing on the promenade, the couple walks holding hands. Tiffany stops abruptly to kiss John from an afterthought. "You see what you've done? You look so darn sharp—everyone remembers you. Once we're married, you're not wearing your uniform outside our home without me. John, do you hear me?"

John kisses Tiffany's eyelids chuckling. "Tiffany, it's you! You're the reason we're remembered. I'm looked at only as the brute who protects you. People think I'm your hired bodyguard."

Tiffany slaps his ass. "You think? You're always cracking jokes, John; you're so silly!" Walking hand in hand, the couple continues to Claude's Jewelers to make another payment toward their wedding rings.

Entering the business, the couple notices an exquisite piece of jewelry in the showcase. "My Gosh, John, who in this world can afford something like this?"

From several display cases away, the business owner looks over the top of his glasses to acknowledge the couple. "Ah me lad and lass, the officer and the complete gentleman. The lad escorts his lovely bride to be. For the love of Mary, to be young again!" Claude shuffles forward. "Forgive an old man for not recognizing sooner. The both of you together, it's brand new every time you come in. It seems time races faster than a bar opening in me Ireland. All this happiness. Gosh, lad, has it been a month already?"

As the men shake hands, Tiffany retrieves a check from her wedding planner's folder. She hands it to John while acknowledging the business owner. "My goodness, Claude, with that kind of introduction, we'll pencil you in as the master of ceremonies for our nuptials. You'll certainly give someone something to think about before they speak."

"Sure, lass! I'll play me bag pipes during the first dance, and we'll drink until either I or the whiskey leaves first." Claude's wit brings laughter to the trio.

John presents the prewritten check, "Well, my Irish friend, that's the third of twelve payments. We still have eight stops with eight payments before this beautiful day ends, yes sir."

Claude accepts the payment appearing puzzled. "Johnny boy, I'm trying to keep up with me mind. I'm confused of sorts. Are you buying jewelry with someone else, lad?"

John pats his fellow Irishman on the back reassuringly. "Of

course not, Claude. I'm speaking of our wedding itinerary. We have a host of other stops to make. Every time we come in to make a payment, we pretty much dedicate the entire day toward our wedding plans. Tiffany finds the day's journey relaxing; better yet, my little angel looks forward to each weekend I fly in from Fort Bragg. I have no complaints."

Tiffany's eyes flutter with the compliment. She joins the conversation massaging John's shoulders. "Claude? I was adamant that John not pay the entire wedding cost. Being the man he is, he wouldn't hear of anything otherwise. Without fail he would get upset every time I wrote a check toward the payment."

Explaining his rationale, John interlocks hands with Tiffany to look into her eyes. Contrarily, Tiffany's forced to close hers, in hopes to ward off the sensation and dampness she feels forming elsewhere. John goes on with his reasoning. "I'm steadfast with tradition. Call me old fashioned or whatever you want to call it. 'Till death do us part' doesn't mean wait until we're married. With the Willoughby way, the commitment began the moment Tiffany accepted my hand. Yes, sir. How's that for tradition?"

Processing John's reasoning, Claude studies the couple momentarily. "Aye, young lad, you're an Irishman no doubt. An old soul with a young heart. Could it be, you're following the path of an old man?" Writing a notation in his invoice book, Claude places the couple's payment in the register. His eyes well with tears as he processes more of John's words. Attempting to cover his emotions, Claude dabs at the lens of his glasses with a handkerchief before abruptly returning them to his face. He shuffles from his side of the counter. "Well there's certainly no argument here." Using both hands simultaneously, Claude shakes the couple's hands. "Bliss to you both forever."

Holding on to the kind man's handshake, Tiffany and John return their sentiments. "Aw, thanks Claude, you're so kind."

"Thank you, sir; we really appreciate you."

Claude leans forward, whispering, "Careful no one hears me words." As if in a football game, the trio huddles. "We gather for celebration. Aye, lad, forget the last payment. It's me gift to you both." Claude exhales to continue in a normal tone. "The good Lord blessed me with father Foley the time he married Martha and me. To this day, over forty two years later, she's the same sweet lass. Being the sweet Irish lass she is, some say its Martha's cooking. Some say it's me good Irish whiskey, but believe! Without the blessing of the heavenly father…." Claude kisses two fingers as he looks toward the ceiling. "Without the heavenly father's blessing, anything brought together won't remain, and any effort to gain bliss will come to naught. For you, lad, the heavenly father has sent this fine lass to hold and honor for all time to come. For you, lass, this fine lad for you to respect and guide you both. This is a blessing from the heavenly father; the same as bestowed upon Martha and me. All glory to the heavenly father for this blessing of God's children. You both pray and ask that he continues to do so. Remember, without him, anything you attempt will come to naught. Enjoy your lives with each other." Claude kisses each of them on the cheek. "The heavenly father is with you both."

The trio's interrupted with the store's melodic chime, indicating customer arrivals. Breaking the huddle, Claude speaks into the couple's eyes. "You two finding each other, remember, a blessing bestowed is a gift from the heavenly father."

A woman's voice interrupts the praising sentiments, "Claude, hello? We're baa-aack."

"Hello, Samantha, has it been thirty days already? Me mind's racing, I can't keep up with all the happiness from everywhere. Give me a tad. I'm just finishing with this fine lass and lad."

Tiffany kisses Claude's cheek. "You're such a sweet man. You made us feel like our wedding ceremony was today. We love you so much. Thanks for everything. John and I can only hope to be as happy as you and Martha."

Claude's face reddens with the compliment. "Now mind yourself young lass! Hurry along with the smart lad; an old man has work in front of him."

Breaking the huddle, John leads Tiffany with an affectionate squeeze of her chin. "Baby, you heard the man. Let someone else get closer to the wedding of their dreams. Come on, let's go." Making way for the jeweler's awaiting customers, John guides his fiancée toward the store exit. As Tiffany moves along, she mouths, "Claude, we love you."

"Aye, and my best to you both. Children, good day!" Claude shuffles toward the new arrivals. "For the love of Saint Peter! How long have you been waiting there? Is this the lad you've spoken of and all?"

"Yes, Claude, it is he, my man of the range. Guntther, this

is the jeweler I've told you all about. Honey, you know how you refer to me as your sunshine? Since we're in sunny California, wouldn't it be nice to purchase our wedding jewels from this nice man, right in this very store?"

Chewing gum, Guntther flashes a smile. "To keep my lil' moon pie smiling, I'd buy every jewel in the Lone Star and then some."

Samantha extends her fiancés hand. "I know you would, honey, but this is Mr. McKinney. I told you all about him on the airplane. He's the distinguished owner of Claude's Jewelers."

Guntther acknowledges in Texas drawl, "Aw, honey, I thought McKinney's was one of them new catalogues on the airplane." He shakes Claude's hand with an overcompensated grip. "To you, sir, I beg your pardon. I say it's mighty fine meetin' you, Mr. McKinney."

Recognizing her fiancé's antics, Samantha interjects with a smile, "Guntther? Turn loose Claude's hand. He's a jeweler, and his hands are very delicate for his craft. This isn't the place for one of your bull-riding competitions, so stop showing off!"

Freed from the cowboy's grip, Claude massages his hand. "Well he's certainly a strong fellow. Nice to meet you, lad."

Guntther's Wrangler jeans hug scrawny legs. Standing wide leg in expensive armadillo cowboy boots, the Texas drawl continues. "Meant no harm, Mr. McKinney. Hell, being from big Texas, Daddy raised all us boys to shake a man's hand looking him in the eye, to make it known you're a man of strength and word. The name's Guntther Scofield, and like the peacemaker, us Scofields is known to be just as sharp with twice the kick. Woo—hot damn." Standing wide leg, Guntther guffaws and struts in place, exposing a huge turquoise-inlaid silver belt buckle. Guntther chews gum, tipping his hat. "Won't find a Texan anywhere more proud."

As if speaking to a disobeying child, Samantha flashes her fiancé a discerning look. "Guntther? What are you doing?" She forces a smile to apologize. "Claude, would you be so kind to excuse us? It seems we need a little time out." Leading Guntther by the ear; Samantha talks to her fiancé as a parent would prepare a child for the first day at school. "Guntther, listen to me, honey. Don't you want to make a good impression? Did you get a shot of espresso when I let you go to the coffee shop alone? You know what caffeine does to you. Guntther, listen to me. If you don't settle down and behave, we won't play the games you like in the bedroom anymore, so stop behaving—now!"

"Aw, what the Sam hell? You can't crawfish on me now. Sam, we agreed, with you picking the ring you want, we'd play our game three times a week."

Samantha reaches for Guntther's ear to twist it. She pulls his face close to hers. "Guntther, stop!"

Preparing himself for a time-out, Guntther whispers a request in Samantha's ear.

The response is hushed. "Guntther, you'll have to behave. Before I entertain 'rope the cow,' you must behave all day, and yes, I'll let you wear your cowboy boots."

Excited by the turn of events, Guntther's rapid gum chewing and herky-jerky posturing resumes as he struts in place.

Guntther slaps his thigh. "Woo! Hot damn! Call Jersey maid and Caledonia! I've come across a heifer that's real ornery and mean. This cowboy's going for a ride, and I won't need my spurs. Ooh wee, look out, Caledonia!"

With a raised finger to her lips, Samantha mouths silently, "Sh-h-h!"

Like a child scolded by his mother, Guntther puts himself back in time-out.

Samantha redirects her attention to feel the buttons on her two-piece pantsuit. Satisfied her wardrobe is intact, she returns to the display counter. Samantha forces a smile. "Claude, I do believe we're ready to purchase that beautiful wedding set."

Witnessing the absurdity from over the top of his bifocals, the astonished jeweler contains himself to give a controlled reply. "Certainly lass; any particular cut in mind?" Selecting pieces from the display counter, Claude compares the stone cuts. "There's solitaire, baguette, Tiffany, and here we have a princess cut."

Overwhelmed with her choices, Samantha claps her hands excitedly. Her voice rises to an excited pitch. "Oh, goody! Honey, come here. Guntther, honey, where should I start?" Samantha points to the display case. "Honey, do you like any of these?"

Claude winks in the direction of Tiffany and John, who have remained at a kept distance of several display counters. Yet unable to determine the dysfunctional couple as a threat, John patiently awaits a sign from Claude to intervene.

Meanwhile, since receiving permission to leave time-out, Guntther returns animated. "Aw, no need to fret, lil' moon pie. Mrs. Guntther Scofield will always have the best Texas can afford." Strutting forward herky-jerky, just as big and proud as the state of Texas, Guntther removes the billfold from his Wranglers. He presents his credit card to his fiancée. "Hell, dahlin', get one of each cut, with encrusted earrings to match. This way whenever you feel like a naughty girl and wanna go for a ride in my pickup truck, you'll be right nice 'n pretty. OOH-WEE, hot damn! I'll tell you, the Scofield name is as big as Texas itself. Line em' up, lil' doggies!" Guntther slaps his leg and guffaws. "If Texas wasn't meant for a man's wife and his pickup, what else would rightly go with Sunday dinner and the Cowboys?"

A soft clap of praise comes from Samantha. "Oh, Guntther, you're so cute when you take control of things. Just you keep that kind of energy for this here saddle. There's a heap of range that needs to be covered in the bedroom tonight, honey. If I don't get you some rest soon and leave you to yourself with a big jug of sassafras tea and your orange juice, how else would you deal with the likes of this dangerous outlaw?"

Witnessing the couple's interaction, Tiffany's mouth hangs agape with uncertainty. As John witnesses the unfolding scene, he stands behind his fiancée with his chin resting on top of her head.

Recognizing an audience, Guntther commences with the herky-jerky strut. His outstretched hand and Texas drawl greets the couple. "The name's Guntther Scofield. How are you folks?" Guntther appraises John's uniform. "Well, just lookee here! We got ourselves a real fightin' man." Guntther nods to

Samantha. "Ma'am."

John extends his hand. "Sergeant Major John Willoughby."

"Well, how do, that there's a real nice uniform, sergeant! So where would they station a fightin' man such as yourself?" Meanwhile the herky-jerky movements continue.

"North Carolina," John answers the overzealous cowboy.

Herky-jerky interrupts with a guffaw. "Hot damn. Fort Bragg?" Slapping his thigh, Guntther commences with the herky-jerk shuffling. "Lieutenant Colonel Amos Scofield, that's the uncle on my daddy's side. He's been a fightin' man all his life. Hell, down in Abilene he's compared with the likes of General Robert E. Lee himself, rightfully so, and being a Scofield by blood." With the informative introduction of his kin, Guntther chews gum to await John's acknowledgment. Meanwhile, his Adam's apple can be seen dancing about his scrawny throat.

John acknowledges, "Yes Lieutenant Colonel Amos Scofield's a fine officer. He's a good man."

Abruptly the herky-jerky movement stops. Guntther looks over his shoulder to the display counter where Claude is sizing Samantha's ring finger. Satisfied with his fiancée's whereabouts, to where he can talk freely, Guntther questions in a hushed whisper, "So y'all getting hitched too, huh?"

"Nine months from today exactly."

Standing wide leg, Guntther's thumbs are tucked inside his huge turquoise-inlaid belt buckle. He tips his hat respectfully. "The hell you say. Congratulations, sergeant major; you both appear to be right fine folk. If you and the Mrs. are ever down near Abilene, Route Sixty-six takes you right through from start to finish. Look for a Scofield's filling station on the highway. Can't miss one. Fill up on a tank of gas, and with your next oil change, you'll get a plate of fresh fried catfish and hush puppies with your choice of soda." Guntther guffaws, slapping his thigh. "Hell, the best damned catfish in all Abilene. Ooh wee, hot damn! Line em' up, lil' doggies! Line em' up!'"

At the display counter, Samantha is close to a decision with her ring selection. "Guntther, honey, leave those nice people alone." Samantha twists her hand to allow the ring's brilliance to reflect in the display mirror. "Claude, this one's very nice; it seems to show more brilliance than the others."

"Guntther, do you like this one, honey?"

Guntther acknowledges over his shoulder, "I'm on my way, lil' moon pie. Just you make sure the diamonds you pick are big enough so when the full moon reflects off them boulders it blinds them bullfrogs just long enough to stay put." Guntther guffaws, slapping his leg. "Texas born and raised! Ooh wee, lil' doggie." Returning his attention to the perplexed couple, Guntther respectfully tilts his hat. "Nice meeting y'all; bye now."

Unable to grasp the reality of what's transpired, Tiffany and John are lost for words. Neither are prepared to return the well-intended mannerisms of the scrawny rooster. In good taste, both refrain from embarrassing laughter. Each looks to the other for choice words to return the pleasantries.

"Nice meeting you as well... good luck to you both."

"Yes, it was really nice meeting you, Mr. Guntther; have a

safe trip back to Abilene."

Guntther, strutting wide leg, returns to Samantha and Claude. "Honey, I was telling those fine folk all about the Scofield name. Hell, I imagine if G.W. were in office, he'd shut down half the state of Texas on account of a Scofield getting hitched." Full of himself, the cocky strut becomes more exaggerated. Abruptly Guntther stops to watch his reflection in the mirror. He turns his body to get a side view. Now admiring the Wranglers cut over his expensive armadillo cowboy boots, Guntther taps his right foot.

Samantha's voice interrupts Guntther's self-admiration. "Honey, come here."

The Texan slaps his thigh with a guffaw. "Ah, Sam, I'm just funning." Continuing the wide-leg strut, Guntther stops at the display counter giving Claude a heavy Texas slap across the shoulders. "Now don't fret or tarry none, Mr. McKinney. The card Samantha holds, that there's the black card. It's just as rich and black as Texas oil, though not quite as big. I'd imagine that card will take care of anything Sam wants. Hell, I reckon five times over before it reached its limit. OOH WEE! Let's all pray for the day the country of America is renamed Texas itself."

Claude winks reassuringly. "There was never a doubt in me mind, lad. The ring she's picked—"

"Thanks for everything, Claude," Tiffany's voice interrupts. "We'll see you next month."

From the display counter, Claude looks over the top of his glasses. He waves, addressing the couple's farewells. "My love to the both of you, my children, and Martha will have cake for next time. Take care."

The store's chime signals as another couple leaves Claude's Jeweler's. Tiffany grabs John's hand to hurry to the escalator. As they descend to the parking level, both simultaneously burst into uncontrollable laughter.

"John, what are you laughing at?"

"Tiffany, I believe I'm laughing for the same reason you are?"

"What?"

"You first."

Stepping off the escalator, Tiffany imitates Guntther's strut. "All that scrawny bird was missing was the rooster's comb on top of his head."

Standing wide-legged John positions his thumbs in his belt buckle as he mimics a southern drawl. "I say, I say, I say, now boy!"

Tiffany chortles with laughter. "That's who he was, Foghorn Leghorn!"

John projects his voice to mimic Samantha, while simultaneously mimicking Guntther's herky-jerky strut. "You've gotta heap of range to cover in the bedroom tonight, outlaw."

Tiffany raises her hand as If she had to reveal something. "Stop making me laugh, John, and we're acting like junior high school kids. Stop, John, I have to pee. We shouldn't make fun of that couple; they were so genuinely happy."

John stops the strutting and mimicking of Guntther to look at Tiffany. "Okay, let's stop."

Tiffany complies. "I agree."

John reconfirms, "I stopped already."

Tiffany agrees, explaining, "I stopped before you did."

John brings clarity with resolution. "It's finished; I'm done."

Laughing together; each points to the other with blame. "You started everything."

"No, you did."

John accepts blame, compromising. "It was definitely a bad thing. Do you forgive me?"

Tiffany nods her head, agreeing. "I'm guilty too. That was definitely wrong."

The couple stands embraced in the middle of the parking level in a world of their own. With no worries of hindrance or reservation, the entwined couple kiss passionately as the public walks around them to enter and leave the shopping galleria.

"John, I love you."

"I love you more, Tiffany."

"John, do you think people are looking at us like we're crazy?"

"Who cares? We're in love, just like the couple in Claude's jewelers. Do you think they even care how the world looks at them?"

"No, John, that was pretty obvious."

"Then why feel any embarrassment? I don't wear cowboy boots or own a turquoise belt buckle."

"John, you're funny."

CHAPTER TWO

*S*ince leaving Claude's Jeweler's, the day's itinerary continued with the scheduled payments to the florist, dressmaker, and travel agent. Right at two o'clock, the couple arrive at the caterer's house for lunch, to be served samples of their wedding menu entrées. From there, their itinerary takes them to Riverside for the weddings horse-and-carriage selection. During their return home, having enjoyed the rush of the day's excitement, Tiffany settles into the cars' soft ride and John's choice of smooth jazz. It has such an intoxicating effect that within minutes she is snoring lightly with John's heavy arm across her body. As his fiancée sleeps, John uses the steering wheel's tuner button to find a news station. The evening's topic of discussion: America being at the forefront of the coalition to counter terrorist attacks on America and around the world.

While listening, John engages the car's turn signal to exit

the freeway. A traffic light at the upcoming intersection brings traffic to a stop on the freeway off ramp. Here a panhandler passively sits and hustles for donations from the awaiting line of cars. Near the panhandler's feet, a homemade cardboard sign has been propped in place by a stake driven in the ground. American vet! Hungry! Will work for food!

Pressing the window switch to roll the driver's window down, John passes the panhandler a twenty-dollar bill. "Here's to you, soldier."

Accepting the bill, the heavily bearded man makes no eye contact with the money's donor. "Thank you, sir," he acknowledges. Appreciative of the contribution, the panhandler offers a six-inch American flag from the saddlebag at the foot of his chair. "God bless you."

A few feet away rests a large German shepherd. The animal wears a sleeveless army jacket with dark sunglasses fixed across its face.

John immediately recognized the distinguished military insignia patch affixed to the jacket's right shoulder. The large shepherd has since risen to sit on its hindquarters. As it pants to keep cool, its tongue dances between its canine teeth. John engages conversation with the panhandler. "I recognized your Screaming Eagles patch. Where were you detailed, soldier?"

John's distinguished dress uniform is recognized. Although appearing worn and haggard, the veteran musters a labored but commanding voice to salute the higher-ranking officer, "Sir! Corporal Zachariah Browning reports! One Hundred First Airborne Division, Third Battalion, Third Brigade. Tour of duty in Vietnam, '67 to '71. Re-enlisted to active duty and stationed at Army Garrison Fort Campbell, Kentucky, 1972 to 1976."

As if validating its owner, the large shepherd acknowledges the significance of the corporal's words with a bark.

John returns the veteran's salute. "Sergeant Major John Willoughby, Special Operations, Eighty-second Airborne Division, Fort Bragg."

Corporal Browning squints to the sky as he folds the twenty-dollar bill. He tucks it inside the lining of his cap. "Sergeant, I know what they explained to us while we were fighting for democracy. After all the fighting a man will ever do in his life, he'll never find more trouble to confront than what's presented to him in his own country. Since the American Revolutionary War, the War of 1812, and Poncho Villa's excursion in New Mexico in 1916, no foreign enemy outside this nation has ever stepped on American soil to attack this great country of ours. On December 7, 1941, Japan did the unthinkable at Pearl Harbor. For over two hours, Japanese planes kept coming wave after wave. Did they ever surprise the sleeping giant! They hit us hard. Like the Japanese at Pearl Harbor, the enemy we fight today brings the fight to us within our own country. Able to strike anywhere at any time, he uses the oldest warfare known to man: terrorism with the element of surprise."

Corporal Browning casually removes a plastic package of crackers from his saddlebag. Putting a few in his mouth, he chews as he dialogues. "After the president pulled the Army out of 'Nam, come to find out the boys returning home were exposed to Agent Orange. The military used it as an herbicide to kill the brush so that the enemy wouldn't have cover to hide. After fighting for my country on foreign soil, I lost my spleen to cancer just two years ago."

Continuing with the cracker chewing, Corporal Browning tosses a couple toward the shepherd. The large animal catches what's thrown its way with a chomp of its mouth. "Atta boy, Otis!" Corporal Browning resumes his saga. "All I have left of any family is Otis here. Since losing my spleen, my army coat's too heavy for me now." He nods to the shepherd. "I've passed it on to another soldier, ol' Otis. What a true purebred! He's never turned his back on me. We sleep, eat, and work together like family. He's been as loyal as they come."

Hearing its name mentioned, the shepherd trots to the driver's window to sit on its haunches. With its ears erect, it looks at Corporal Browning to whine for further instructions.

Seated in his chair, the corporal's left leg is crossed over the right at the knee. Going about with the cracker chewing, small pieces expel from his mouth as he communicates with his shepherd. "Otis, he's just met you; he needs time to get used to you, boy." Corporal Browning gives a nod. "Otis likes you, sergeant. He doesn't mean you any harm; he just wants you to rub his chest."

John pets the large shepherd's head cautiously. As his confidence builds, he talks to the animal while rubbing its coat. "Oh, yes, what a good boy you are. He's a fine animal, Corporal Browning."

The veteran winks. "I couldn't find a truer friend."

Swallowing a cracker, he directs a command. "Fall back in line and join ranks, boy!"

Following orders, the shepherd removes its head and huge paws from the driver's window. With an abrupt about-face, it trots back and settles at the corporal's chair.

"Atta boy, Otis!" The shepherd is rewarded with a solid whack in the chest. Corporal Browning directs attention to the sleeping occupant in the passenger's seat. "Is she your wife, sergeant?"

Admiring Tiffany's natural beauty, John beams with pride to whisper, "Indeed, corporal, very soon to be indeed."

Blaring car horns interrupt the conversation in choruses of honks, as both lanes of awaiting cars continue on to the main boulevard.

"Honk."

"Keep moving, asshole!"

"Honk"

"Merge with the fucking traffic!" The car behind John veers into the right lane to pass.

"Honk"

"Asshole! Get his fucking phone number."

"Honk"

"Just throw him a quarter and get the fuck out of the way!"

As another car approaches, the driver's middle finger is seen through the windshield. Rolling slowly to a stop, the car's window opens. A woman yells to the trio, "You fucking jerks. Fuck off!" As the car speeds away with its tires spinning, a quick bark comes from Otis.

Corporal Browning resumes his saga. "As I've said, you'll never have to go out of your way to find it. There will always be a heap of trouble simmering in your own country." Finishing a cracker swallow, corporal browning continues. "Sergeant major, when I served this country, I wasn't attached to anyone, nor did I have anyone to spend my life with, so I re-enlisted on active status in the Army. In the end, I returned with nowhere to go or anyone to go to. That's when I got my shepherd." The corporal looks to the sleeping occupant in the passenger's seat to make his point. "I never gave myself the same opportunity. You're ahead of the game; you have someone to spend your life with. Ten-hut!" Corporal Browning salutes. In the customary formality when saluting, the corporal's right hand remains positioned until the higher-ranking officer returns the salute.

"Currahee!" Sergeant Major Willoughby salutes, returning the Screaming Eagle's motto. "At ease, corporal."

Pressing the console's electric switch, John closes the car window to proceed within the flow of traffic.

Awakened by the commotion of car horns, Tiffany's voice is heard from the passenger's seat. "John, were those people honking at us, honey?"

With his thoughts remained at the freeway off ramp with the corporal and Otis, John dialogues to himself. "So much more could be done for them."

"For who, honey? John, were those people honking at us or for the traffic signal to change? Next time use the Arlington off ramp, honey; there's hardly ever any traffic there, and it's faster."

Reaching for Tiffany's hand, John lightly massages her palm. Being sensitive to his touch, Tiffany attempts to remove her hand. John applies just enough downward pressure to prevent her escape. Continuing the mischief, John heckles with puffs of air toward Tiffany's face.

"Woman, be still. I need to hold you. It's been a whole day already, and you're still trying to get away from me. You must enjoy making it hard on yourself."

Squirming in every direction to escape John's touch, the seatbelt restrains Tiffany's attempts to move. John puffs more air toward her face, which leaves Tiffany's ears tingling. To elude the sensation, she squirms and twists her body.

Managing to free her hand, Tiffany covers her left ear and bends it, in an attempt to dispel her ear's sensitivity. "Stop it, John! You know how sensitive my ears are."

"Tiffany, with you everything's so sensitive. Which will it be, your hands or your ear? Believe me, you'll run out of energy before I'm finish with you, so stop fighting the feeling."

Covering her left ear, Tiffany protests with laughter. "Stop it, John!" During the same time, she protects her left hand from John's touch by placing her left leg on top of her hand. "John, you're harassing me. We'll get a ticket for reckless driving. Pay attention to the road, John!"

"No worries, Tiffany, bothering you is definitely worth the ticket. Just you explain what you were doing before the officer writes it." Using his index finger, John pokes Tiffany in her left side. "When we're pulled over, I'll simply explain you were itching, and I was helping you scratch where you couldn't reach.

Now be still, Tiffany; you need to be touched by John."

"Oh, no you don't, Stop it, John!"

John taunts, chuckling. "Oh, yes, I do, baby, and this needs to be done." Tiffany's kneecap is squeezed.

In a panic, she unlatches the seatbelt to jump about a foot out of the passenger's seat screaming, "John, stop! That tickles."

Abruptly the playful antagonizing ends. "You're asking me to stop?"

"Yes, John."

Changing strategy, John points his right index finger. "Okay, listen carefully. If you want me to stop, just tell me where I shouldn't touch you." John playfully pokes Tiffany in her left side. "Should I stop touching you there?"

Tiffany screams, covering herself. "Yes, John."

"Or should you not be touched here?"

After Tiffany's left kneecap is squeezed she submits, "Okay, John, okay!"

Threatening a probe with his right index finger, John relents to admit, "Tiffany, baby, you're right; I should listen more."

Anticipating another probe. Tiffany covers herself, "Stop it, John!"

John antagonizes, "Baby, that's what I'm trying to do. Are you sure you don't want to be bothered? I can't hear you."

At this point, Tiffany's body is exhausted from laughing. Though sensitive to John's touch, she tries not to squirm as he reaches for her left ear.

He asks, "Baby, can I have a kiss? Are you listening, Tiffany?

I need to hear it from you. All you have to do is repeat ten simple words to overcome what's making you so very uncomfortable. Repeat after me and simply say, 'Yes, John, I want you to stop touching me, please.'"

Bewildered, Tiffany's unable to respond.

John points his index finger playfully to instigate, "Okay, I don't know if you understand, because you're not saying anything."

Tiffany answers quickly, "John, I heard everything you said. Please stop." Going on the offensive, Tiffany grabs John's right hand to prevent him from pointing his index finger.

Countering, John removes his left hand from the steering wheel to threaten another probe. "Did you forget this one, baby?"

"John, stop it; I'm going to pee on myself."

John returns his hand to the steering wheel to instigate, "Oh no! This is a rental; we don't want that. Tiffany, they'll charge me if it's not returned clean."

Preparing herself for more badgering, Tiffany remains tensed in the passenger seat.

Contrary to what she's expecting; John redirects his focus to the road. Driving several blocks, he proposes a quiet ultimatum. "Tiffany, if you really want me to stop, then prepare yourself for what I'm going to ask for next."

Tiffany grabs John's right index finger. "Okay, John, enough, stop playing."

With Tiffany tensed with expectance, John expresses, "Come on, baby! Surely you've thought of a sweet resolution to all this madness already. As smart as you are, you probably had it figured out yesterday." Removing a hand from the steering wheel, John points to his right cheek with a request. "Please hurry up and put one right there."

Unprepared for the unexpected, Tiffany exhales with relief, kissing John's cheek.

Receiving the affectionate peck, John chuckles. "See there, for the last twenty minutes you've had yourself all worked up, thinking I was going to put my tongue in your ear. That's what you get for running. Thanks for the ride, lady."

John continues the drive chuckling. "I've never seen you so frightened; I was only leading to a sweet kiss."

Outdone, Tiffany massages the back of her fiancé's neck guardedly. "John, you're so silly. You're lucky we didn't wreck."

Proceeding toward their destination, John resumes listening to the all-news radio station. The topic continues with caller discussion: Should America wait for coalition support before committing U.S. troops to respond to terrorist attacks on America and around the world?"

The first caller responds: "What bothers me is America policing the world and protecting the freedom of others. Why is it when America's attacked, every freaking country we've sent troops to restore order in their own country looks at America as the bully getting our just desserts? That's bullshit! In the future, they should take care of their own problems. America should be protecting America first for Americans."

Caller number two responds, "This is America. Since when does America need permission to retaliate on any enemy who has committed atrocities on American soil? This is god-damn Pearl Harbor all over again. America needs to strike back. This country has always stood alone against tyranny. Since when do we talk or negotiate with criminals? 'Deeds, not words!' That's why America had the One Hundred First Airborne. Currahee!"

The next caller rationalizes, "The president has clearly shown restraint and good judgment by requesting involvement of a united front against Al-Qaeda. This is reminiscent of The Big Three united against Nazi Germany in World War II, but on a much grander scale. With the united coalition, we also present a united front. We send the message terrorism will not be tolerated anywhere in the world. I agree wholeheartedly with the president."

While in the midst of caller discussion, the couple has arrived at Tiffany's apartment. John turns the radio down with an inquiry. "Tiffany, is there anything you'll need before we head in? Our show comes on tonight. I don't want any interruptions once *America's Best Performer* starts."

"Well, John, it depends. How demanding will you be for dinner? Do you have a taste for chicken alfredo or the shrimp scampi?"

Pressing the car's electric door lock switch, John unlocks both doors. "Okay, that was simple enough. Thanks, Tiff! We're in for the night with no interruptions. Great!" John opens the door to exit.

"John, you didn't answer. Which is it going to be? I need to know which to prepare so that I can prepare for the show. You know we always watch the show together. Quit being silly!"

John smiles as he walks around the front of the car. He opens the passenger door with his answer. "Baby, I have faith in you. Trust me; you'll manage." While extending a hand for Tiffany's exit, John asks, "The microwave and the stove burners … are they functional?"

"Yes, John, you brought the stove new; everything's working. What does that have to do with your choice for dinner?"

John spins Tiffany into his arms. "One of the many reasons I appreciate you so much, is because you're always willing to go the extra mile." Before she's able to respond, John kisses Tiffany with an explanation. "All that's left to decide is whether you want to boil the frozen bag or defrost it, after you remove it from the package."

Tiffany punches her fiancé in the chest; she screeches, "JOHN!"

John counters by pulling Tiffany into his embrace. Her protest is silenced with a kiss.

Being difficult, Tiffany bites into John's lower lip, clenching it with her teeth. "Say you're sorry, John!"

John chuckles defiantly. "Never!"

Tiffany increases the pressure in her bite, forcing John to submit.

"Okay, okay, you win! I'm sorry."

Tiffany maintains her bite. She questions, "You're sorry for what, John?"

John answers in a tone a little higher than usual, "I'm sorry for the teasing, Tiffany. I'm sorry for everything."

Tiffany releases her bite to pout playfully. "You better be sorry."

John licks his lower lip along the embedded grooves of Tiffany's teeth marks. He feigns being frightened. "Tiffany, please don't hurt me. You're an animal unleashed when you don't get your way. I'll do anything you ask; just please don't bite me again."

Tiffany clanks her teeth, threatening to bite. "Willoughby! What's it going to be for dinner, the shrimp scampi or the chicken alfredo?"

Conceding defeat and smiling, John walks toward Tiffany's apartment with his arms raised. He repeats his name as if preparing for enemy questioning. "Private Willoughby, United States Army!"

After inserting her door key, Tiffany opens the door to point toward the interior, directing a command. "Willoughby! Report to the mess hall to wash the pots and utensils that are to be used for the evening's meal, which will be served in the officers' dining room at seventeen thirty hours!"

Enjoying the role play, John salutes. "Sir, yes, sir!"

Tiffany grabs a handful of John's ass to direct another command. "Willoughby! After you've finished preparing the meal, report immediately to the officers' shower to your commanding officer. As your duty, you are hereby compelled to ravage her until you're directed to do otherwise. Is that understood, Willoughby?"

John salutes smiling. "Sir, yes sir!" Lowering his arm, he ends the salute to turn in about-face toward the bathroom.

Within his first step, another command is shouted.

"Halt! Parade rest! At ease, sergeant."

Tiffany approaches from the rear. Continuing the role play, she reaches around his waist to find the stiffness in his crotch. "Very good, sergeant major. To take advantage of your blatant breach of defense, I'll engage this next operative using a hands-on approach." Tiffany squeezes the hardness. "Feeling rather frisky in your uniform, are you? I'd say you've definitely been a bad boy! As I discern the shape, hardness and logistical positioning of this dynamic weaponry, as your commanding officer, I conclude a campaign of rigorous amphibious maneuvers in the shower as the assault plan to expose the enemy's flank."

John turns his head to Tiffany, stunned. "Now where did you learn that? What type of scripts are you reading these days?"

Tiffany sticks out her tongue to admit, "I have friends that tell me things too, you know!"

John puckers his lips to smooch a kiss. "A little Ms. Tease a-lot is what you are. Tease and run, tease and run; hello, I'm Tiffany Adams, would you like to play tease and run?"

"John, you're the one with the harpoon bulging in your pants. Look at that thing! You can't even hide it!"

Embarrassed, John reaches for a couch pillow to cover his crotch, "What do you expect? You're the one grabbing and reaching for things, Tiffany. You started this! While you're throwing rocks in the volcano, you're meddling with the fire that comes with it! Remember that, now." Tossing the pillow back to the couch, John loosens his belt to reposition the hardness in his crotch. Mischievously, he gives Tiffany his Dudley

Do-right grin. "I'll have you know I was quite the track stand-out in high school. Around campus I was known as ol' reach."

Tiffany squints her eyes disbelievingly. "John, you have flat feet. There's no way you ran track."

"Tiff, I'm telling you, I was a pole vault champion!"

"John, really?"

"Yes, really! Hear me out; I'll explain my feats. After the fourteen-foot mark in the first and second heats, I choked. In the next competition after flopping twice, I was on my third and final attempt. I took off running in perfect form toward the crossbar. My head was raised and my hands were spaced evenly with good over and under grips. I was twenty yards out and closing in. Fifteen, ten, five, three, and just as I reached the vault pit, my jock strap tore. I'll never forget that sound, 'boi-yoi-yoing!' What do you know? Mr. Peterbilt down there hit the track field hard and heavy. It left an impression in the vault pit you wouldn't believe. I swear, it was the same diameter as the vault pole."

"John?"

"Really, Tiff! I'm telling you, as I projected up I was in perfect form. I cleared the twenty-foot mark easily and set the national record in that heat. Was I ever embarrassed, but after everything was said and done, the local paper ran an article referring to me figuratively as the heat's pole position. From that day forward I was known around campus as ol' reach."

Realizing she's been hoodwinked, Tiffany throws a couch pillow at John. "Okay, already, you got me. I can't believe the stories circulating around the officers' dining room. John, you're a mess!"

The couple's shenanigans bring Lucky into the living room. Seeking affection, the tabby purrs as it rubs its body against Tiffany. With persistence, it goes from one leg to the other until Tiffany picks it up. "Did bad Johnny awake you? You heard that nasty story too? Don't worry; we'll make sure he keeps his pants on. Neither of us wants to look at that scary thing anytime soon, huh Lucky?"

As Tiffany gives Lucky affectionate kisses, John strokes the tabby's eyebrows. "Sorry to wake you, Lucky. I'll make it up to you with a piece of raw shrimp. Wouldn't you like that from bad Johnny?"

Cradled in Tiffany's arms, the tabby closes its opal eyes, dismissing John's proposal. Tiffany spins away. "Don't even try to talk your way out of making dinner. It's your day in the kitchen all weekend, Mr. Smooth Talker, and since when are you called Johnny these days?"

"Oh my, Tiffany, I've yet seen you so insecure about our relationship. Is this the iceman cometh? You're questioning who calls me Johnny? Tiffany, that was supposed to be a joke with Lucky."

Continuing with the rubbing and stroking of the tabby's fur, Tiffany arches one eyebrow in thought. She raises her dimpled chin with nonchalance. "No, no iceman cometh here. I wanted to make sure to whom I should make the request of potatoes au gratin to be included with the dinner you'll be preparing. Very fine, thank you. Should I be speaking to John or Mr. Johnny?"

John walks toward Tiffany smiling. He stops within

inches of her to whisper. "Well, Ms. Adams, it depends on what you're looking for. If it's the soldier you're after, send all requests to Sergeant Major John Willoughby. On the other hand, about the cooking requests, be adventurous. Mosey on around back and ask for Johnny. He'd obliged to any fixings you like." Stepping closer, John rubs his lips lightly across Tiffany's eyelids. He kisses her lips to whisper, "All you need to do now, Ms. Adams, is determine which of us will sleep in your bed tonight. Will it be John or Mr. Johnny?"

Tiffany becomes mesmerized with the kisses and whispering, to the point that she cradles Lucky with her eyes closed.

John's chuckling returns her to the living room, where she immediately opens her eyes to punch him. "That wasn't fair John; you tricked me!"

John laughs it off to walk toward the bedroom. Now snapping his fingers, he begins to motion his head in a rhythm that's out of sync with his rhyme. Without shame, he appears silly in the attempt:

1730 hours, Sergeant John Willoughby's preparing the meal.
After the shower, Johnny's closing the deal.
When we cuddle under the covers, you'll meet Johnny in his prime.
The shows John's to steal, and Johnny love you long time.
Counting the rounds will be your job; no doubt you'll be warmer.
Meet Sergeant John Willoughby; I'm America's Best Performer!

Appearing ridiculous, John abruptly flashes his Dudley Do-right grin.

Awestruck from John's goofy uncouthness, Tiffany doesn't know how to respond. Lost for words, Tiffany has a shocked expression to where her mouth is slightly open.

John breaks the silence, defending himself. "What, you didn't know I had it in me? You're not the only one watching the music awards. I'll give any of those guys a run for album of the year!"

Tiffany's eyes become large with shock. Not knowing what else to say, she mouths, "Oh my god! Now you're watching the hip-hop music awards too? John, do you wear your uniform when you watch the show? Did you feel you had street credibility too? Really, John, really?"

CHAPTER THREE

Together the couple enjoyed their meal of chicken alfredo. Then since, John has showered and now sits on the living room couch to sprinkle foot powder between his toes. As he works the powder into his feet, he wiggles and stretches his toes while dialing the message center to retrieve missed calls. In Tiffany's visit to the bathroom, she turns on the showerhead to allow the bathroom to steam. In between time, having creamed her legs with hair remover, Tiffany sits on the tub's rim with a damp towel to remove the excess hair remover.

John's voice is heard from the living room. *"America's Best Performer* starts in ten minutes, Tiff!"

Tiffany acknowledges over the shower's streaming water, "John, I've programmed the DVR to record honey; just make sure the power light is on."

From the living room the message center's automated voice is heard. "You have one urgent message and two new messages.

Urgent message received today at 12:27 p.m."

Beep!

"This message is for Sergeant Major John Willoughby. By orders of Special Operations Command, you are to report to base command Fort Bragg immediately."

Beep.

"Message received today at 12:30 p.m."

"Sergeant Major Willoughby, this is Special Operations Command Sergeant William Shackleford. You've been directed to report back to base command. We're being airlifted soldier!"

Beep.

"Message received today at 5:00 p.m."

"John! It's First Sergeant Rawlings. Have you heard the buzz going around? Everyone on a three-day pass or leave is being called back to base command. We're pulling out. The joint chiefs of staff met with the president. John, it's going down. The president's making the announcement in the morning. He's sending two thousand US troops! Special Operations are being deployed ahead of the united coalition. We're flushing out Al Qaeda! We'll be the first ones there to kick Al Qaeda ass! Whoa!"

Beep.

"There are no more messages."

The message center's automated voice has brought Tiffany into the living room. Clothed in her bathrobe, she stands motionless behind the couch. Both she and John have heard the messages, but neither speaks.

Tiffany nervously adjusts the towel covering her hair. "John, what does all this mean, and where would you be going?"

"From the sound of things, we're going to war! No one knows for sure until the president announces whatever is to be. One thing's for certain, soldiers are being deployed; as to where remains with the president's announcement."

The light on the DVR has turned green, indicating the recording of *America's Best Performer*. Tiffany walks around the couch to sit next to John. Parting her bathrobe, she continues with the hair remover and the damp towel. Neither looks to the other; in dumbfounded shock, they both watch *America's Best Performer* blank faced. Within the same time, the bathroom shower is heard over the silence. Tiffany moves closer to her fiancé. She asks, "John, what about our wedding?"

Keeping his blank gaze to the television, John places his arm around his fiancée reassuringly.

"It'll be all right, Tiffany!"

Tiffany validates her concerns with further scrutiny. "The ring and Mr. McKinney. We've made all of the arrangements, John."

John reassures, "Everything will be okay. Tiff, let's not put worry into what we've planned. Nothing's definitive until I'm briefed upon my return to base command." John breaks his gaze from the television, kissing the top of Tiffany's head. He pulls her closer, giving a reassuring squeeze. "Nothing's going to get in the way of our day, nothing!" The couple continues watching television over the lingering tension. Unable to shake the anxiety, John regroups to restructure his travel plans with a cellphone call.

The answering party's voice projects from his speaker phone. "Traveling Airlines, Sandra speaking. How can I assist you today?"

"Hello, I'm Sergeant Major John Willoughby. I've recently arrived in Los Angeles, and I've just been notified of an emergency that forces my departure sooner than what was anticipated."

"Sergeant, would you know your flight ticket number?"

Breathing heavily, John acknowledges, "My flight ticket number is FZXC eight zero three four WYSX."

"Thank you, sergeant; I have to place you on hold momentarily to bring up the screen." The service representative continues the call confirming booking and flight departures. "Sergeant Major Willoughby, thank you for your patience. Flight one nine two three, round trip from Raleigh, North Carolina, to Los Angeles International is scheduled to depart a direct flight on Wednesday, January 8, at seven p.m., arriving at Raleigh-Durham on January 9 at 1:30 a.m. The next direct flight departs this evening at 11:45 p.m. from L.A.X., arriving at Raleigh at 6:30 a.m. There's another direct flight departure from L.A.X, scheduled for tomorrow afternoon at 12:30 p.m., arriving at Raleigh at 6:45 p.m. Which flight would you like in place of your original departure date, sergeant?"

John hesitates. Tiffany's eye's well with tears as she watches her fiancé expectantly. John gives his answer squeezing Tiffany's hand reassuringly. "Thank you for your assistance, Sandra. I'll have to go with tonight's flight at 11:45 p.m.

CHAPTER FOUR

*K*abul, Afghanistan. It's been ninety days since America initiated the coalition's campaign against terrorism. Within that span no coalition casualties have been reported. Al Qaeda has yet to launch a major military offensive; rather it has engaged coalition forces with sporadic skirmishes and fire fights. Nonetheless, the American show of force has been impressive. Five platoons of the fourth infantry have been detached and positioned in a perimeter of defense surrounding the American embassy. In the outer perimeter of the city, a combat outpost has been detached in a triangular formation, serving as the first line of defense. Reveille's been announced. As the embassy's detachment prepares for chow, platoons of thirty personnel are rotated to and from the mess hall to thwart any breach of defense.

As foreigners on indigenous soil, the heavily geared platoons appear out of place for the region's climate. The indigenous people wear garments lightly woven from the customary fabrics of cotton, linen, polyester, or nylon worn in a loose fit with sandals to both shield and expel the region's intense heat. Though the regions indigenous people have been clothed in this manner for thousands of years, coalition forces have been briefed and trained for imminent perils, and the region's clothing is somewhat perceived as suspected vessels for terrorist attacks. Nonetheless, the treaties of humanitarianism protect both the residents and land from reckless and misguided warfare. Therefore, the indigenous people come and go about in their customary clothing unmolested, unless seen committing acts of terrorist aggression.

It's sunrise, and the first of the five calls to prayer are heard throughout the region. Throughout the day, the men of the region make their pilgrimage to the mosque for dutiful prayer to Allah. Attired in perahan tubans and wool pashtun caps, each carries with reverence the book of faith, the holy Koran, which is wrapped and protected in flannel cloth. Over the muadhdhin's call to prayer, the daily activity within the infantry's command post has also commenced. Sergeant Major John Willoughby is seated in the passenger seat of the Humvee transport. He's being driven to the region's combat outpost near the remote village of Wanat, located in Konar province. Within just a few blocks of leaving the command post, the driver of the duo, Corporal Wilkinson, coasts the Humvee to a stop, allowing passage for a procession of goats being led by a young goatherd. The high-strung animals pass around the Humvee without incident in bleating chorus. Proceeding forward, Corporal Wilkinson navigates the duo through the narrow roads leading to the outer region of Wanat. Within another few blocks, the Humvee coasts to another stop to afford passage to a group of women and adolescent girls.

As with the Muslim tradition, in public the faces of women and adolescent girls are covered with the formal hijabs, or veils. Continuing, they make their way dutifully to the marketplace during the blessed month of Ramadan, to gather items for the feast at dusk. Midway up the road, a flock of goats run in a ruckus of confusion in every direction. Their goatherd, who looks to be between fifteen to seventeen years of age, flees in terror. In his pursuit is an assailant who wields a large stick. He yells in Afghani Wanetsi dialect, "Coward! I curse you to die a thousand deaths!" In his flight the goatherd trips and falls between the panicked animals. Closing in on his quarry, the assailant now stands over the victim to unleash deliberate solid whacks to his head. Abruptly the assailant stops the attack to look in the direction of the Humvee. Redirecting his focus, he hurls obscenities and curses at his captive audience before landing the large stick repeatedly across the goatherd's back. Returning his attention to the Humvee, the assailant raises his fists clenched in defiance. He shakes them toward the duo as if challenging them to intervene. While the assailant animates his hostility toward the Humvee, the goat herder balls into a fetal position to protect himself. The assailant continues his assault with an onslaught of kicks and stomps before delivering a well-placed kick to the ass of his quarry. Lying sprawled and helpless in the dirt, the goatherd moans, "America, I've done nothing, please help me!"

Corporal Wilkinson grips the steering wheel, questioning his commanding officer. "Shouldn't we do something, sir? He's likely to kill that boy."

Sergeant Willoughby uses his binoculars to survey the road and surrounding buildings in the Humvee's direct path of travel. He answers. "Corporal, that would be a negative, the directive for the rules of engagement reads that unless there's insurgent aggression, we're to stand down. We are not to intervene with cultural issues."

Corporal Wilkinson acknowledges, "Yes, sir!"

As his assailant hurls his fist challenging the duo to intervene, the goatherd seizes the opportunity to break away. Continuing his flight in terror, he yells for the Humvee's protection. "America, I've done nothing; please help me!"

Being outrun by his quarry, his assailant ends the pursuit within twenty yards of the chase.

Overwhelmed by his narrow escape, the goatherd falls and tumbles face first. Though stunned from the fall, his fear quickly overcomes the disorientation. The goatherd rises to run toward the Humvee's occupants. Within a few strides, he collapses within several feet of the Humvee. Blood oozes from his head with his plea. "Please, America, I've done nothing!"

Corporal Wilkinson looks to his commanding officer. "Well, sir, I believe we're required to give some medical attention. I'm referring to the protocol in the Geneva Convention."

Witnessing what's played out before them, Sergeant Willoughby directs, "Corporal, that's a negative; stand down."

Corporal Wilkinson sighs in disbelief. "Yes, sir!"

Continuing, the Humvee inches forward.

In his struggle to rise, the goatherd refuses the Humvee's passage. He has now affixed himself to the vehicle. "Please, I'm being punished for talking to Americans!"

Corporal Wilkinson looks to his commanding officer. "What am I to do now, sir?"

Sergeant Willoughby continues to look through his binoculars. The assailant is witnessed clenching his fists while hurling curses and obscenities toward his quarry. Noting the assailant's proximity to the narrow road and surrounding dwellings, Sergeant Willoughby questions, "What's with this asshole? He beats his chest and talks a good game, but he won't come forward to finish him. He's called this guy's mother and her descendants everything but a child of God. He knows the lay of the land, and he knows we won't get involved with cultural disputes. The question remains, corporal, why won't he finish him?"

After gaining a foothold on the Humvee's hood, the goatherd makes a desperate plea. "Please help me; I am a friend to the Americans!"

From gut instinct, Sergeant Willoughby barks a panicked order, "Corporal! Back out now; get the fuck out of here! Back out, corporal!"

Corporal Wilkinson slams the gear shift into reverse. The Humvee lurches violently, causing all four wheels to spin.

Securing his grip, the goatherd is now sprawled across the windshield. He looks into the faces of the Humvee's occupants giving praise to the god of the Muslim faith. "Allah akbar! Allah akbar!"

Sergeant Willoughby screams a command. "Corporal! Stomp the gas pedal as you turn the steering wheel, then hit the brakes! When he falls off, drive over his deceiving ass. Make it happen now, corporal!"

In an attempt to throw the goatherd from the Humvee windshield, Corporal Wilkinson stomps the gas pedal. He turns the steering wheel a quick spin in both the right and left directions before locking the brakes. In doing so, the wind's velocity raises the front of the goatherd's garment, revealing several explosives strapped to his body. Corporal Wilkinson's eyes bulge with fear as he fights to maintain control of the steering wheel. His voice distressed, he pleads to his commanding officer, "Oh, have I fucked up here. Sir, shoot him! Please shoot this motherfucker! I really have us fucked up here! Holy shit, don't let me die in this country."

Gripping the windshield, the goatherd reached under his garment to detonate the explosives. Sergeant Willoughby fired off four rounds from his officer's firearm. Too late! Just before his death, the goatherd praises the god of the Muslim faith, "Allah akbar! Allah akbar! Death to all capitalist infidels!" Executed with perfection, Al Qaeda strikes using a brilliant ruse. First a flash, followed by four explosions. The searing shrapnel cut through metal and flesh. With it came the smell of burnt flesh and the smoke of molten metal.

Losing consciousness, Sergeant Willoughby talks toward the bright light. "Tiffany? Oh my god! I promised Tiffany everything would be all right. I promised Tiffany..."

The bright light brings Tiffany's voice. "John? What about

our wedding? What about… everything we've planned…John, how long will you be deployed?"

As the bright light fades to complete darkness, sergeant Willoughby ceases to recognize anything.

CHAPTER FIVE

Tiffany's cell phone alarm awakes her at 5:45 a.m., giving her an hour's window for showering, eating breakfast, and leaving a bowl of finicky mignon for Lucky. During her weekly work schedule, it's out the door at 6:45 a.m., to where she takes the brisk fifteen-minute walk toward her 7:00 a.m. shuttle. This morning there is an exception to her usual modus operandi. Tiffany remains in bed. Yawning lazily, she collects her thoughts before rising and stretching.

Walking through her morning ritual, Tiffany turns on the shower's hot water to allow the bathroom to steam. Fifteen minutes later, she enters the shower to an array of body washes and shampoos. Making her toiletry selection, Tiffany leans back into the shower wall to allow the oscillating force of the showerhead to rinse the body wash and shampoo into streams toward the drain. Tiffany steps out of the shower to stand directly under the heat lamp to wipe away the steam from the bathroom vanity. She now goes through her ritual of daily pro-active self-maintenance.

Having utilized the shower's steam for a facial, Tiffany inspects her complexion for imperfections of facial hair or blackheads. She then critiques her eyebrows. Their natural fullness and arched appearance complements her facial features, to the point that an actress auditioning for a cat woman role would be willing to claw for them. Smiling, Tiffany inspects her teeth and gums for discoloration. To ensure optimum maintenance, she flosses regularly before brushing her teeth and gums with an electric toothbrush. With the preliminaries out of the way, Tiffany takes a rinse of mouthwash to admit, "Ah, squeaky clean; it does it every time." Motioning toward the vanity, Tiffany applies a roll-on deodorant while re-adjusting the towel fold at her breasts. Continuing through the hall into her bedroom, she opens the dresser's center drawer to select a panty and bra ensemble. She steps into her panties and releases the towel fold to connect her bra straps. Now standing before the dresser mirror in her lingerie, she notices her tabby's reflection.

Tiffany speaks into the mirror. "Lucky, you're always looking good, aren't you? You're easy to please too; no fussing, no fights; you're awesome! A half bowl of finicky mignon and bottled water keeps you looking like a million bucks, even as you sleep. Look at how you shine with your new rhinestone collar. You appear so regal. Hands down, you're definitely the cat's meow!"

Tiffany breaks from the mirror to face her bed to look at Lucky. Sleeping comfortably, the tabby sleeps with its paws turned inward as it snores. Tiffany asks, "Am I lucky enough to have some of your shine rubbed on me, today?"

Lucky's eyes open to translucent ovals of green and amber. As if considering the request, the tabby rises from the bed comforter to nudge its head into Tiffany's body. Tiffany lifts the purring tabby, giving it pampered smooches. "Oh, thanks Lucky! It's just the assurance I need before today's audition, subtle confidence; it's sexy! It says, 'I'm here; I have purpose, and I'll leave after I've made my point. Thank you very much; nice meeting you!"

Returning the pampered tabby to the bed's comforter, Tiffany uses her finger to adjust its rhinestone collar, questioning, "Lucky, do you have to be such a cutie pie even in your arrogance?"

Back within its sanctum, the tabby's ears are laid back as it purrs. As if its rhinestone collar bestowed royalty, the tabby's eyelids are half closed as it twitches its tail with carefree content.

Tiffany steps away from the bed with a whisper. "A spoiled mess is what you turned out to be; Lucky, shame on you."

Continuing into the kitchen. Tiffany prepares for a breakfast of cold cereal and nonfat milk. She collects a cereal bowl from the cabinet to sit in the breakfast nook. After meticulously selecting a perfect banana from the tabletop basket of assorted fruit, she pours nonfat milk atop her favorite cereal. While eating breakfast in her lingerie, Tiffany looks over her studio pictures affixed to the kitchen wall. She's recognized a few she's included with her portfolio for today's audition. *Interesting* she thinks. Generally the portfolio picture overplays the subject, since it's airbrushed and enhanced. In Tiffany's case, her portfolio pictures are dead on, with no disparity between what's submitted and her actual appearance. Bobby, Tiffany's agent, always submitted a set of both prints with her portfolio, one with touchup and one without. In her mind, Tiffany recites Bobby's rationale verbatim.

"Tiff, you're a natural, like Sally Field and Sophia Loren. They didn't need any of that stuff. What little makeup they did wear enhanced their natural beauty. Believe what I'm telling you, kid. You're with a good crowd! I always submit both sets to show what you're working with, to showcase your versatility!"

Finishing her breakfast, Tiffany selects an apple from the fruit basket. She wipes it off, thanking her agent. "Bobby, during the two years you've represented me, I've done six commercials and twenty extra appearances. It seems I qualified for my SAG card in no time. In a few hours, I'm doing my first major read for a movie role! It's meaningful dialogue, mind you. Bobby, you've been really good to me. Woo, Bobby, you rock!"

Comparing her photos with her agent's rationale, Tiffany bites into the apple. Its crispy tanginess stimulates her taste buds with every bite. The crunchy sound brings Lucky into the kitchen.

"Oh, Lucky, did I awake you? I'm sorry. I got excited is all. I have a read today. Aren't we very lucky?" Tiffany laughs. "I know. Bad joke." Lucky meows. Tiffany picks up the spoiled tabby to nudge faces. "That was a very bad joke. Lucky, you know how much I love you."

Returning Lucky to the floor, Tiffany talks to the finicky

tabby. "See there, aren't you glad I disturbed you? It was time for your wonderful breakfast!" As Tiffany pours milk in its bowl, the tabby meows while twitching its tail to inspect the bowl's contents. Tiffany returns the milk to the refrigerator before she leaves the kitchen. "Lucky, enjoy breakfast. I'll be back in a few hours or so. I'm going for a walk!"

CHAPTER SIX

At 8:30 a.m., Tiffany has donned headphones with her sweat suit to begin her weekly power walk regimen. For today's trek, she listens to a special format in her CD player. Her journey begins at the intersection of Leimert Boulevard and Garthwaite Avenue. Trekking westward to Stocker Boulevard, Tiffany ascends the three-mile incline toward Fairfax Park. Within minutes of her trek, an abrupt change in the traffic signal interrupts Tiffany's rhythm, forcing her to momentarily walk in circles and S patterns. With the signal's change she proceeds across the busy intersection. Continuing her westward trek, Tiffany changes directions south onto Fairfax avenue to enter Fairfax Park.

The distance to the park from Tiffany's front door is a seven-mile round-trip journey, generally returning her home within two hours. Today's an exception. Tiffany's preparing for an audition. Methodically rehearsing her character's dialogue, she wears headphones. In Tiffany's diligence, she's listening to the dialogue opposite her role, to cue her for when her dialogue commences. As she articulates, Tiffany transforms the power walk to a slow gait. When her character's dialogue ends, she resumes the power walk full thrust.

Trekking through the park, Tiffany's power walk takes her past a trio of men at the baseball diamond. The first of the trio acknowledges, "Hello again, young lady! I was just about to leave, but I'll use your inspiration and follow you around the track. Please don't be in a hurry, because you're definitely doing me a favor."

The second of the trio comments, "Wow, what was your name again? Both you and your sweat suit's very cute! Would you slow down a bit and explain why the woman I married doesn't look like you?"

The last of the trio is more creative in his pitch. "Excuse me, young lady. I happen to be both lost and lonely. Is it possible you can help me find the way into your heart?"

Undeterred in her focus, Tiffany maintains her stride, giving a diplomatic wave of acknowledgment to the familiar faces. "Hello, guys!"

The power walk makes a transition from the paved cement onto the dirt field area of the park's walk path, to where several people are in motion at staggered intervals. In one segment, an older gentleman works out as he jogs. When arriving to the curved sections of the track, he turns sideways to shadowbox through its curves. In another segment, two women work out in spandex attire. Walking in conversation with large shirts covering their derrières, both women carry small plastic dumbbells. Stopping periodically, each rotates the dumbbells in a forward and reverse motion of the arms. In another span of distance, a woman runs with her dog on a leash. The dog owner appears to be in better shape than the prized animal she's coaxing around the track. Upon the completion of a lap, the dog begins to wheeze as if having an asthma attack. Winded, it struggles and attempts to sit as its owner continues to run. To force its owner to stop running, it pulls its head in the opposite direction and begins to poop as it walks, farting as much as it wheezes. Its thoughtful owner removes the poop from the walk path to dispose of it in a plastic bag. Shortly thereafter, the exhausted animal is offered bottled water from its owner's cupped hands.

"Connie, take all the time you need to recover. It's all my fault you're feeling sluggish and heavy. I'm to blame for everything. It's the leftovers and gravy I've been pouring over your food; that's why you've been so bloated lately! I'll change your diet right away. Yes, precious, take your time. We'll stop on the way home and get the non-dairy yogurt. Connie, would you like that?"

Meanwhile, Tiffany has completed the first of three laps on the walk path within good time. Unknown to her, she's being trailed by friendly Frank with the receding hairline and comb over. Frank's the manager of the travel club's touring department. Harmless, Frank passes his business card regularly with the reassurance, "I'll get a good deal on any car you want. Yeah, sure, the dealer's price! Have you seen my Porsche? You won't believe the deals I come across. Join me for dinner, and we'll go over the particulars."

A regular on the park's walk path, Frank remained in a time warp. His hair comb over was from the 1970s era, like the 1972 Porsche Targa he drove. As Tiffany goes about her trek, friendly Frank has paced himself to stay within ten to fifteen feet behind her. Peering through bifocals, friendly Frank has been watching Tiffany's ass the entire time. Focused on her audition preparation, Tiffany has yet to notice the sixty-something-year-old man who proudly sports the throwback 1970s era powder-blue short-shorts. Possessing a slender build at five feet, eight inches, Frank resembles the actor Don Knotts. Consumed watching Tiffany's ass, friendly Frank isn't prepared for her sudden transition to the slow gait. To keep his kept distance, Frank is forced to abruptly stop. In an attempt to appear as though he stopped casually, Frank fumbles with a handkerchief to wipe the lenses of his bifocals. For the park regulars, friendly Frank is the motivation for the women wearing oversized jogging suits, and without a doubt the sentiments are the same for the women covering their derrières with shirts. However, when all is said and done, friendly Frank's antics are harmless, and he continues to be tolerated.

As the dialogue for Tiffany's character comes to an end, she resumes her power walk full thrust. Her pace quickens with zest as her hips roll from side to side. With her back aligned straight, pumping both arms, Tiffany brings each elbow to a ninety-degree angle in time, much like the wheels and strut rods on a locomotive. Caught off guard, Frank's not prepared for Tiffany's sudden explosion of energy. Fumbling as he puts on his bifocals, Frank struggles to keep within Tiffany's pace. Previously, as he watched Tiffany's hips roll, Frank's pace was even and consistent. In his effort to close the gap, Frank is now forced to run. With his long uneven stride, he appears winded. He actually looks like Don Knott's sprinting to the finish line. After struggling to catch up, Frank now runs alongside Tiffany. Breathing heavily; he downshifts several gears to match her pace.

Frank catches his breath. "Hey, Tiff! I thought it was you. How's it been going? I see you're being consistent with your workouts; you've been going really hard!" Frank struggles to keep in stride. "You should reward yourself every now and then, you know? By the way, I keep a table at Monty's Restaurant on Wilshire two nights a week. Consider it an open invitation anytime you like stopping...."

Unknown to Frank, Tiffany's character's dialogue has commenced. To articulate her lines, she transitions her power walk to a slow gait. Feeling dismissed by Tiffany's sudden change in character, Frank's expression eclipses from securely convincing to perplexed embarrassment. Frank widens the stride in his power walk to distance himself. Continuing, he peers through his bifocals with his chin held high, as if he had never approached Tiffany with a conversation. Genuinely focused and disconnected from her surroundings, Tiffany has no knowledge of either Frank's invitation or of his perturbation. Nevertheless, she continues on the walk path to methodically articulate.

As Tiffany goes in and out of dialogue, she continues through the park's winding declines and ascents. With the juniper trees coming into view, the walk path levels. Tiffany recognized the muscular man positioned at the pull-up and dip bars.

From this strategic point, Dale the personal trainer gains maximum exposure. Taking full advantage of both his nice looks and polite demeanor, Dale self-advertises his well-defined specimen, being shirtless. With a business card in hand, Dale smiles with an offer. "Tiffany, you're looking a little winded. The next time you do cardio, give me a call. I'll show you a breathing technique and massage your calves. No charge for the first fifteen minutes."

Undeterred, Tiffany points to her headphones with an acknowledging wave. "Good morning, Dale!" Continuing her trek, Tiffany leaves Fairfax Park to proceed north onto Stocker Boulevard, from where she continues to powerwalk in the eastward direction. When within a few blocks of her apartment, she allows her body to cool by walking the remaining distance at a regular pace.

CHAPTER SEVEN

$\mathcal{A}$pproaching the entrance to her apartment complex, Tiffany notices Trisha, the mail carrier, in the foyer. Pending Trisha's route coverage, the two friends have talked upwards to thirty minutes while Trisha placed mail in the recipients' mail slots. Trisha's affable personality and congenial smile always left a lasting impression. She's Tiffany's only friend in the apartment complex, yet Trisha doesn't live there. As friends, the two are perfect for each other's personalities. Tiffany, outside of auditioning for roles, is a something of an introvert. Naturally shy, she avoids engaging new people. Contrarily, Trisha's a ham in every recollection of their history as friends. Tiffany revisits a scenario where Trisha declined an offer to accompany her to an audition.

"Girl, no. Auditions are your thing! If I were to audition for a role, it would be in line for free passes for the all-you-can-eat buffet! I don't have the time you have to power walk. Why do any of that? Save that foolishness for you little women. I walk far enough as it is, delivering mail. Now don't get me wrong, I will put on spandex, but not for what you're doing! Huh, I'll be wearing it to be comfortable just to compete in the same event with the other big girls. We'll all stampede together to the Hawaiian all-you-can-eat buffet." Tiffany and Trisha both explode in laughter.

Having Trisha as a friend was as natural as looking in the mirror and overlooking your flaws. Whenever the friends talked and wherever the conversation led, Trisha had a way that relaxed Tiffany when she needed to confide. Trisha offered everything the wealthy insecure willingly paid their high dollar shrinks to tell them, without pretending to have listened patiently. Honest and uncompromising, Trisha refused to carry herself as a self-conscious woman. She neither entertained what others thought of her, nor did she yearn for their trivial validations. Case in point; Trisha would eat a quart of butter pecan ice cream in a single serving, just to give weight-watching onlookers something to talk about. In addition to her headstrong attributes, she was fiercely loyal to whomever she befriended.

Tiffany enters the apartment foyer. "Hello there, Trisha."

Involved in closing the mail drop's face plate, Trisha turns the key in the opposite direction to lock it in place. Acknowledging Tiffany's voice, Trisha retrieves the mail satchel, beaming with excitement. "Tiffany, girl, I was just on my way to your place. I think it's your lucky day."

"Trisha, you're funny. You're only trying to set me up again." Tiffany removes her headphones. "You say the same thing every time before handing me a handful of bills. Lucky's the name of my cat, remember? For me, lucky is when my bills are put in another mailbox for someone else to pay. So, thank you, Trisha, but how lucky am I really?"

Trisha produces a stack of mail to make her point. "Girl, why are you always crying when you have it good? Have you received any certified mail to acknowledge your check being garnished? Think about it."

Tiffany admits, "Well, it's not that bad, yet."

Trisha speaks her mind. "You do know there are a lot of folks that wish they had the blessings you're having, Tiffany." Trisha refers to the bundle of mail in her hand. "See here, you're lucky you're not in this stack. These days, creditors are beyond asking for payment. They're outright taking money from people and using the law to do it. The people in this stack are the ones that should be crying the blues." Trisha hands Tiffany her mail. "Here, girl, read it and cry with your prima donna ass."

Tiffany goes through her mail to read the senders' names, "Very funny, Trisha. You're fun-nee." Recognizing a letter from John, Tiffany's eyes flash to Trisha. Her radiant face exudes energy and purpose in the same manner a desert springs to life after a flash flood. Tiffany jumps with excitement. "Yes! It's been six months since I heard from John. Oh, my god, I can't believe it!"

Tiffany abruptly stops rejoicing. After a moment of reflection, she comes out of oblivion excited. "Bless, you, Trisha, you're a true friend! You knew I wouldn't have checked my mail box for several days. You wanted to make sure I received John's letter today, didn't you?" Tiffany hugs her best friend. "Thank you, so much."

As Tiffany opens the letter, her face reveals the emotional roller coaster of joy and insecurity that a woman would have for an intended husband. Overtaken with surprise, Tiffany stops short of reading John's letter in its entirety. Blushing with excitement, she harmonizes a familiar tune she replays continuously every Sunday morning.

Sunday mornings are dedicated to reminiscing the days and events she and John shared. As Tiffany celebrates her joy, though she's not much of a dancer, she manages a two-step maneuver while harmonizing her favorite song, "Missing" by the group Everything But the Girl. Tiffany ad libs the lyrics, waving John's letter.

"It's been half a year, and now you've come to me again.
I've been so unsure, I didn't think you'd write anymore.
Since you've been gone, I've cried, I've lost my friend.
Now being blessed with grace,
You've reappeared from some other place.
And I've missed you, yeah, I wanna dance out in the rain.
Oh I've missed you, yeah, I suffered emptiness with pain.
Oh I love you, yeah, my life will never be the same."

Witnessing Tiffany's emotions unfold, Trisha stands by expectantly. "Okay, what's he saying? You two have been living this *Officer and a Gentleman* movie for over a year now. You receive a letter today, and now you're singing and dancing in the street? Tiffany, what's up? Is the wedding today? You're getting married this evening when I get off work, right? Hey, we're girls with everything else, so what's up? Don't clam up now, after you've been crying every day for six months. Okay, girlfriend, start any time you're ready. I'm listening."

While processing what she's read in John's letter, Tiffany abruptly regresses into a blank stare. As though she were hypnotized, Tiffany appears as if she were a little girl being questioned, like one seen in the movies, a little girl who twists from side to side at the waist as she holds a lock of hair in one hand, while holding the bottom of her pretty dress with the other. Tiffany answers like the little girl in a trance. "Trisha, Trisha, Trisha! Do you really expect me to share my joy with you so soon? You're being selfish!"

Abruptly, Tiffany comes out of the trance to stick out her tongue. "I'll tell you everything the next time you bring good news part two. No, really Trisha, I'm on my way to audition for a lead role. I need to get going, and I promise to tell everything after the audition."

Trisha swats Tiffany's hand playfully. "Hold on, Ms. Barbie, you're not going anywhere yet. I'll pass on what's happening with you and your Ken doll. We're girls! You wanna thank me? Just hook me up with the melt-in-your-mouth man at the park! The one you have no business knowing anyway, and we'll be square."

"Who?"

"Hoot what? Now you're an owl?"

"You know damn well 'hoot' I'm talking about. Mr.

chocolatey sprinkles, that's who, the one that keeps giving you the business card I never seem to get. The pretty man at the park with those big pretty piano teeth, the one who wears no shirt, the man you have no business looking at, that's who."

Tiffany laughs. "Not Dale."

Trisha snaps her fingers in agreement. "Hoot, that's him, delicious Dale! The man's so fine, I couldn't remember his name. Tiffany, hook a sista up! Girl, waking up to him with a cup of coffee, I could drink, dip, and eat him all at the same time. Don't play; you know the big girls don't hold back at the dinner table."

Tiffany's nose turns red from embarrassment. Both friends exchange a slapping high five. ""Trisha, okay already! I have to get to the audition. I'll call you later." Tiffany backs up, holding her stomach from laughter. "Stop!"

Trisha returns a bundle of mail to her satchel questioning, "Audition? Will Mr. chocolatey sprinkles be anywhere in the vicinity? Girl, if he is, with all that chocolate, uhm, uhm, uhm! I'll have spandex gripping this big ass with the quickness. I'll roll up there to audition for *The Real Biggest Loser*. Don't play with Trisha's emotions, because Trisha will set it out there for real. I'd give up a week's worth of chocolate turtles, the diet re-fills, and the double chili cheeseburgers. I'll even starve myself for a month for the opportunity to be trained, just hoping for an accidental feel of Mr. chocolatey sprinkle's ass. Now don't read me wrong, because I'm nowhere near desperate, but I am convinced with what I want. Tiffany, girl, hurry up with it! Walk with me to the mail truck, and I'll drive your boney ass to the audition myself. Don't play with my plate. I'll kidnap his fine ass with the quickness. He'll be in my house strapped to the bed like in the movie *Misery*. Watch out!"

The friends give another slapping high five. Tiffany holds her side to laugh. "Trisha, come on. Stop it. I can't keep doing this; I need to get focused. There's no way I can go into character now; you've taken my energy away."

"Okay, Barbie, you're serious?"

Tiffany holds her sides to refrain from laughing. "I'm trying to be, if you'll let me."

Trisha repositions her mail satchel. "You're going Hollywood on me with this one, for real? Okay, where's the audition being held, girl, where?

Tiffany teasingly fans John's letter. "Bobby said I was to report . . . where? Oh yeah, I think it was, where was it again? I hope I haven't mistaken, they may not have the read where they did the last time."

Waiting expectantly for Tiffany's answer, Trisha asks, "Girl, where?"

Tiffany fans John's letter. "Yep, I'm sure of it. I'm certain; with all the preparation and planning, I became confused. Trisha, have you ever had to go through anything like this?" Before revealing the location, Tiffany stops the playful fanning of the letter. "I'm going to North Hollywood Studios, YES!"

Trisha cackles at Tiffany's wit. "Okay, you did that. Be careful of how you treat the messenger missy, especially the bearer of your good news."

Tiffany explains her wit. "I wasn't seeing stars, Trisha, I was being silly is all."

"Tiffany, girl, you don't have to explain anything. I know what you meant. Just save all that good energy for what's ahead. Click those heels together and handle your audition business. In other words, Dorothy, get that bony ass on down the yellow brick road."

Laughter explodes.

Trisha walks away to continue her postal route. "See you later, Dorothy! I'm sure I'll get an earful tomorrow. Remember, if Mr. chocolatey sprinkles is anywhere in the area of that audition, girl, call me. I'll run to wherever you are and bite his fine ass. I'm not playing. If he's there, they'll have to serve a restraining order to keep me away."

Tiffany backs up with laughter. "Oh, Trisha, no. Girl, bye. I Love you."

CHAPTER EIGHT

Tiffany remained at the mail drop to reminisce the last weekend she and John were together. The letter's scent triggered her yearning even more. It's unmistakably, the same fragrance left behind on her pillow and sheets whenever John visited. Opting not to wash her treasured extension, Tiffany preferred the scent to dissipate over time, believing the natural oils in John's skin enhanced its erotic fragrance. Until John returned, her extension of him remained embedded in his bathrobe and safeguarded in her bedroom.

Now that her wheels were spinning, Tiffany critiqued the envelope. How was John's name written compared with hers? Did he spell her name neatly, and what font style did he use? Was it the same for hers? Was her name written as though he were still in love with her? Why was the letter addressed as Tiffany Adams? Why wouldn't John use the foresight to address it as Tiffany Willoughby? *Wow!* Tiffany admits, *Trisha's right! Maybe I am acting like Dorothy, though this isn't a dream, and when I awake, John and I won't be in bed together in Kansas.* Tiffany reasons, *Just as Dorothy had her dog Toto, Tiffany has Lucky, her finicky tabby. Both were faithful pets accompanying their owners during a time of tribulation. In Dorothy's instance, she awoke from a dream to be reunited with Toto and her family. As for Tiffany, she dreamed to be reunited with John and for their lives to continue together with Lucky.* Tiffany returns from thought to click her heels together. "Well, Trisha, you can't say I didn't try."

While scrutinizing the letter's appearance, Tiffany noticed a disparity of two weeks between the date on John's letter and the Army's postmaster's date of receipt. There was also an additional month's delay before the letter reached America for delivery. While in the midst of recalling John's explanation of the mail transportation protocol, Tiffany's cell phone rings.

"Hello? Tiffany speaking."

"Tiff, it's your hard-working agent, and I've got great news."

"Hi, Bobby! I certainly hope so, and you don't have to remind me to be on time. Before you ask, I know my lines; I've studied everyone's lines."

"Tiff, that's great, and I know you're ready! Tell me you stood in front of the mirror while preparing for your read. I can't say it enough, it'll have you much more relaxed when you're called. Seeing yourself as you perform, you'll be that much more polished during your takes. You think any of this will help you, Tiff?"

"Thanks, Bobby! Yes, I'm definitely ready, and I can't wait

to audition. I'm looking beyond the casting performance to the callback. I even downloaded the dialogue to rehearse my lines whenever I powerwalked. Bobby, you'll see when we get there. I'm like so really prepared!" Tiffany notes her watch excited. "It's eleven o'clock already! Bobby, my read's in less than four hours! What time will you be here?"

"That's my reason for calling! I bumped your read time up by two hours; I put you at the front of the line! Tiff, we've raised the bar. Who loves you, kid, any guesses? With Bobby as your agent, you're going places!"

Bonk Bonk! The sound of a car horn interrupts the conversation.

"Look out your window. Do you see a taxi parked there? I paid for it already, tip included! No worries. Have I said it already, kid, we've stepped up our game! Consider this audition our coming-out party. We'll use North Hollywood as a stepping stone to your future. When we're finished teasing them with this audition, Tiff, I'm thinking a world premiere! We're going there in style, kid!"

Tiffany interrupts with a whine. "Bobby! How could you move my read two hours earlier without first telling me? That's way too soon. I'm not in my apartment yet. I just walked into the building foyer. Bobby, I'll need a little time to unwind. I haven't yet put my wardrobe together, and my curling irons are still missing!"

"No worries, Tiff; you have everything you need! Trust me, your performance separates you from the rest. You'll do fine. I'll meet you there."

"Bobby, wait! Hello? Bobby? You can't just hang up!"

Bonk Bonk! The taxi horn sounds.

Tiffany turns around in the foyer to acknowledge the driver. "Hi there, you're early! I need a few minutes to shower, and I'll be right out!"

"Are you Ms. Adams?"

"Yes, I am!"

The driver returns a thumbs up. "Your agent requested a cab. No worries; we're good!

Tiffany closes the foyer's glass door to hurry toward her apartment. Inserting her door key, she opens the door, placing her mail and mini disc player on the table. Lucky rises to stretch in the living room to meet her with meows. Tiffany steps over the tabby to avoid stepping on it. "Yes, it's good to see you too. I can't pet you now. I'm in a hurry Lucky, show time's much sooner than I was prepared for. Bobby tricked me!"

Hurrying to the shower, Tiffany turns on the hot water to allow the bathroom to steam. In her return to the living room, she takes an inventory of her audition bag to think aloud. "Bobby, how can you change my read time? Where would I be if I hadn't packed last night?" Tiffany notices the CD player and John's letter on the living room table. She questions, "Look at me." I'm moving so fast I forgot I placed you there." Kissing John's letter, she places it in the audition bag. "I'll need my John with today's good news. Okay! Let's get to the shower."

Removing her clothing, Tiffany leaves a trail of her workout attire leading to the bathroom. The first to appear are her running shoes and socks. In another pile she leaves her jogging suit and sports bra. Just before entering the bathroom, Tiffany's panties appear at the threshold. Before stepping into the shower, she reaches for the toothbrush and toothpaste. In the same motion she grabs her shower cap from the sink countertop. Brushing her teeth as she showers, within ten minutes Tiffany's covering her body with a towel. After applying a body splash and underarm deodorant, she sprints to her bedroom to find a panty and bra match. From the top of the dresser cabinet, Tiffany sorts through her jewelry for a pair of classy mother-of-pearl earrings. While securing the earring clamps to her earlobes, she walks into the bedroom's wardrobe closet. Within a few seconds, she's selected a white blouse and skirt ensemble. With the opening of the adjacent shoe closet, she comes to another immediate choice, selecting a pair she has yet to wear. Tiffany kisses the shoes with praise.

"John, these lovely shoes were one of your last gifts just weeks before you were deployed. With you being stationed so far away, I am really in the dumps over you not being here. On a brighter note, today I was definitely surprised with your beautiful letter. Within forty-five minutes of receiving it, I'm making it a point to wear one of your lovely gifts for today's audition. My god! White pumps and mother-of-pearl earrings! John, I wish you could see me. You're everything to me, and I'm ruined only because of you." Tiffany sighs. "As sweet as the memories may be, none of them will bring you back today. John, I gotta get going, honey!" Tiffany talks into the mirror at her reflection as she begins to dress. "Well, I certainly look the part. I'm definitely feeling the part, and I'm leaving here prepared for it. Bobby, no worries; I won't let you down." From the hallway, Lucky's meows are heard just as the tabby appears in the bedroom. Tiffany picks up the tabby, giving kisses on its nose. "Aw, was that your approval, Lucky? Thanks for your support! You're probably asking why you haven't been included in the audition bag with John's letter. Truth is, I'm very lucky to wake up to you every morning. I'm twice as lucky to have you meet me at the front door. I look forward to your purring for affection each time I return from work. How can one girl be so lucky?"

Bonk Bonk! Two short bursts from the taxi horn interrupts Tiffany's praise. Returning Lucky to the floor, she opens the living room window with an update. "No more worries; I'm walking out in twenty seconds!"

Hurrying to the wall mirror, Tiffany gives herself the once over. Her skin supple and smooth, with its natural glow, she appears to be ten years younger than the birthdate on her driver's license. Removing her shower cap, Tiffany works the hair mousse through to her scalp. Within moments, she's teased her hair into a French-fashioned tapered pageboy. With another glance in the mirror she brushes her eyebrows back in place. Satisfied with her appearance, Tiffany returns to the window with another update. "I'm walking out now!" As she collects her audition bag from the living room table, Tiffany pauses to give homage to the photos of actresses on the walls throughout her apartment: Marilyn Monroe, Ava Gardner, Sophia Loren, Raquel Welch, Lena Horne, and Lauren Bacall. Tiffany admits, "Ladies, much like yourselves, I'm not asking for anything other than a chance. I'm very grateful for the opportunity, and I give special thanks to every one of you for your inspiration. I can only imagine to have been there as a fly on the wall, as you remarkable women talked of your roles and the roads you traveled. Your accomplishments are immeasurable! You've all experienced the moment, the shine, and the awards. Speaking of which, today I received a special piece of what's wonderful in my life. I put it with my other piece of wonderful, and I'm fortunate to have both pieces at the same time: my John and Lucky!" Tiffany blows a kiss from her hand to the wall of photos, "Bye, girls!"

CHAPTER NINE

*H*urrying through the apartment complex, Tiffany comes upon a disagreement between two men in the apartment foyer, Donte, an African American male, and Paul, a white male several years Donte's senior. Although the trio was never formally introduced, Tiffany recognized Donte as a resident of the apartment complex. Privy to Trisha's unsolicited scrutiny, Tiffany's learned that during high school Trisha and Donte were best friends. Trisha was a member of the cheerleading squad. Donte wanted to be a cheerleader, but instead became the pep squad captain. Bar none, Trisha admitted, Donte out cheered and out danced both the pep and cheerleading squads combined. Tiffany surmised Paul as the male opposite Donte. According to Trish's intelligence, Paul is very married, extremely wealthy, and pays Donte's lease with a cashier's check every year.

With her presence not yet noticed, Tiffany witnesses Paul

postured to present a bouquet of flowers. Opposite Paul, Donte has his arms crossed in refusal of the gesture. He flickers and rolls his eyes upward toward the foyer's chandelier with exaggeration.

"Flowers? Are they being presented as something meaningful, Paul? I suppose you come wrapped with a cute ribbon with the bouquet as well?"

"Donte, this isn't the time for one of your vanity tantrums! A lot more's involved here than your self-centered issues. Do you really expect me to leave home and disregard the emotional attachments? Believe it or not, there's a grey sky for everyone involved here."

Donte places a hand to his mouth as though appalled. Continuing with the theatrics, he bats his eyes erratically, giving a light clap. "What do you mean now isn't the time? When might the right time be for Paul to leave? I'm confused! Will the timing ever be right? There's a sensitivity issue here, that's for sure, but now isn't the right time to deal with this?" Placing his hands on his hips, Donte snaps both fingers simultaneously. "Whatever happened to courageous Paul, the man I fell in love with? Where's the man that swept me off my feet? You're definitely not him! You've seem to have lost touch with our paradigm. Together in love! Paul, wasn't that our story?"

Tiffany forces a cough to make the couple aware of her presence. "Ahem! Excuse me, coming through!"

Paul breaks his focus from Donte to give a hesitant look to Tiffany. Awaiting Paul's response, Donte remains appalled with a hand covering his mouth.

Paul addresses Donte under his breath. "Please, don't go there. I neither respond nor react to pressure. I broker the deals, remember?"

Playing it off as if she hadn't witnessed what transpired, Tiffany quickly exits through the foyer's glass doors to enter the awaiting taxi. In her hurry, unknown to Tiffany, John's letter has fallen from her audition bag and remains in front of the apartment complex. The taxi pulls away. Within four blocks into the journey, Tiffany thinks aloud, realizing she hasn't given the driver a destination. "Excuse me, I didn't tell you where I was going!"

The taxi driver speaks into the rearview mirror. "I'm sorry I passed on the formalities. You were moving so fast, I didn't get a chance to assist you. Hello, Tiffany! I'm Chris. I'm told you have important business to handle before 12:30 p.m., and North Hollywood Studios is the place for you to be."

Tiffany does a mental rewind of Bobby's telephone call. "Oh, I'd forgotten. Bobby did mention something. You do know Bobby, right?"

Chris talks into the cab's rearview mirror. "Absolutely. We're lodge brothers."

Settling back into the rear seat, Tiffany interlocks her hands as if she were an obedient student sitting at a desk. "Okay, we're on our way; it's happening. Yay!"

Within another few blocks, the taxi comes to a stop, allowing a woman walking her dog to cross at the crosswalk. Chris directs a comment to the dog owner. "Beautiful Yorkie. He's what's called a teacup, right? What's his name?"

Strolling confidently, the dog's attractive owner wears designer tennis attire. She responds smiling beautifully. "His name's Randy, and he's the toy breed. Teacups are a little smaller; they're bred to be under seven pounds. How did you know he's a male?"

Chris offers, "He didn't squat. He raised his leg when marking his turf. I've raised dogs for years; believe me, it takes one to know one."

Chris is all smiles as he continues to watch the dog's attractive owner cross the intersection. From behind his dark glasses he gives a thumbs up. "Pretty lady, to both you and your nice dog! Enjoy the rest of your day." The cab proceeds on.

Chris directs his conversation into the rearview mirror. "Tiffany, wasn't that a beautiful dog?"

"Yes, it was very beautiful. I wonder how they ever came up with a breed that small."

"So do you own a dog, Tiffany?"

"No, I've always been lucky enough to have a cat."

Chris chuckles. "All righty! To the lady and her cat!" Repositioning the rearview mirror away from Tiffany, Chris adjusts the taxi's radio volume just enough for jazz to be heard. "Ms. Adams, enjoy the scenery. It's a nice day out; we should be at North Hollywood Studios in forty minutes."

During the scenic drive along Highland Avenue, Tiffany's mind raced in every direction. She's back and forth in her thoughts of John, Trisha, Bobby, the audition, and John's letter. Every scenario that led to the cab ride flashed in euphoric blur. The first to play out was John's conversation the weekend of his unexpected return to Fort Bragg.

"Tiffany, you won't believe what I happened upon through casual conversation. I've found the quaintest little church for the wedding. I'm sure you'll like it. While we're out this way, I'll drive by there on our way home. If it's to your liking, we'll make a payment to hold the date for our ceremony."

How could she ever forget that pleasant afternoon? With John every afternoon was just as pleasant. Since their last evening together, she's taped every *America's Best Performer* program for his return. Tiffany comes out of the scenario questioning, "John, when are you coming home? Lucky and I miss you."

The next voice in Tiffany's head belongs to the bearer of her good news, Trisha!

"You go girl; it's your lucky day. Well, what's he saying? You two have been living this *Officer and a Gentleman* movie for over a year. Tiffany, where's the audition? Okay, Dorothy, click your heels, and ease that boney ass on down the road and then handle your business, girl. You wanna thank me, hook me up with Mr. chocolatey sprinkles, ha hah!"

Bobby, Tiffany's agent, has the next rented space in her mind. In this scenario, Tiffany's reassured of her future. "Kid, we can't miss; this one's the windfall. After this read they'll circle like buzzards, trust me. You'll be booked tight for the next six months with no breaks between gigs. We'll put Japan on notice first. Beyond the rising sun will be requests across the globe for a world premiere."

Preoccupied with the scenarios, Tiffany has yet to notice

her arrival at her destination. The taxi driver's voice returns her from her haze of thoughts.

"Ms. Adams, North Hollywood Studios."

As Tiffany refocuses her mental direction, Chris stands at the rear passenger door to unload her audition gear. "Chris, thank you. I hadn't realized we arrived. My goodness, where'd the time go?" Tiffany reaches in her purse. "It was kind of you to wait at the apartment. Just a moment, my wallet's in the bottom of my purse."

Chris waves off the gesture. "Ms. Adams, that's not necessary. Bobby's taken care of everything. I can't accept your money. We're good. By the way, I heard you rehearsing your lines. Good luck! Well, you don't need any of that' you're ready. I listened to your rehearsal. You seem to know every character's dialogue. Ms. Adams, you've certainly done everything on your part. It's amazing! Whoever this John guy is, I hope he's as prepared as you are. If he isn't, you'll definitely embarrass him. Good luck to you both."

Blushing with the compliment, Tiffany nervously smooths her eyebrows into place. "My goodness, what did you hear? I hope I haven't embarrassed myself."

Chris shuts the cab's rear door. "No way. The way I heard it, my understanding in listening to you rehearse, Ms. Adams, you've come prepared. Truthfully, had you not auditioned, it would have been a miscarriage of talent. Bobby said the right words when he spoke about you. You're definitely a natural."

Chris returned to the driver's seat with the reassurance, "Ms. Adams, handle your business in there; you're ready!"

The taxi drives off. Tiffany doesn't enter the studio until the taxi drives out of sight. She acknowledges under her breath, "Bobby, thanks for everything, and thank you, Chris, for those kind words."

CHAPTER TEN

At 12:20 p.m., Tiffany walks into the vestibule of North Hollywood Studios. Before entering into the lobby's electrifying atmosphere, she stands momentarily to take in what's before her. Immediately noticed are the different circles of actresses who have strategically placed themselves with the hopes of being noticed by the industry's movers and shakers. In the unspoken mind of every actress or groupie, there's a silent prayer for an edge, perhaps a callback for a private read with the director for a one-on-one exclusive behind closed doors. As the actresses speak among themselves, every ear listens attentively for her audition number to be announced. Recognizing familiar faces, several actresses are heard wishing the best for others, offering affable smiles and high-fived blessings of good fortune. In spite of the gestures of camaraderie, when an actress is called to read, she competes to be cast for a role; therefore it's every woman for herself. As Tiffany proceeds

around the different circles of contestants, she gets a lesson on genuine congeniality.

In this instance an actress waves excitedly for another's attention. "Is that you, Samantha?

"Hey, Sandy! Long time no see. How long has it been? I was just asking about you. After your read let's hang out for a while. We'll have to bring each other current on what's been happening in our lives. Smooches!"

With Samantha on her way, Sandy mumbles within her circle of friends, "Oh, my god! Is she auditioning with those terrible hair extensions? She looks like the alien in *The Predator* movie. Was Samantha authentic or what? She definitely earned that star on Hollywood Boulevard for this one."

Another actress comments, "I hope the director paid his health premiums; if not, it'll be ugly. He's likely to have a heart attack when she steps into the audition room. Who would weave something like that in their hair? She looked like she had a hyena sewn in her head."

Snickering laughter's heard within the group.

In a different circle another scene plays out. One member of a group acknowledges an actress within another party. "Wendy? I see you made it. Wow, I thought we were riding together. When you didn't call back, I made other arrangements."

"Arlene, yeah, sorry about the miscue. My cell phone battery went dead. I had to recharge it, and you had already left by then. Have you been called to read yet?"

Ignoring Wendy, Arlene gossips within her circle, "What a real live skank! What she did do was turn a few dozen tricks to pay her phone bill. No doubt she took a whore's bath in the sink afterwards, before turning another trick, so she could be dropped off here. Believe me, I know Wendy. As I speak she's looking for another trick to ensure she'll have a nasty ride home. It amazes me how low a desperate skank will go to get ahead. Well, since we all know what not to do. Remember, ladies, protect yourselves at all times, and never leave a trail of condoms to the guilty. In this industry people will pillow talk with you at night, just so that they can testify against you in the morning. Poor Wendy should have learned that by now."

Patiently continuing through the crowded lobby, Tiffany comes upon the line leading to the ladies room. As she awaits her place in line, she overhears a conversation between actresses.

"Hi, I remember you. Didn't you read for the role of *Twisted Sist*er?"

"Um—which role?"

"*Twisted Sist*er. I was standing behind you as you were called to read. Were you cast for that part?"

"I do remember. She was the dope fiend sister who ran away from home to join a convent. She kicked clean from heroin and changed her life around. She went on to become the mother superior and cleaned up the neighborhood, right? That one was a goody. Did you read for that too?"

"I did, but what a perfect role it became for you; you nailed it. How did you prepare for your lines? You were so relaxed, I hope I'm called before your read for this role. Good luck!"

With praise comes the scandal.

"Did you hear that bitch? 'What a goody!' What da fuck is

that supposed to mean, and who in the hell is she supposed to be? She pulled a role out the air like she's chewing bubble gum. Fucking bitch, who does she think she is?"

Laughter comes from within the circle of scandal. During the same time, the awaiting line to the ladies room moves ahead. Tiffany overhears another group in conversation as they exit the ladies room.

"Christie? Has it been that long?"

"Geez, how time flies when you're busy! When I heard you were reading for the role, I wasn't surprised. Really, Christie, I've seen a lot of your work."

"Thanks, Jenny. I've worked my ass off for years. Being out of the country for so long, it's about time for a reward here and there. Call me! I mean it Jen; maybe we can put a lil' something together to get you going."

Jenny forces a smile. "Christie, really? Wow, is next week good for you? I can't believe this! They say everything happens for a reason. Truthfully, I had passed on this audition because it was a last-minute thing, but my agent talked me into going for it. So yeah, Christie, Tuesday is a good day for me. You know that saying, 'iron sharpens iron.' I'll be there; let's do it Tuesday."

As the two circles continue beyond the awaiting line, Tiffany overhears Jenny's reaction.

"Can you believe that high-powered bitch? She's surprised she got the part? Surprised my ass! I'd be surprised if there weren't a cast member she didn't screw in all the movie sets she's worked. Will there ever be any shame in that whore's heart?"

Jenny's friend chimes in, "Tell me about it. To a degree we're all guilty. I'm sure that starting out, who hasn't buffed a few helmets here and there? But to sleep with the same person twice after landing the role, it's against the code totally!" Laughter's heard within the group.

Reacting from the candid small talk, Tiffany avoids eye contact with the other actresses. Flush with embarrassment, she removes herself from the line to the ladies room. Attempting to block out the surrounding negativity, Tiffany hums a melody as she walks toward the studio's casting receptionist.

"Hi there, I'm Tiffany Adams, I'd like to check in. My agent, Bob Smithers, rescheduled my read to a much earlier time, from three o'clock to one."

The casting receptionist refers to the list of names and read times. "Ah, there you are, Tiffany Adams. Thanks for checking in on time. Here's your audition number. Simply peel the number off and place it on your lovely blouse." She admits, "You have quite the charmer for an agent, young lady. Is Bob showing up today?"

Tiffany answers, "I certainly hope so."

The receptionist continues admiring Tiffany's blouse. "Chiffon's one of my favorite fabrics, and you've matched your blouse perfectly with your pearls. Remember, young lady, when it's time for your read, you're doing what you prepared yourself to do. That gives you twelve minutes. Good luck."

Tiffany responds excitedly, "Thanks; I should get going. I'll need to find a cubbyhole to rehearse my lines." Tiffany steps away from the reception table to look around the crowded venue for an area to focus. Before going into character, she removes the script to articulate the dialogue. For every few lines she reads, Tiffany closes her eyes to recite them from memory. As she comes out of dialogue, her eyes open to an image of a man twirling a cigar.

He exhales a smoke cloud toward the ceiling. Had he been critiquing Tiffany, he revealed neither admiration nor contempt in her performance. With his arms folded comfortably, he appeared to be in thought. Abruptly the cigar twirling stops. As though to have found sound reasoning, he resumes to puff his cigar to exhale smoke rings. "Perfect! You delivered a perfect read."

"Excuse me, were you talking to me?" Tiffany questions.

The cigar twirling man continues, "The role you're rehearsing for, it's perfect for you." He remains in his comfortable posture, and the twirling of the cigar resumes with more smoke rings.

Uncomfortable with the unsolicited criticism. Tiffany's perplexed expression telegraphs her next words. "What, who are you supposed to…"

"That was a good read. You're perfect for it. If you deliver the same energy when you're called, the role's yours." He exhales cigar smoke. "Trust me, if you're able to stay relaxed as you are here, you'll take the role."

Tiffany's voice rises to question, "How do you know what will happen? What are you saying? Who are you?"

With his arms now folded across his chest, the cigar twirl continues with a smile. "Hey, kid, it's not like that. Every so often I come out for a smoke break. From time to time an actress will rehearse in the same spot you're rehearsing in now. I'm merely enjoying the goings-on with a cigar. Believe me, young lady, there's nothing else behind it." He looks to his watch. "The next read's at one o'clock. Going by your audition number, that makes you one of the next reads. That's ten minutes from now. Remember, deliver in the audition room in the same manner you delivered here." Exhaling cigar smoke, he offers a reassuring wink. "Stay relaxed and deliver your performance. I'll be seated in the director's chair. Good luck!" In his return to the audition room, the cigar smoking man whistles to the tune of "Strangers in the Night."

Tiffany self-consciously questions, "Was he eyeing anything exposed?" Covering her breasts she feels at the buttons on her blouse. Using both hands, Tiffany flat irons her skirt in hopes it hadn't crawled. Satisfied there's nothing to be embarrassed about, Tiffany retrieves a mirror from her vanity case. She looks over her appearance, scoffing at the bizarre encounter. "Director? Yeah, right, then what was he looking over here for? The studio's full of groupies; they're not hard to find. Everything in a groupie he would ever want is here. Walk by the line at the ladies room, buddy; listen to those accolades. I'm guessing he thinks he impressed me with his nonsense. What a pervert! I can imagine what he thought was perfect. Who other than a groupie would fall for those corny lines? Give me a break!"

Tiffany stops her rant momentarily to note the lobby wall clock. It appears animated, as if to become larger. She further frustrates herself to rant, "Five minutes until the read. Ha. Am I to be impressed with that one, buddy? Even the receptionist knew what time the read starts." Returning the vanity case to her purse, Tiffany raises an eyebrow to dissect the cigar-smoking man's conversation. "Until you get what you want, I'm sure you'll be willing to do a lot more than talk. How many others have been perfect for the role? Geez, how many times have I heard that? Which was perfect, my skirt or blouse? He gave me the creeps is what he did." Covering her mouth to control her outburst, Tiffany looks over the congested lobby to admit, "Listen to me. I've gotten so carried away I sound like the rest of the monsters here."

Redirecting her thoughts toward meditation, Tiffany closes her eyes to focus. Unable to go into her character's dialogue, she breaks from meditation to whine, "John, I brought you here today for support, and now I can't think clearly. I'm getting my character's lines confused with your letter. My goodness, John! Whoever thought hearing from you would work against me?" Closing her eyes, Tiffany collects herself to count to ten. She exhales with her characters dialogue.

"Harold? Please don't equate the time we've known each other as a bargaining tool against the virtues of my chastity. Clearing the air of any confusing thoughts that may have misled you, there's no possibility of us ever sleeping together. I'm not for sale. I will admit your proposal was beautiful; however, I cannot accept. Your beautiful ring should be given to someone with the luster in her heart that the ring clearly exudes. Harold, that special woman's out there waiting for that special someone, and hopefully you'll find each other…"

Tiffany breaks from character. "John, this isn't fair! You're keeping me from concentrating, I can't think about anything but you and our days together." Tiffany acknowledges, "I'll reread John's letter. Focusing on something nice will take the edge off." With the opening of her hand, Tiffany allows the script to float to the floor. She self-talks while rummaging through her audition bag. "John's letter will release this anxiety instantly. I need to feel his words to get through this." Contrary to Tiffany's expectations, John's letter is not among the bag's contents. Becoming impatient, she empties the contents onto the lobby's floor to search the audition bag's compartments.

"Where did I put you? You were just here. How do you expect me to react, John? We haven't talked for six months, since that unexpected phone call rushed you to the airport. Today I received your letter, and now I'm right in the middle of an audition. John, I'm completely overwhelmed! Is this what two people being in love feels like?" Returning the contents to her audition bag, Tiffany exhales frustrated.

"This isn't fair! There's just too much going on, with your unexpected arrivals and departures. John, where are you?"

With her audition bag in tow, Tiffany maneuvers through the crowd to re-walk her studio entrance, but the letter is nowhere to be found. The frustration returns her to the awaiting line to the ladies room, where she canvasses the sections of groupies and actresses. Nothing! Meandering through the crowd with no direction, Tiffany exits the studio to revisit the cab's drop-off point. Re-entering the studio, she asks for directions to the dressing room. In her confused state of mind, Tiffany overlooks the logic that she never entered the studio's dressing room upon her arrival. She makes an inquiry of the dressing room occupants. "Hello? I've misplaced a very important letter. Has anyone here found or seen a white envelope?" The occupants shake their heads to the negative.

During the same time, the casting assistant makes an announcement via the studio's speaker system: "Casting number eight! Tiffany Adams, first read."

Hearing her name announced, Tiffany freezes momentarily. "They're calling me! Surely someone in this room may have seen the envelope I misplaced?"

The casting assistant's voice interrupts. "Second call! Casting number eight, Tiffany Adams, first read."

The dressing room occupants continue to go about their wardrobe change in silence. Tiffany's frustration returns her to the lobby's congested shark tank. She's now back in the midst of everything that makes her uncomfortable: groupies and actresses positioned with audition numbers to where they want the eyes of the director focused. Every actress or groupie receives an audition number. The significance of where the numbers are placed matters most to the less talented. Worn shamelessly, blouses have numbers positioned to reveal inviting cleavage on flawless boob enhancements. Speckled here and there, several are glued on midsections above tight-fitting Daisy Duke shorts, leaving nothing to the imagination toward the deeply revealed camel toe. Within earshot, a Barbara Eden-look-alike shows off her new bubble butt, which happens to be the latest gift from the married doctor. As she poses to reveal her latest asset, her very visible G-string is seen through the sheer material of her *I Dream of Jeannie* ensemble. In her creative resourcefulness, her audition number has been placed across the small of her back to direct attention to the silhouette of her perfect bubble butt. Appreciative of her good fortune, she shares openly with the have-nots around her. "Being wealthy, he's able to afford everything he wants, and he gives really nice gifts. Neither I nor his wife complains about the arrangement. Everyone's happy! I never knew having a bubble butt would complete my life to such a degree. My popularity is now off the charts. I'm noticed doing the simplest of things, like conveniently washing my car, and do I relish the attention! Out of nowhere, college guys are constantly inviting me to their frat parties. Before the bubble ass, I never had college guys coming on to me. So there you have it. Mine is a living testimony, ladies. Having a bubble ass definitely opens a lot of doors. I don't know why I waited so long. Had I known, I would have gotten the bubble ass with my boobs fifteen years ago."

The lobby's electrifying ambience changes immediately with Tiffany's anxiety. As she makes her way toward the audition room, facial expressions quickly form to mouthed reactions of "WHAT?"

In her bolt past the lobby fountain, a group of actresses react with ridicule. One actress who happens to be chewing gum blows a bubble. When it pops she signifies, "You're going the wrong way, honey. Poor girl, it must be her first audition. No worries for the Sunday school teacher's role! Believe me, Pauli

Pure-bred, won't anyone here fight you for that one; you're a shoe in!"

Snickering high-fives are exchanged within the group. The next actress to comment has a nasal New York accent. Placing a cigarette to her mouth she signifies, "It's probably the pressha! Someone promised her a SAG cawd, and after all the 'head and quickies' in the broom closet, she's found out it's a fake." Laughter explodes.

The next offered synopsis comes from a Shirley Temple look alike. She twists a golden lock of hair with her forefinger. "I've seen this reaction before; it's the Xanax wearing off. Poor girl; she should have chased it with espresso shots. My grandpa gave Xanax to my brother to punish him whenever he pissed the bed. It made him so drowsy, he would have to lie in his piss puddle until the next morning. Then grandpa would kick my brother's ass for trying to hide his pissy blankets during the night."

Faces within the group look to the Shirley Temple look alike in awed silence. The silence ends with Shirley Temple blowing another bubble until it pops.

Shortly thereafter, the casting assistant's plea is heard throughout the studio. "Casting number eight, Tiffany Adams, last call! Please report to the audition room."

Tiffany works her way through the lobby's contestants toward the request. "They're calling my number! Sorry, excuse me, can I get by please? I'm coming!"

"Last call, Tiffany Adams!"

Movement within the crowd brings forth Tiffany's voice,

"I'm trying to get there! Excuse me, coming through!"

Within several moments, the casting assistant makes another announcement. "Casting number nine, Cathy Ogolsbie, first read."

From within a circle of contestants comes the triumphant yell of "Whoa, yeah, baby!"

Several seconds later, an actress sashays across the lobby to make her bid for the role. Within moments the casting assistant's instructive voice is heard from the audition room, "Five, four, three, two, one, read."

As soon as contestant number nine stepped into the audition room, her presence within her circle of friends was already forgotten. The lobby's electrifying buzz resumed with the never-ending drama among actresses and groupies. Witnessing the window of opportunity closing before her, a distressed Tiffany walks hurriedly toward the exit. As the crowd parts way, Tiffany's anxiety forces her to cover her face. Tiffany's screeching voice breaks the silence. "John, my god, what have I done with you? I need you! Where are you, John? I can't get through this without you. Excuse me...coming through! Sorry. Thank you. Can I squeeze by, please?"

The lobby's commotion has brought the director and casting assistant from the audition room. Witnessing the distressed woman work her way through the sea of actresses, the casting assistant talks while gesturing with his hands. "What the fuck was that? A meltdown and a brain fart together? Look at her audition number. She's number eight. She doesn't respond for her read, but here she's running through the studio like someone shot a freaking starter's pistol. Where in the hell is she going? Maybe we should have made an international language announcement. Un-freaking believable!"

Removing a cigar from the breast pocket of his suit, the director twirls it in thought. He supports his left elbow by resting it on top of his right hand. "Where in the hell is she going? Vladimir, I've asked myself the same question. Do a good public service announcement for the film. Reference her cast number and contact her agent. She's the one we've been waiting for."

Vladimir questions quizzically, "You're suggesting I locate that atrocity? She's a screaming banshee is what she is. She turned down the role to scream for the leading man from who knows where. I'm sorry, the request for her is undoable. It's totally despicable."

Tiffany continues screeching in her flight, summoning a man who has yet been seen or heard. "John, you can't write after six months and then disappear in the same day. I can't wait for another letter. I need you. No one has seen you anywhere. John, I'm not ready without you. I can't think straight. How am I to get through this without you?"

The distressed woman before them wears a very nice white ensemble with pearl earrings. In her flight, her distressed voice is heard while her body appears to run in an encapsulated bubble. In astonished silence the sea of actresses look at what's before them.

The director continues with the twirl of his cigar. "As the casting director, Vladimir, I feel the request is very doable. She's exactly the energy we want for the role. She has everything, and everything we're looking for in an actress is leaving the building with her. Have you witnessed anyone here deliver the energy she has?"

"Yes I have! I meant no sir, I haven't until you mentioned it."

CHAPTER ELEVEN

*K*elly walks her Yorkie terrier through a neighborhood of richly green manicured lawns. In the midst of making his territorial rounds to sniff and scent mark, the toy dog strains against its leash. Going from tree to bush before stopping at an apartment complex, it poops in the grass parkway. Within the same time, two kids wearing backpacks approach from the rear. To allow the toy dog to relieve itself, the backpack duo steps off the sidewalk onto the curb area of the street. As the duo passes, one kid flows a rap beat while the other flows its catchy lyrics.

As her dog finishes with its pooping business, Kelly maintains its leash with one hand. Using the opposite hand she retrieves the poop, giving praise. "Mommy's Randy has done it outside again? What a good boy you are! You're such a good Randy for Mommy." During the time Kelly retrieves its poop, Randy stands on the curb to sniff and bark at a letter lying on the street surface.

"Randy? What's Mommy's little boy fussing over?" Being naturally high strung, the Yorkie whips its stubby tail frantically. Barking excitedly, the toy dog strains at its leash to get to the letter. Kelly animates her voice with praise. "Wandy's excited. Has Mommy's Wandy found something? You're such a good Wandy for Mommy." Kelly retrieves the letter from the street surface rationalizing, "One of those kids may have dropped their letter." She yells to the duo ahead of her, "Hello, guys, I believe one of you may have dropped something."

Being fully absorbed in their hip-hop aspirations, neither person in the duo responds. Since bypassing Kelly and Randy, the backpack duo is in the midst of giving an excellent performance to an imaginary audience. Without breaking the rhythm in either's stride, the duo crosses from one side of the street to the other to trade off mimicked microphone performances. Just as her effort to return the letter goes unacknowledged, Kelly recognizes the letter's distinguished fragrance. It's unmistakably one of her favorite designers in men's cologne. Kelly's infatuated with the fragrance to the point that it would be recognized from the grave. She opens the letter teasingly. Within moments, she's consumed in reading someone else's business. Randy meanwhile continues in perky vigor to sniff at selected areas to scent mark.

The sound of music diverts Kelly's attention from the letter. To her surprise, Randy's patrol has returned them in the midst of the backpack duo that performs street side to an audience of three girls. The duo flows lyrics to music from a parked car in the driveway of a residence. Kelly declined offering the letter, concluding the writer overshadowed any lyrics the duo could express convincingly in relation to a monogamous relationship. True, hip-hop told its story with rhyme and reason. What the letters writer expressed was beautiful poetry, and he expressed himself without the record sampling and drum machines. He was expressing his love to a woman from far away seemingly, and the music he used to convey his feelings were the words themselves. The way he put together what he was saying was off the charts.

A woman's admonishing voice disturbs Kelly's processing. "Raymond! Boy, turn that damn music down in my car!"

The middle-aged woman has witnessed five kids dancing and flowing hip-hop lyrics in front of her residence. Not impressed with their street-side performance, she directs her attention to a Chrysler parked in the driveway of her home. "Did you hear what I said, Raymond? Turn my car stereo down."

As the backpack duo delivers its flow, the car's occupant prepares to present the rap's hook. Unknown to him, the resident's owner has stepped off her porch to get the occupants' undivided attention. She yells toward the direction of the car. "Boy, turn that damn music down!"

The street-side performance comes to a stop. The hip-hop kids acknowledge the woman's presence with a simultaneous greeting. "Hello, Ms. Cranberry."

The car's occupant becomes aware of the imposing presence, only after the group no longer dances to the tune of the car stereo. He turns the radio volume down immediately. "Hi, Mom!"

"Hi mom? Boy, don't play my car stereo that loud, and stop beating on my dashboard like you're playing a damn instrument." Ms. Cranberry directs her attention to the group. "Don't you kids sass me none either. Why aren't any of you at home with your families? Out here doing the devil's work is what you're doing, bringing nothing but shame to your parents, especially you young girls. Just carefree and happy with nothing to do, giving your lives to the devil is what you're doing. When was the last time any of you went to church?" Ms. Cranberry directs her comments to the car's occupant. "Raymond, you should know better than anybody. Get your big lazy butt in the house and mop that nasty floor in your bedroom! I shouldn't have to tell you how to live clean. As big as you are, I never have to tell you twice when to eat, now, do I?"

Laughter explodes from the street. Ms. Cranberry speaks over the ruckus. "Raymond, move your big butt! You're out here with that nonsense talk, beating on my dashboard like you have nothing else to do. I'll tell you what potty mouth; you come inside and clean every toilet in this house."

Raymond's friends reiterate Ms. Cranberry's mandate. "Mop your nasty floor and clean the toilets, Raymond!"

Disinclined to follow the request, Raymond exits the Chrysler shrugging his shoulders. "Dang, Mama! Do you have to go big on me in front of my friends?"

Ms. Cranberry walks inside her residence continuing with the admonishment of her son. "Boy, who do you think you're questioning? Get your big ass in this house and don't knock over my juice with those funky feet of yours. Where's your mind, Raymond? You're out there running my car battery down playing that damn sinful music, when you know I need my battery to start my car for church in the morning."

Raymond's friends remind him of their presence with a heckling chorus. "Get your big ass in the house and clean those toilets, Raymond!"

Obediently Raymond walks up to the residence porch. From under his breath a sigh is slightly heard. "Damn!"

Ms. Cranberry's admonishing voice is heard from inside the residence. "I heard that, Raymond! Keep up that sass talk, and you'll be in one of those boys' homes! Then you'll be around kids like the ones you're beating on my dashboard talking that trash talk about. I never allowed you to talk like that. You weren't raised that way, Raymond. Whenever you weren't in church with me, you were definitely in church service with your grandmother. You've been going to church since you were born, so cut out all that rappin' and foolishness of having another life! The Lord's Prayer will give you all the strength you need. Come in here and recite it before you start working. Don't let anybody steer you wrong, Raymond; you've always been a good child. In the morning we'll sit together during church service. Right after bible study, you and I will have a long talk with the youth minister. Mark my words. You'll follow the good Lord or you'll find somewhere else to live. As God is my witness, you know I didn't raise any fools in this house, Raymond."

Raymond shrugs his shoulders, abandoning the thought of remaining with his friends. "Moms is going big. She's on one!

She's all turned up over the big revival the church is having next week. I still wanna flow that hook; it's tight. So I'll have to get back with y'all after next week with the beats."

Reluctantly Raymond walks inside the residence, leaving Ms. Cranberry's Masons jar on the porch. Being cleverly entertained by the hip-hop kids, and to have witnessed the scene at the Cranberry residence, Kelly is all smiles. Continuing her walk, she resumes reading the letter as Randy pulls and strains at the leash. Randy's discovery quickly becomes Kelly's good fortune. Kelly reacts to a hot flash, fanning her face. "This man is truly amazing. Mister, the way you talk and how you put it together, I'll have to sit on a block of ice until I'm able to think straight." After having her moment, Kelly continues to delve into someone else's business.

Hello baby!

There are no excuses for not writing or calling sooner, but please know I have thought about you every time my eyes have blinked. As I struggle without you, my days here are the complete opposite from where you are with yours. I love you. Please accept my apologies for not acting on my thoughts to just up and quit my post and fly home to be with you forever. Damn, I miss you!

Held captive by her infatuation, Kelly closes her eyes to rationalize. "I can't stop reading. There's fire and passion all through it, and he even used a few metaphors to turn the wheels.

Who gave this man all the right words? He's so expressive with emotion." Kelly looks to the sky. "It would indeed be heavenly to recreate my husband to communicate like this. Should I have enough time during the span of my life, please accept my prayers for my husband's head and mindset to be the next place for divine intervention." Kelly opens her eyes to realize Randy's patrol has returned them home. "Oh lookee; Mommy's Wandy's brought us home safe already, and Mommy wasn't paying any attention. Thank you, Mommy's Wandy! Mommy's so happy she has her Wandy to help her." Continuing to her residence door, Kelly immerses herself in the letter again without realizing it.

She inserts her door key, only after Randy's bark returns her from the letter's transfixed effect. Bending at the knees, Kelly unsnaps the leash to reward Randy's ego.

"Aw, somebody's jealous? Don't worry; Mommy still wuvs her Wandy. You're Mommy's little boiee! Mommy will always wuv her some Wandy. Wanna eat-eat? Your mommy has something nice for him. Does Mommy's Wandy wanna eat eat?"

Kelly rises to continue Randy's reward to the kitchen's pantry. The Yorkie prances excitedly in side-to-side motions as it follows Kelly, in anticipation of the half scoop of Premium Plentiful for its meal. Finished with Randy, Kelly walks to her desk. She contemplates resealing the letter and mailing it to the intended address or doing otherwise.

Kelly reasons, "Wow, this address is close by. I'll leave it in the residence mailbox the next time I walk Randy. That would be the right thing to do, no questions asked.

I've righted my wrong, and everybody's happy again." Kelly scrutinizes the letter's addressee. "Tiffany Adams? No, I definitely don't know her. Since she lives so close, I can't risk being seen returning her mail. She'll know for sure it's been read. No way! I'll take it to the grave before admitting I illegally opened and read someone else's mail." Foregoing the risk of embarrassment, Kelly chooses her first option. Intending to be politically correct, she removes an envelope from the desk to rewrite the address. "I'll simply put it inside another envelope and mail it after I finish reading it." The writer's magnetism has rekindled the romantic fire within Kelly. In an afterthought she clears her conscience. "Though it's difficult to admit, Tiffany's letter has passion's fire blazing for my husband. I never imagined expressions from a stranger would be so therapeutic for my relationship, so this is difficult to accept for anything other than what it is, another woman's letter. It's not like the letter is written to me, and neither will I beat myself up with guilt. I haven't done anything to jeopardize my husband's trust. After ten years of blissful marriage, I still love Paul unconditionally. Since reading Tiffany's letter, I appreciate him even more, so don't judge. I'm just making the necessary adjustments to turn up the fire. Thank you very much for the clarity, Kelly." She chuckled at her rationale.

Kelly displays her elegant wedding ring. By turning her hand, she allows the light's reflection to dance off the ring's brilliant facets. Marveling at the impressive six-and-a-half-carat princess cut stone, Kelly feels at the twenty-carat necklace at her neckline to admit, "Pieces like these speak for themselves. Everything a man wants to say to a woman has been said." Kelly plans for the evening ahead with a thought.

"Tonight Paul and I are going to have a nice comfortable evening at home. When he walks through the door, his favorite dish will be waiting for him. He'll be so excited, no doubt he'll want to thank me. I'll be conveniently in the bedroom styling my hair while wearing my sexy lingerie. Scented candles will be placed everywhere in the house to create the perfect ambience. We'll have so much fun; I can't wait for Paul to get here. We'll drink wine and listen to love songs before I give him a striptease. Paul will really love that; he should! Every pole dance class I ever enrolled in is payoff in our bedroom tonight. Yes, he'll definitely be entertained, and then I'll go to him and ask for what we both want. We'll knock boots like teenagers tonight."

Kelly relaxes in the Jacuzzi while listening to one of her favorite R&B artists. While enjoying the near darkness of the bathroom, she takes in the aroma and glow of cupcake candles. As she sips wine, a half-empty wine bottle rests on the floor among white rose petals. In her thoughts, Kelly has definitely created the perfect ambience she envisioned for their evening. Within her sanctum of wine and candles, Kelly has read the letter repeatedly. Each time she finds more fuel for her desire to pole dance for her husband. In her return from fantasizing of what lies ahead, Kelly rests the letter against the tub base to sing along with the R&B artist.

Who needs to stress at work
To grind it out for another dollar?
When I spend time with you,
Every day shines bright with hope,
Like fresh exotic flowers.
True love is our bet, and aren't you glad
That we are winning?
We hardly fuss and fight, our fit is right,
With us there's no pretending.
It's real, our love,
A day without you in my life
Is much too much.
We'll both pray it never stops.
Oh my love...

Reaching to the Jacuzzi's rim for her wine glass, Kelly sips the sweet nectar, transfixed within the dancing flames of the cupcake candles. Nearby, Randy takes in the bathroom's ambience from the floor. Kelly looks to her Yorkie, smiling.

"See how good Wandy's made Mommy feel? Wandy's found Mommy and Daddy more happy. You're such a good boy! Daddy will be home shortly, and Mommy's going to make him some happy too, thanks to our little man. I'll be sure to tell Daddy what Wandy found us."

Kelly smooches her lips to blow Randy a kiss. "Thank you, Wandy! With a sip of wine, Kelly sings along with the R&B artist.

With our love, a day without you from the start
Is much too much.
Together we'll pray it never stops,
Our sweet love.

CHAPTER TWELVE

*G*wyneth is penciling in the daily crossword puzzle when the phone rings in her office. She answers the call talking through the speaker phone. "Unspoken Matters, can I help you?"

The caller questions, "Is Paul available? I was directed to your company as a referral, with the understanding Paul would help me with my credit situation."

"I'm sorry, Paul's not in the office at this time, but he does check his messages throughout the day. Would you like for me to connect you to his voice mail?"

The caller continues, "Because of my circumstance, my credit's shot. I don't have a callback number to leave. I'm unable to qualify for a house phone, cell phone, or any other means of communication; that's why I'm calling you. Is there a supervisor available to explain your credit-repair process?"

"You're speaking with Gwyneth Buchanan, the office

manager. Our company policy requires an office visit for your initial consultation. With respect to confidentiality, Unspoken Matters will not disclose its process over the phone. We offer office consultation visits on either Tuesday or Thursday from one to four p.m."

"Okay, one-thirty Thursday is good for me. I'm traveling from Agoura Hills, which is a forty-mile trip one way. Before I invest the time and mileage, I would like to know if I meet the criteria. Is it possible to speak with someone at the next executive level?"

Gwyneth declines respectfully. "I'm sorry; you'll have to speak with Paul initially for your consultation. His discretion dictates how your case will be assigned to a credit specialist."

Meanwhile in close proximity to the call, Danny Jenkins sits comfortably reclined in an office chair. He challenges his motor skills playing a videogame on the wall-mounted television. Between maneuvers, he over hears Gwyneth's conversation in the adjoining office. Danny pushes a button on the phone to include himself in conference call. "Hello, Daniel Jenkins speaking. Your call has been forwarded for executive direction. I understand you've spoken with our intake manager, and you may have a few unanswered questions. Being at the next executive tier in this corporation, I'm afforded latitude and flexibility when dealing with the delicate intricacies of Unspoken Matters. May I ask with whom I have the pleasure of speaking?" Awaiting the caller, Danny removes the Ruben's cube from the elaborate desk to quickly align the correct sequence.

"Mr. Jenkins, good morning, my name is Karrie Washington."

Danny quickly straightens up in the chair to acknowledge, "Damn, is that right, like the actress, Cary Washington?"

"Mr. Jenkins, excuse me. I'm not following where you're going with this."

"Uh, pardon me, Ms. Washington, and I can clear that up." Danny continues with the video game. "What I meant to say was is that spelled with the letter C or K? I'm merely ascertaining with whom I'm talking. Please be advised, this company will never judge any of our perspective clients. Now back to the question at hand, if your name's spelled with that expensive letter K, that's cool. Know what I'm saying? Shoot! With Karrie Washington's money, why bother with credit? You can buy any damn thing you want and still have room to throw a little sumpin' sumpin' to the next man.

"A lil' help is always appreciated. Look at it as helping out the less fortunate; ha hah, yes, that would definitely be me." After the wrong move with the videogame, Danny has a slip of the tongue. "Now I'm really out here fucking up! Uh, excuse me, I got carried away. I was handling other business at the same time." Danny clears his throat. "Ahem! Now back to the professional I'm known for. Okay, here we go. Unspoken Matters. It goes without saying, send it, and Danny will help you spend it. Know what I'm saying? And no worries; this entitles you to have it exclusively your way, every day, all day. Danny performs willingly whatever requests you send his way, and for the record, as long as you're willing to pay, the kid is definitely good at what he does."

Danny looks at Gwyneth with a wink. "Tell me, Ms. Washington, have you ever heard game spit like this? We are talking Unspoken Matters, so take your time answering. There's definitely a shock value included with this here. With that in mind, I'll let you have a moment without the brain freeze."

Uncomfortable with Danny's unprofessionalism, the caller responds after a moment of awkward silence. "Excuse me, Mr. Jenkins. I didn't grasp any of what you've just mentioned."

Danny backtracks, explaining his humor. "Oh, no no, no, no pun intended. What I meant to say Ms. Washington, was how is your name spelled? Is it with the letter C or the letter K?"

"Mr. Jenkins, to sort out any confusion, its Mrs. Washington and with the letter K, as in K-a-r-r-i-e."

Seated in the executive chair, Danny uses his feet to spin the chair into rotation. After several spins, the chair returns to the point where it began. Danny looks to the office wall using his best friend's wedding photo to fuel his wit. "Marital bliss. Absolutely, Mrs. Washington. My wife and I have also enjoyed a dream marriage for twelve years, and that's without any medications, not even Viagra. Nope, if we remarried today, we wouldn't do anything different. Ha hah, I'd say we've been working it pretty well, yes sir."

"Kudos on your marriage, Mr. Jenkins, but does your company have a rating with the Better Business Bureau?"

Gwyneth shakes her head in disbelief. "You do know Paul will kill you for this."

Danny dismisses the threat with a roll of his eyes. The

call continues. "Our company's rating? Well, you certainly were the one doing the calling, weren't you? Didn't nobody steer you wrong, and you've definitely come to the right place. Unspoken Matters; that's the business. We don't speak on anything else, just come with it, and we'll handle it. That's how we get down around here. Good money in place gets bad credit erased absolutely."

Danny looks at Gwyneth, offering a wink. "I'll tell you what, Mrs. Washington, you come on Thursday at say one-thirty, and bring either cash or your checkbook. Be advised, we run every check through Tele-check, so don't half-step with excuses. We keep it professional around here. Know what I'm saying? And don't even think about using a credit card. That's the very reason you were referred to us. We'll repair your good name for a small fee of three hundred dollars per line of deletion. Here the game is sold, not told. You'll have to come in for consultation for the rest of the business. Pardon the expression, but we handle what others can't. Unspoken Matters, you dig?"

There's momentary silence before the caller responds disbelievingly. "Mr. Jenkins, what did you just say? You lost me."

To offset the caller's irritation, Danny clears his throat. "Ahem!"

Gwyneth shakes her head with disbelief. "Danny, you don't know who you're talking to, and you're going to jail."

Danny waves Gwyneth away dismissively. "Mrs. Washington, out of nowhere I was called for direction on another line, and we seem to be experiencing technical difficulties at this time. So yes, as we've discussed, one-thirty Thursday would be your initial consultation. I'll have the intake receptionist pencil you in as we speak. Are there any other unanswered questions I can assist you with?"

"Yes, you didn't mention whether your company's fees were negotiable."

Danny sips from a soda can using a straw. Meanwhile the slurping suction is heard through the phone.

Danny continues matter-of-factly, "Damn, listen to you whine! Your credit's jacked up and you want to negotiate the fees too? You might as well ask for that slurping sound leaving the soda can. You sure can be frugal when you wanna be. Frugal was what you should have been when you were spending the bank's money, but since you now recognize you've made serious mistakes managing your money, and you did come in good faith, I've made an executive decision to look the other way on this one. I'll knock off ten percent when you come in for your consultation. Now isn't that the executive thing to do?" Danny continues with the slurping suction leaving the can.

The caller's irritation continues. "Mr. Jenkins, I'm not feeling comfortable with any of your explanations. I'll have to talk this over with my husband. I have a gut feeling your company's not the right place for my business. Setting aside the referrals, does this company have a Q.A. /Q.C policy in place?"

"A Q.A. /Q.C? What the hell is that supposed to mean? Is that like the free lunch tickets we used to get in school? Haven't you heard, the Republicans cut out all the programs for minority businesses, so we won't be able to help you with anything free. This company is unable to offer the convenience of coupons to do business. Like everywhere else, you pay as you play. Ha hah, yeah, it's plenty rough out here."

"Mr. Jenkins! I'm referring to quality assurance and quality control, the measures of good faith that ensure your company is in compliance to do business with prospective clients. Does your company have such a policy in place to ensure its business integrity?"

"Oh, that's what you were saying? When you went to using those alphabets, you lost me. Yeah, we have quality control and the other things; we have all that. That's why we're having this conversation. Your credit isn't happening, and you were referred to this professional company for our professional services. We offer relief from those 'Unspoken Matters.' Ha hah! Girl, I'm sharp with it. I'm on that A-game. Don't even think of getting around me; I'm way ahead of you and anybody you thought about going to. Game over! Say it and be done; you like the way I put it down. That shit was tight, wasn't it?"

The caller doesn't respond.

Danny attempts to rekindle the conversation. "Hello? Hello, Mrs. Washington? Please don't let my direct approach scare you off. I'm known to push a hard line. That's why your call was put through for my executive discretion. We let it be known around here that with this company, Unspoken Matters, the executive tier goes hard in the paint. Every customer gets what they pay for, along with the prompt professionalism you've experienced since I've personally handled your concerns myself. Mrs. Washington, I'm hoping you're feeling all this. We go out of our way to campaign for paying custom-ers; we go hard."

There's a moment of silence before the caller responds. "Excuse me, Mr. Jenkins. I don't recall any of this information mentioned with the referral to your company, nor do I feel comfortable making this decision by myself. Give me a mo-ment to include my husband."

Over the top with his sales pitch, Danny pops his collar. A soft suction is heard as he runs his tongue along his teeth. With complete satisfaction in himself, Danny whispers to Gwyneth reassuringly, "D's about to close the deal. It's all day every day, in whatever venture I parlay. Commission baby! Whenever D's playing, best believe the other side's paying. Whatever I touch shits money. Watch how I handle player; I'm smooth with this here."

There's silence with the call. Danny's simpleminded rheto-ric has left Gwyneth's mouth agape with disbelief. Danny gives a reassuring wink before resuming his senselessness, "Yes, sir, this be Danny Jenkins, executive director of Unspoken Matters. Silence is golden and time is money; once we repair your bad credit, all that appeared gloomy returns bright and sunny. Ha hah, player, let's talk about it. How will you be spending that paper? Will it be cash or check? However it will work for you, let's get it done."

A male's voice condemns Danny's mindless wit. "You mindless mother fucker! What the hell are you doing, and you're talking like you're sitting in my office. Please tell me your funky feet aren't on my desk."

Danny has been seated comfortably in his socks with his feet resting on Paul's executive desk. Caught off guard, he damn near breaks his neck from spinning the executive chair in the opposite direction.

"Paul! I'm sure glad you interrupted that call, because somebody was playing and bullshitting on the other line. I had to hold it down and make the company look good, so I answered the phone in your office to handle it, because Gwyneth didn't know what to do. Paul, what happened? I thought you were at the golf tournament. How many holes did you play?"

"Danny, put Gwyneth on the phone."

The office manager stops penciling the crossword puzzle. She whispers to Danny, "I told you, stupid. I'm right here, Paul. I told him; he doesn't listen."

"Gwyneth!"

Gwyneth answers giving Danny a burning look, "Yes, Paul?"

"Who's in charge whenever I'm away from the office?"

Gwyneth rolls her eyes to Danny. "You put me in charge, Paul."

"Gwyneth, exactly! You're in charge. Fire Danny. I don't want to look at him when I return to the office."

"I can't fire him, Paul; he's your best friend."

"The hell you can't."

Danny yells into the phone, "Paul, you heard her. I'm your best friend. You're firing your best friend? Damn, you fired me eight times this year already. How in the hell do you fire your best friend eight times in the same year? I'm going to the

EEOC this time. You're firing me because I'm a black man. Explain that one to the government."

"Danny, shut the fuck up. I'm a black man myself. I'm firing your ass for being simple!"

"Yeah, but you're black and rich now, and being rich don't count. You and the wife got that Tiger Woodie thing going on. Being rich put you and your wife beyond being black a long time ago. People are inviting y'all everywhere, and I'm still the only black friend you and your wife have, and you wanna fire me? Do it, and I'll tell Kelly the truth. I'm not lying, Paul. What? What was that you asked Kelly? Why haven't I been coming around? No, I didn't, and who said I moved out of town? Your husband's been lying to you. Kelly, he fired me again; excuse me for cutting this short, but I'm about to have a nervous breakdown just thinking about it. The shit I went through was excruciatingly painful, and I don't want to talk about it and relive that bullshit Paul put me through."

Paul breathes into the telephone frustrated. "Gwyneth, can you shut that simple silly fucker up? I can't think with him running his mouth. I need a fucking Valium just to deal with him. Gwyneth, have a cab come to the office and send my Valium with it to the country club. Now back to Danny. Gwyneth, fire him! I don't want to look at that simple silly Willy Jack in the box. He shouldn't be anywhere near the office to irritate me either. If he won't leave willingly, he's trespassing. Call security to remove his ass. Gwyneth, why is he answering the phone? His only public contact was to contest delinquent credit reports. What's wrong here? Have I put the wrong person in charge? What's going on?

Gwyneth shakes her fists toward Danny. "Paul, he's your best friend. He doesn't listen when you're not around."

"Oh, is that right? Is he listening now?"

Gwyneth balls up her crossword puzzle to throw it at Danny. "Yes, Paul, you have his un-divided attention."

"Good! Now that I have you both listening, Gwyneth, open the office door and point toward the exit. Danny? Figure it out and get somewhere; just keep running until you disappear."

Gwyneth covers her mouth to laugh.

Danny yells into the telephone, "Paul, you can count on me. I'm on my way to the country club. I love you, man. And I don't believe any of that shit you've just said. I'll be there in forty-five minutes. Don't worry about nothing!"

The call ends. Danny looks to Gwyneth smirking. "This shit's for grown folks, and believe me, Paul's not playing. He'll fire your ass quicker than you can spell Guinevere, or however the fuck you spell your name. Just because you come to work and are on time every day, you're not fooling anybody in this office either. I bet your people in Ireland don't know you're working for a black man. So don't try to explain a damn thing otherwise, because you're not slick either. I'll call immigration on that ass quicker than stank on shit. I'm not playing! Just you try to tell Paul I said any of this shit."

Refusing audience to a fool, Gwyneth looks over her glasses to respond matter-of-factly, "You heard the man, simpleton. Get your frail ass to the country club and pick up the boss. You're becoming quite an actor. Have you've been watching a lot of TV? That show *The Wyre?* You sound like one of its characters. You know we watch that show in Ireland too. Your 'I'm from the hood' facade is weak, homey. You need to tighten up your game before you get caught up and wreck yourself."

Gwyneth becomes the instigator with their role reversal. Danny looks on disbelievingly with his mouth agape with chagrin. "Now you're playing the dozens too? White girl, who in the hell taught you to talk like that? Don't even think about telling Paul I said that shit either. I'm not bullshitting. Paul's serious this time; he's likely to fire me again before I pick him up."

Danny arrived to the country club within thirty-five minutes of Paul's request. Recognizing his best friend sitting in a golf cart, Danny made an attempt at being professional by assisting Paul with his golf gear. Paul overlooked Danny's gesture with scathing instructions directed toward the trunk of the car.

"Don't try to talk to me! Just open it up and drive to my residence. When we arrive, I get out of the car, you pull the fuck off, keep driving, and forget everything about me. When you're as far away from me as humanly possible, I'll pray for divine intervention to keep you away. I'll pray that my life will be beautiful again without your irritating simple ass. Now being a simpleton, you're not expected to know your ass from a hole in the ground. So I hope I haven't talked over your head in making so much sense, you stupid mother fucker."

Danny accepts the hostile reception standing motionless. "Paul, no worries, I won't bother you or say shit to irritate you either. Bullshitting on the telephone—I admit that shit was childish. I deserve everything, and however you're feeling about me, from here on out I'll do my job. As we speak, I'll shut the fuck up and just drive; you can believe that. I need my eighty-hour work week. My landlord's already looking for an excuse to evict me. My sister reminds me that I can't move in with her every day, so don't worry about me fucking up a good thing. Believe me, Paul, I appreciate this job."

With Danny's pledge to do the right thing, Paul entered the vehicle to secure himself with the seatbelt restraints. As the commute begins, he made several attempts to call Kelly to determine whether he should pick something up from the market before arriving home. With all call attempts going directly to Kelly's voicemail, Paul put the inquiry aside to make a music selection from his iPod. Now settling back comfortably into the car seat, he listens to smooth jazz through his headphones. Meanwhile the commute comes to a traffic signal stop at the intersection of Slauson and Fairfax Avenue, where Paul noticed his favorite deli. With Danny's shenanigans silenced, Paul watches the turnstile of traffic entering and leaving the deli to notice two very attractive women. Paul makes a mental note of Danny's uncharacteristic demeanor. Danny made no effort of pursuit. Had the day's circumstance been different, he would have been unrelenting in his quest for their acquaintance. Danny was a silver-tongued beast when it came to the women he described as "the fine specimens with the fabulous backyards." Whether they were in the deli parking lot, reserved VIP sections at concerts, or someone's wedding, it didn't matter. Anywhere and every-where fine specimens congregate, Danny would have initiated an introduction.

With the signal change, the flow of traffic resumes. Danny proceeds.

Unknown to Paul, Danny voiced the missed opportunity with one word: "Damn!" Impressed with Danny's self-discipline, Paul closes his eyes to continue listening to the headphones' smooth jazz.

In afterthought, his mind drifts to a recent scenario with Danny and beautiful women. "Hello, young ladies, there's no need for either of you going out of your way. Any questions I may have had, you've answered already, and believe me, I'm very satisfied. What's in your beautiful backyards sings the sweetest of songs. Everything I've been raised to live for is chasing you around. What I truly relish and hold dearest to my heart, you're sitting on. Should my vision become weak, I'll wear the best of bifocals for my sight. Were I to live as an old man and became sickly, I pray 'Lord, up until the day you call me, don't deprive me of looking at a woman's beautiful ass, forever and ever.' Were I to be called home while doing so, allow me a simple headstone not to offend, 'Here lies a good man creaming and dreaming!' Yes ladies, I'm really a very nice guy. I would love to be included with the festivities. I'm Danny."

The commute comes to an end with their arrival at Paul's residence. As soon as the car comes to a stop, Danny, as though employed as a chauffeur, opens the passenger door. He immediately goes to the trunk to retrieve Paul's golf gear. It's an awkward moment; both men have kept their word by not communicating with the other. Paul acknowledges Danny's effort with a gesture of giving dap, or bumping fists over a handshake. "Thanks, dude."

Danny hugs Paul. "I love you too, man."

Paul relents with the gesture, "D, whatever happened at the office has blown over. Meet me here in the morning; it's all good."

Danny returned to the driver's seat with an expression of somberness. Deceived by Danny's feigned emotion, Paul shut the driver's door. "Danny, it ain't nothing. Everything's still good; we'll talk about it in the morning."

Danny's wit unfolds. "Yeah, man, believe me. I'll be here first thing, right after your wife cooks my breakfast." Danny laughs at Paul's gullibility, shaking his head, "Damn!"

Paul cut through Danny's shenanigans with a comeback, "See, there you go; we talked about this earlier. You and that bullshit. I keep telling you, Danny, but you go back to talking that Walt Dizzy anyway. That goofy shit will get you fucked up every time. Dealing with your stress has me a lil' slow today. Regardless of what I'm going through, Danny, you're stuck stupid every day of the week. Mark my words, if you were in the desert and became lost, no one would either find or come looking for your simple ass. Wanna know why Danny? There are a million rocks in the desert just lying around basking in the sun. You and your entire family belong out there in the middle of all of them, just as aimless with no direction. Because everyone in your family looks up to you, here's the part that makes you the man. While in the middle of the desert having your family reunion, not one of you dumb mother fuckers has enough sense to know where you are. To impress the rest of the simpletons related to you, you went big and went all out with the trimmings. There's plenty of yellow potato salad, them good pork ribs with the homemade barbeque sauce, ham, baked beans, and those good deviled eggs your sister makes. Everybody's drinking red liquor and dancing, and then out of nowhere, every one of you goes to clapping and doing the down home, just cuttin' up out in the middle of the desert clapping and carrying on. Even the grandmothers from both sides of the family are doing the electric slide. Everybody's whooping and hollering and acting out like there's no tomorrow. As soon as the ham and ribs are gone and the liquor runs out, you all go to scratching and itching. Come to find out your entire genealogy's been out in the desert for over a week. Not one of you simpletons has yet to realize this wasn't a tour bus trip you won. It was the decent people that live near you who took up a collection. They paid for that bus going to the desert in the hopes not any of you Simple Simons would find your way back. Now wasn't that shit funny, Danny?"

Danny's smirk vanishes with a laugh. "I can't mess with it, Paul. You put that one together pretty tight. All bullshit aside, I should be here by the time you're done with breakfast."

Shouldering his golf bag, Paul turns about-face to walk toward his residence. He looks to Danny with an acknowledging nod. "You just stay with the bullshit, don't you? All that's required is keeping it real. Believe me, Danny, it's not that hard. Have your simple ass here on time in the morning; it's back to business as usual."

Danny puts the car in gear, agreeing, "Baby boy, I heard that. Believe me, ain't nobody playing with it around here either."

Danny drives forward only to make an abrupt stop. With a perplexed expression he backs the car in reverse. "Damn, Paul, I knew it was something we both forgot."

Paul falls for the ruse, retrieving his house keys from the golf bag. "I have them, Danny; I'm good."

Danny's expression quickly changes from "Paul, you forgot your keys," to "I got that ass again." Danny chuckles, irritating his best friend. "Nah dude; that one's too easy. This one's for the wife. Tell Kelly, I want biscuits, jelly, and bacon with my eggs."

Realizing Danny's got him again, Paul concedes the setup grinning. He gestures with his middle finger. "That was some real funny shit, and you're fired again. Funny's a bitch isn't it? It has to be, because you look in the mirror every day to make sure you're just as equally stupid as your reflection."

Both laugh within the camaraderie of friends. As Paul continued toward his residence, Danny drives away with a promising pledge, "Boss man, back to business in the morning, and no worries about me being on time, either. I'll be here eating breakfast before you piss away that hard on."

Paul dismisses Danny under his breath. "How many times

do I have to tell you, you simple bastard, everything is fair game but the dick. I don't care how many years we've known each other, we don't cap on the dick. I'll never be comfortable with the dick talk, okay? Fuck you."

CHAPTER THIRTEEN

*A*fter checking the mailbox for the day's mail, Paul continued up the walkway of his residence. He removed newspapers and flyers that have been recklessly thrown from trucks or vans throughout the community. Noticing his neighbor's yard and driveway are piled with several weeks of the same unsolicited materials, Paul vents his irritation as he unlocked the door to his residence. "Why solicit on another's property without the owner's consent? Who reads any of this, and why throw more of the same meaningless bullshit that's still piled from the previous twenty weeks? Where's the logic in that?" After opening his residence door to a mixed aroma of cupcake candles, and food, Paul's temperament quickly changed when Randy met him in the living room with a welcoming bark. The toy dog pranced from side to side excitedly, whipping its stubby tail before writhing into the carpet to patiently wait for Paul to rub its stomach. Paul brings his golf gear into the residence with a smile, before closing the door behind him to rub the toy dog obligingly.

"Hey, lil' Daddy. You're all fired up? Tell me about it. Is it good to be seen? I know that's right. This woman has you spoiled to where you've never seen a rough day in your life. Rough's what I had today, and you don't want any part of that. Where's Kelly, huh? Where's your mommy?" Paul moves his head to the faint sound of music coming from the bedroom. "Okay, I know where mommy is. She left you out here, and you're in your feelings about that. Is that why you're excited to see me? Did you eat, lil' man? I know you ate. That woman will definitely make sure you eat and forget everything about me. Am I right? Remember the cardinal rule. Kelly was mine first! From the kindness of my heart I brought you home as a gift for my woman. She's my woman, Randy. Are you cool with that? That's a good lil' guy. That's Paul's lil' man! Now let me get to what smells good around here."

Without further ado, the toy dog trots to its kennel to rest on the newly purchased pillow bed. Paul continued toward the kitchen's delectable aroma. He whiffs expectantly, "it smells like . . . I won't say. I'll open the pot and have myself a party." Standing at the kitchen sink, Paul washed his hands using hand soap from the soap dispenser. He dries his hands quickly using paper towels before closing his eyes to take in more of the aroma. He removes the pot lid. "Halleluiah! Gumbo with steamed rice. Kelly wants to make babies tonight!" Paul licked his lips expectantly to admit, "Baby, I know you put it down in this one. I'm sure glad you didn't invite anybody else to help me enjoy this occasion." Paul dialogues toward the bedroom. "Kelly, thank you for appreciating your man … Baby, are you hearing me?"

He spoons through the gumbo pot to sample a taste. "Mm, mm, mm, good lord! Baby, where are the crackers? You really set it out there with this one. Chicken sausage, king crab legs, colossal shrimp, and oysters with just enough rice and okra. Yeah, man; Kelly, it's definitely going down in here tonight. Just tell me how many babies you wanna make?"

Paul returns the pot lid to walk to the living room to undress. As he placed his clothing on the couch, he dialogues. "Don't worry, Kelly, I won't go about this like a savage. Before I get my nibble on with that good crab and shrimp, I'd like to say I truly cherish the blessing you've put before me. To make sure I'm primed and ready to go, I'll unwind and relax in the Jacuzzi. Are you joining me, baby?" Paul has removed his clothing with the exception of his underwear. To celebrate his favorite meal he begins to shadowbox while giving commentary. "Watch me; it's going down, it's going down! DOWN GOES FRAZIER! DOWN GOES FRAZIER! Watch me, I'm too fast and too pretty." After throwing several combinations, Paul huffs and puffs in exhaustion. In good humor he redirects to the bedroom. "Kelly, you should have seen your man handling things out here. I'm fast, I'm ready and can't possibly be beat. I'm a bad man." Leaving the living room, Paul praises his favorite boxer with his hands raised in victory, "ALI! ALI! ALI! I'm a bad man."

Entering the bathroom to an aroma and glow of cupcake

candles, Paul immediately noticed the white rose petals placed around the Jacuzzi's rim and floor. Within the ambiance, a bottle of wine and a half-empty wine glass sits on the dual sink vanity. Standing motionless with surprise, he recognized the music in the bedroom to be one of their favorite R&B artists, Michael Collins. Paul directs to the bedroom where Kelly remains enthralled in its ambiance. "Baby, you've been buying lottery tickets? You must be feeling good news, because you've definitely set it out there with all this." Paul looks at his mirrored reflection to flex his chest muscles. He talks over the music. "Kelly, you've been talking to your sister again? No doubt she convinced you to go with that procedure to have twins. Don't deny it! With all the shrimp and oysters in that gumbo, you must really feel like working that thang. Baby, I'm feeling you on all that. Talk to me, and I'll talk back. I know what you want. You should've ordered a case of Viagra, and it would have been a lot cheaper than that pot of gumbo. Since you're feeling it, I'm telling you now, what your girlfriends do with their dudes is their business. I'm not knocking anybody on what they do to get them to feel like they should, just don't you try putting your finger in my butt. I'll never get down like that, so don't waste your time trying to convert me. You should already know; ain't a damn thing changing about that, either. I'll make my own damn gumbo if I have to. Are you hearing me, baby?"

Paul picks up the half-empty wine glass to swallow its remains. "Kelly, why didn't you wait for me, baby? We could have enjoyed everything together." Awaiting a response, Paul refills the wine glass to take another swallow. He admits, "She's in the bedroom enjoying a Michael Collins concert, and I've been talking to myself the whole time. Listen to that; the woman doesn't have a clue I'm in the house." Feeling the wine's effect, Paul continues to watch his physique in the mirror. He talks toward the bedroom. "Everything's all good, and we're both feeling it. You do you, and I'll do me, until we meet and do each other in the bedroom. Kelly, baby, you've said it all in the kitchen, and Paul's not mad at anybody. Your husband's feeling like Tupac in this joint. Yeah!" Paul begins to dance in place. Between sips of wine, he picks up rose petals to gently blow them from his hand to watch their return to the bathroom's floor. While in the midst of folly, he inadvertently finds a letter at the tub's base. As the voice of the R&B artist croons in the bedroom, Paul sips wine while reading the letter. His expression now vacant, he looks into the rose petals strewn about the floor. As though he were watching the scenario of the letter being played out before him, Paul looks into the glow of candles positioned around the tub's base and rim. In one hand he holds the letter, while the other clenches rose petals gathered from the floor. Speechless, Paul appears distant and stiff. Meanwhile, the crooning voice of the R&B artist continues within the bedroom's ambience.

Whenever I close my eyes, I see your lovely face,
The very thought of you gets me feigning.
When you're nowhere near, my heart beats out of place,
I can hardly sleep with senseless dreaming.
To protect myself, I don't want anyone else,

But your loving arms to ever hold me.
With you the right card was dealt, your true love I felt,
I was blessed the day you chose me.
From the depths of the seas, to the branch tips of the tallest trees,
No stone went unturned until the day I found you.
After searching the world for you, I'm no longer feeling blue,
I have both the clay and what's left in the tray,
From where God shaped and made you.
It's real our love, A day without you in my life,
Is much too much . . .

Kelly remains in the bedroom awaiting her husband's arrival. She's created the bedroom's ambience by programing the disc player to play continuously. Seated at the vanity mirror, Kelly patiently wrapped the ends of her hair with delicate tissue paper before rolling and locking each in place. Sipping wine with the crooning of Michael Collins was the perfect combination she envisioned for the evening ahead. After giving it some thought, it's been a while since they've been in the mood. For married couples of ten years or more, the mood's love bug isn't lost, but rather its spontaneity is suppressed. That I-want-you-right-now feeling seems to fade and lose luster in time, like unpolished silver. Spontaneity is kept harnessed and reserved for the politically correct place and moment to tell someone how you feel about them. Spontaneity's fire; that's what Kelly felt after reading a letter written by a stranger. Speaking for the record, Kelly was neither turned on nor had lustful intent toward the letter writer. Needless to say, she's thirty-four years old and very capable of controlling her emotions and urges.

While enjoying her wine, Kelly joked about it earlier, but aren't people inspired by reading a stranger's written feelings? It happens all the time. People buy cards for weddings, birthdays, anniversaries, baptisms, and other occasions. Every card is written by an unknown person presenting his or her feelings to others, yet the people buying the cards aren't bothered by what they've read to be another's words or sentiments, as in the instance with Kelly, after reading the letter intended for Tiffany. Kelly reminisced how she and Paul expressed their love before and during their first five years of marriage. Truthfully, Kelly never lost her love bug for Paul and neither was she complaining. Paul had come through as he professed in their wedding vows. The sticky of the matter was Paul's success. Their lifestyle attests to her husband's success, but being successful kept Paul fighting what he feared most: failure. With Paul's fear of failure, the spontaneous fire they experienced during the first five years of their marriage had fizzled. If Kelly were to wave a magic wand, she and Paul would be together being very spontaneous. They'd revisit their honeymoon in Tahiti to enjoy a relaxed excursion. As they walked in sandals on the beach, Kelly would wear matching sarong and thong ensembles. They'd venture to restaurants to enjoy a glass of wine with their meal of conch and garlic noodles. Finishing dinner, Kelly would sit in Paul's lap to flirt with spontaneity. After positioning her sarong like a picnic blanket, Kelly unzips Paul's pants while kissing him passionately. Relishing her uninhibited freedom, Kelly pulls her thong to the side to guide her husband to enter her. She then spoon feeds him his favorite dessert, peach cobbler with vanilla ice cream. Coming out of her orgasmic euphoria, Kelly sips more wine. She giggled with an afterthought.

"Ooh, Daddy! That was nasty. People are watching us, but don't worry, Daddy! I don't care. I'll give you your dessert just the way you like it." Embarrassed, Kelly blushed to release a girlish sigh. "M-m-m!" With another sip of wine she purged her naughty thoughts. "Ooh, Daddy! Daddy, you ought to be ashamed for having me think something like that. That was too much for TV."

As he watched Kelly's theatrics unnoticed, Paul stands at the door of the bedroom wearing only his boxers and socks. Getting a glimpse of her husband in the vanity mirror, Kelly smiles to say, "Hi, Daddy." Taking full advantage of the crooning of Michael Collins within the bedroom's ambience, Kelly exudes flirtatious confidence in her body language as she walks toward her husband.

Embracing Kelly, Paul lightly massages the back of his wife's neck to kiss her earlobes. Reciprocating her husband's affection, Kelly runs her tongue along his lips and face to gently bite his ear. Carrying the sentiments of their embrace, Paul has visible lipstick residue on his cheek and bare chest. Gazing into her husband's eyes, Kelly uses her finger to brush his thick eyebrows back in place. She says, "Daddy, I heard you talking all through the house. I didn't answer because I wanted you to come find me. I had everything you would want in the kitchen. What else were you looking for, Daddy? Was it your lil' pretty pumpkin booty?"

Controlling his demeanor, Paul holds his thoughts to search Kelly's eyes. "It's the first thing I do when I come home, baby. I look for pumpkin booty. When I didn't see you when I walked in the house, I had to make sure you hadn't escaped. Everything's' laid out so pretty. The food; the house smells pretty. You're in the bedroom looking pretty and listening to pretty music. After seeing the pretty flowers and candles in the bathroom, I felt pretty. Randy even ran to me like he was having a pretty moment. I pretty much saw everything in the house that's pretty but my pretty wife, so you can understand why I became nervous when I didn't see you, right baby?"

Embraced, the two move slowly in a side to side motion to the crooning of Michael Collins. Embedded in Paul's chest, Kelly continues. "H-m-m, h-m-m, Daddy, you're funny. You missed me?"

Paul confesses in a whisper, "That's all the time and every time. I even miss you as I sleep. Daddy especially missed his lil' pretty today. It's coming to a point. I'm forced to tie strings to you before I sleep; that way whenever you move, I'll feel it and put you back where you're supposed to be."

Kelly removes her face from Paul's chest. Gazing into her husband's eyes, she questions, "H-m-m h-m-m. Is it all the time or only when I don't have one of Daddy's favorite meals ready, hmm?"

Paul kisses his wife's delicate chin with his answer. "Cupcake candles, and chilled wine? That's how I had to campaign to get next to you. You even have the Mike Collins thing working in the bedroom. Kelly, you must want me to ask you to remarry me. Look at you all dolled up. You're going out and didn't invite me?" Holding his gaze, Paul gently cups each of Kelly's cheeks; he kisses her forehead to ask, "Baby, is today my birthday?"

Kelly responds whining, "Daddy, I don't want to talk about your birthday now." As the couple remains embraced to rock in a side-to-side motion, the R&B artist crooned within the bedroom's ambience.

Paul affectionately pulls Kelly's face into his chest. He admits, "I'm a cautious man, and you know I put what's in your heart over your beauty when I married you."

Kelly answers, mesmerized. "Baby, I know this."

Paul closes his eyes with a confession. "Everything I wanted in a woman, I have in you. Honesty, sincerity, and loyalty. There was never any doubt with us, right baby? Bar none. You and me, all or nothing."

Kelly's eyes are closed. Being deep in her emotions, she snaps her fingers in agreement. "Preach Daddy! Till death do us part and after we transition to the dirt, I'll follow you. Don't stop talking now, Daddy!"

Paul's whisper continues. "That's what I'm talking about. I'm blessed to have a woman that has my back, and she knows how to look out for her man. You're just too good for me. Baby, you know I love you?"

In complete surrender in her husband's embrace, Kelly answers in a mesmerized whisper, "I love you more, Daddy!"

As the couple kiss passionately, Paul retrieves the letter

from the waistband of his boxers. He drops the bomb. "Kelly, what the fuck is this?" Presenting the letter, Paul appears cold. He asks, "Is something wrong, because you look surprisingly fucked up, and why would that be? The whole stage is set. Scented candles with chilled wine and Michael Collins. Everything's damn beautiful. Now you really look confused. What's the matter, baby? Shouldn't I have that look on my face? It's no secret. Kelly, you had me fucked up when I walked through the door."

Taken aback by Paul's emotional flash, from a newly-wed couple holding hands in the convertible while driving under romantic clear skies at thirty miles per hour, with the sound of empty cans tied to their car, to Prepare Yourself; don your night goggles as you enter divorce court, but before firing your weapon, adjust its sites to ensure your target is your ex-spouse. Perplexingly frozen, Kelly attempts to clarify the misunderstanding.

"Baby, Randy found the letter. It was lying in the street. I picked it up only because Randy found it. I was going to read-dress it and re-mail it but …"

Paul's sarcasm overplays Kelly's explanation. He talks matter-of-factly toward the bedroom ceiling. "Oh, she has good game. If anybody stupid catches you cheating, they'll believe this bullshit, especially if that somebody's your husband. Don't worry, the shit's foolproof; believe me, it works. When you're caught, drink a glass of wine and simply tell whoever the clueless motherfucker you're cheating on, that you found a letter written to a complete stranger, and somehow it just came the fuck home with you and laid itself on the floor. Don't forget to mention the scented candles and the wine you just happened to be enjoying, while listening to Michael Collins as you relaxed in a Jacuzzi full of rose petals. Whoever pulls that off with a straight face, believe me, they're a bad motor-scooter. They could just about sell Thanksgiving to a pilgrim without Pocahontas and the good horn of plenty."

Paul hands the letter to Kelly. "Here, baby, I believe this belongs to you."

Kelly's knees become weak. Unable to stand, she kneels on the bedroom's bamboo floor to plead, "Paul, let me finish telling you—"

"Finish telling what, Kelly? Telling the story or reading your script?"

"Paul, don't you want to know what happened? Let me finish—"

"Oh no, I've got the story, Kelly; it's so crystal clear I'll finish it for you." Paul continues the scathing sarcasm miming an MC presenting an award. "The award for best actress in a melodrama goes to … you've guessed it!" Paul motions his head to Kelly to clap as though she were being honored. Abruptly he stops to raise his hands to an imaginary audience, as though requesting silence to enable him to make his next presentation. "The award for the most simplest of simpleton's you'll ever meet in your entire existence as a human being, goes to …? It's everybody's guess, her husband, Paul. Can we have a warm welcoming round of applause for this dumb simple clueless mother fucker?"

Paul commences to clap with deliberate exaggeration.

Overcome with grief, Kelly cries to escape the blistering badgering. Clenching the letter, she places her face in her hands to plead, "Paul, please stop it; you're not allowing me to finish."

Paul's obnoxiousness stops momentarily. He reasons, "Kelly, you're right, an adjustment would be proper. Ahem!" Paul clears his throat to look around the bedroom as if looking for someone. The sarcasm continues. "I beg your pardon. Like most of the time you're on point with your logic, Kelly. How silly of me to have overstepped my boundaries. From recollection, I believe this is the part of the drama where the other guy steps in and gets the girl." Kneeling to face Kelly, Paul gently removes the letter from her clench with an offer. "Baby, let me help you out here; it's the least I can do. You look as though there's something really heavy on your mind." Within the bedroom's silence, Paul closes his eyes to sing along with the R&B balladeer's enchanting voice.

As I looked to the sky, I couldn't believe my eyes,
The moon and stars were out to witness.
For my special night, thanks for sharing your light,
You know I've come to state my wishes.
As I make my move, I winked at the moon,
I'm prepared to say it all for you.
To spend my life with you?
Name something I wouldn't do?
For the moon and stars to see,
I stand before you on bended knee.

Please accept my plea, become my Mrs.?
Were the world to be gained, living without you
Would be too much pain,
My heart will never beat the same truth.
But what remains, there's love to blame,
I refuse to live my life without you.

Paul abruptly walks out of the bedroom leaving Kelly teary eyed.

She sobs, "Paul, please listen and hear me out. I love you. Why would I do anything to hurt you?"

As though he left something behind, Paul does a flash return to the bedroom. "Kelly, did I mention earlier? The gumbo is screaming. You really put your foot into that one. Thank you." Exiting the bedroom for the second time, Paul closes the door behind him. He resumes chiding Kelly from the living room. "Kelly, I know how much you respect privacy, so I shut the door. Now you can go back to your wine. When you start feeling its buzz, just gaze in the mirror to fantasize about the guy who wrote the letter. But Kelly, I'd turn the music down, because the guy? He probably wouldn't want to compete with Michael Collins. Oh, by the way, the wine? That was a very good choice. Did you pick that one with me in mind, baby?" Paul retrieves his clothing from the living room couch to dress. After stepping into his shoes, he confiscates Kelly's car keys from the kitchen countertop. "Even if my car weren't being serviced, I think I need to be the one riding around in the Mercedes for a while." Randy barks in objection from the kennel's pillowed bed. Paul gives the toy terrier an informative wink. "Lil' man, stay in your lane! I brought the car like I brought you and everything else around here. You need something to do? How about watching the house, and don't open the door for strangers." As Paul makes his exit with the sound of locks securing the residence door, Kelly's faint sobs continue in the bedroom.

Immediately the toy terrier trots to investigate. With its head slightly cocked and its ears raised, the toy dog waits expectantly for the bedroom door to open.

Since leaving his residence driving his wife's car, Paul has driven to a nearby liquor outlet to purchase a cigar and a pint of vodka. The store clerk assists him with his order.

"Will there be anything else with your purchase sir?"

"Yeah; pass me two cups and a small bag of ice."

CHAPTER FOURTEEN

$\mathscr{L}$eaving the liquor outlet with no destination in mind, Paul drives several miles before stopping. He pours vodka over ice to sip in thought over what transpired at home. Treachery wasn't in Kelly's makeup, and no one anywhere could have told him anything different about his wife, yet as of an hour ago, Paul is his best witness to speak against Kelly. Without a doubt he read the letter's ink. Whoever the dude was, he was smooth with expression. Kelly was twice as guilty because she was definitely feeling the letter, but what rattled Paul, Kelly wasn't one to stray. So how did dude get to her? Whatever the scenario, Paul had a huge void in his ego. He reasons, "Who could I call to vent with that wouldn't judge me for appearing foolish?

Damn, how would I say it? I don't talk to her mother; she's not allowed at our house, so I can't knock on her door and say, "Hello, we both know I can't stand you, but could you tell me anything about my wife and her lover?" I can't get down like that. It would seem that I cared. I'd appear hurt and butt sore, like I was being all sensitive and shit.

I don't know where to go. I can't call my mother for advice; we recently had an argument over her minding her business and not mine.

Paul disregards the cup to take a swig directly from the pint. As the vodkas burn traveled down his throat, another thought comes to mind. "I can't believe Kelly, but what I do believe is a lil' get back is in order, before I have divorce papers served on that ass." Paul dials his best friend's phone number.

It's answered immediately, "Danny speakin', what it do?"

Paul adjusts the volume on his earpiece. "D, what's happening with you?"

"Paul? Hey, about earlier today, I know you're still mad. That was some childish shit I did in your office."

"Danny, don't worry about it; we're good. You got a minute?"

"You're the one doing the calling, Paul; what's happening?"

"D, you won't believe this shit. If I hadn't witnessed it myself, I wouldn't have believed it in a thousand years."

"Damn, Paul, that's a long-ass time! What the fuck could you have seen that's bothering you enough to want to talk about it right now? You saw the mother ship or some shit? That ain't nothing! Whenever I smoke that boo-bonic bomb-ass bud, I see shit like that all the time."

"No, Danny, it's not any of that; it's Kelly. When you dropped me off, just as I stepped in the house, Randy met me at the front door. So I pet him and we chopped it up, you know, 'Lil man, you're a good boy' and all that. Bam, the gumbo hit me. I teased myself with a few spoons of shrimp and sausage. Danny, it was the bomb. Kelly had those aroma therapy candles going all through the house. She even had my Michael Collins CD crooning in the bedroom. I was feeling it, and I'm yelling through the house, "Kelly! Kelly, baby, I'm home." She's not acknowledging me. I then make my way into the bathroom, figuring I'd relax in the Jacuzzi to relieve some of that work stress."

"Right, Randy always meets you at the front door, and as fine as your wife is, Kelly still cooks at least four days a week. When I picked you up from the country club you were listening to jazz all the way home. That's what you normally do, and you get in the Jacuzzi every day, so what's all the hype?"

"Danny, that's what I'm trying to tell you. I never got a chance to get in the Jacuzzi. You know why?"

"Paul, I don't have a clue. You reached in your briefcase and took the Valium instead of the Viagra pills?"

"Danny, hell no! The lights were off in the bathroom. Kelly had cupcake candles lit all around the Jacuzzi; she had white rose petals everywhere. Instead of getting in the Jacuzzi, I finished off a bottle of wine with a wine glass on the floor."

"Damn, why didn't you say all this shit before? Kelly wants to have a baby. How many? That's a good thing, Paul. Kelly knows what's up; she's going through with it before you start getting grey hairs on your nuts. Believe me, after those grey hairs start poppin' up, your sperm count starts playing out. Congratulations, Daddy! Today's women really don't want to go there after thirty-five years old. Most of them opt for the adoption thing after that. You ever hear about that Down syndrome shit? I read up on that, and the shit's serious. It has kids being born already senior citizens. I'm telling you, the shit's fucked up, but anyway, you and Kelly are ahead of the game. So how many lil' Kellys and lil' big heads should the world be expecting?"

"Danny, please, I'm trying to tell you what happened. Just shut the fuck up and be serious."

"I'm being serious, Paul. I've heard everything you've said. You and Kelly's expecting a big-head bambino."

"Danny, you really are a silly mother fucker. Believe me when I tell you, being simple comes easy to you. Are you listening to what I'm saying?"

"I'm listening, man."

"Good! Then shut the fuck up and hear this. Danny, Kelly's been stepping out on me."

"Stepping out on you? Damn! Now I understand why you've been coming to work so upset. You're having serious problems. Now you see, Paul, you see? I never, ever trust them. Believe me, we won't even bullshit each other with trust. They're trying to work me, and I'm trying to work them. It's all fair exchange in the game; that's why I'm having it my way, all day, every day, and believe me, everybody's satisfied, and I might be a lil' fairer than most. Hearing it from you makes it official. 'Trust them not, even if you do marry them.' Why even portray that *Little House on the Big Prairie* shit? It's all overrated with contracts and stipulations. That's the shit that kills you. Fuck all that! Marry them and work all your life to take care of them? What for? To die from stress and aggravation? Paul, you and I share a common quality."

"What quality do we share, Danny?"

"Shee-it, it's no secret! Paul, you're a freak like me. So you already know what it is; that's why you've been so miserable lately. Dude, they stop giving head once you marry them. I can't figure that shit out either. That reason alone is enough for Danny not giving anybody a ring. I'm staying ahead of the game. Ha hah, yeah, man! That's why I refuse to do any melo-dramas, all that crying and carrying on, they're just setting you up for that engagement ring. See, now you understand my po-sition. With Danny it's either action flicks or horror movies, and guess who's buying the popcorn. Believe me, player, Danny boy will never go out like that. They already know what it is."

"Danny!"

"Come on with it dawg, I'm listening?"

"Explain what the fuck you've just said that makes any sense, and how would it help me with what's going on with Kelly? No, no, don't answer; you'll just fuck up again."

There's silence between the two.

Danny breaks the vigil with more senselessness. "Paul, I wasn't going to speak on this. One of the reasons for your prob-lems is your lack of patience. People are afraid to talk to you; that's why you have Gwyneth answering the phones and me doing the credit deletions and picking you up and shit. I think maybe I should get a raise for being your therapist and for all this personal coaching. You know what I'm saying?"

"Danny, the only person rightfully afraid of me is you, simpleton. That's only because I know you're full of shit. So shut the fuck up before I lose my trend of good thinking. Thank you, with your simple silly shit. See how easy we get along when you let me do the thinking? Don't answer that. Meet me at the Hotel Where We Rendezvous in two hours, and bring a few choice females to go along with the vodka. I'm feeling like about two or three fifths."

"No shit? Paul, say no more; I'm there already with the bizness!"

"Danny, you still have your dispensary plug with the granddaddy product?"

"I got it like that continuous. It's continuous, and I can feel my eyes getting tight as we speak. Now that's the way I like hearing you talk. Paul, reactivate that player's card, baby!" Danny pounds his chest with his fist. "You see why we're boys? You already know the get-down. Long and strong, all night long! Welcome back at it, player!" Danny pounds his chest. "Know what I'm saying P? Know what I'm saying? Your boy P? Your boy ain't went nowhere."

"Danny!"

"Admit it P, when you wanna do the damn thing, you know who to call."

"Danny?"

"I'm listening, P."

"Danny, don't show up with any hood rats. That includes your baby's mother or any of your cousins or their home girls! They're all the same to me. I've been through enough bullshit today, and I'm not entertaining any more problems. Danny, listen to me. I mean it; that's WORD!"

"Damn, P, you're hard on the hood rats. There's at least one in every family, whether she's somebody's wife, your partner's sister, or neighbor's granddaughter. Shee-it, all the hood rats I know have character. Hood rats compete for the player with the biggest cheese to get them out of the neighborhood. Hood rats are down with the struggle. I'm not bullshitting. I'm looking for one now! P, relax; I'm bullshitting. I've got this handled, besides as particular as you are, if you were to step out there, you would wear at least three condoms. Am I right?"

"Danny, why do I waste my time fucking with you? If I have to go beyond my bedroom, you're damn right I'm wearing a sleeve."

"P, that's what I'm talking about. Then what difference does it make? We just wanna get our socks blown. Believe me, you know like I know, can't nobody anywhere at any time, work that ass like a proper hood rat."

"Danny, not right now, you silly bastard. Say another word, I'll fire your simple ass for listening to my problems, and then I'll fire you again for being stupid and asking for your job back."

"Okay, okay, P, don't get back on that page; I need my job. Don't worry about nothing, I'll be there in two hours."

"Danny, don't play me with the bullshit, and I meant what I said about the hood rats." The call ends. Taking a swig of vodka, Paul opens the cigar canister as he contemplates calling Kelly. After several moments of the cigar's enjoyment, a woman walking a toy dog distracts the notion. Paul watches the dog and its owner in thought, as if Kelly were walking Randy.

"Kelly's trying to have a baby?"
Baby? Baby? Baby?
"You can't trust them."
Trust them! Trust them! Trust them!
"She had wine chilling."
Chilling! Chilling! Chilling!
"I wouldn't have believed that shit in a thousand years!"
Years! Years! Years!
"You know I married you for what's in your heart."
Heart! Heart! Heart!

A bark from the toy dog returns Paul from thought; he then taps his unattended cigar in the ashtray. As he watches the woman and the toy dog make their way, he checks his cell phone for missed messages.

"Damn, two hours before the Hotel Where We Rendezvous hookup. Kelly could at least have texted to offer some gumbo."

CHAPTER FIFTEEN

*W*hile sitting in the parking lot of Big Lester's strip club, Danny does a mental rewind of the conversation with Paul. "Danny, don't play me with the bullshit, and I meant what I said about the hood rats!" Danny self-talks, "Come on, Paul, you can't have it both ways. This is the best it gets on such short notice. You're the one having problems; besides these girls are pretty close to being decent, so technically they aren't hood rats. Just deal with it, player." Rummaging through the car's glove box, Danny comes across a box of breath mints. He puts a few in his mouth expectantly. "All shit! I'm feeling refreshed already. I wonder if this is an indication of what lies ahead." Closing the glove box he notices the box of Big Shot condoms. "Damn! I forgot all about these. It seems I have a little work to put in before the expiration date expires, ha hah! Danny boy will get you there for sure, baby, and we'll both come and have fun at the same time." As he exits the car, Danny feels at the money outline in his pocket to admit, "Yeah, man, the honeys aren't too quick to say no when you have it like this. Big paper allows you to have it the way you want it, and tonight a big dawg wants a whole lot; whatever a good time costs." Continuing toward Big Les's strip club, Danny acknowledges a member of the security team. "That's right, a player's in motion, so give it up and recognize. Yes, big baby, I see Big Les has everybody on their A-game tonight. Everybody better do what they do, and keep that ass in the parking lot doing it, handling that bizness. There won't be no hanging around the buffet table or kicking it in the back of the room to watch all that ass go to wiggling and jiggling. Yeah, what's happening with it, Train? Give it up big baby!"

Acknowledging Danny, the burly security guard removes his earpiece to bump fists giving dap. "D-boy, what it is?"

"I'm good with it, Train, and you already know the move, big baby. It's another one like the other one, with just enough conversation to leave the tab for another's obligation. I'm not passin' up nothing. Anything moving gets charged to the game, player; know what I'm saying?"

"I'm feeling you on all that, D-boy. You recognize anybody else from the turf?"

The big guard nods to another security guard, this one's even bigger than Train.

Danny looks in the direction of Train's nod. "Shee-it, your folks is hooked up too? What's happening, Big Cheddar? When'd you get home? Don't even think about robbing anybody; don't entertain any of that shit. People got tired of you robbing them, Cheddar, and they put cameras everywhere for your big ass. Don't be up here fucking with Big Lester's money, either. Run to the penitentiary on a violation if you want to! Lester will come there and kick your big ass. Cheddar? Take off the damn penitentiary glasses scaring everybody. People spending honest money don't wanna see your institutional ass wearing penitentiary sunglasses. Who the fuck in their right mind will walk past you to spend money with their dick hard? Shee-it, not with your institutional ass behind them. You're in the wrong line of work. Hook up with a paralegal and serve eviction notices, Cheddar; you'd be rich. Imagine your big ass at somebody's door. 'Hello?' 'Who is it?' 'Motherfucker Big Cheddar is who it is. I'm here offering options. One, un-ass all the rent you owe, or two, hurry the fuck up and get some-where. Make a choice before I go to stompin' you out with this size fifteen!'

"Cheddar, you and all that damn black, believe me, my heart goes out to the strippers you escort to their cars. Every one of them will pee on themselves driving home. I'm not bullshitting. They'll be on Facebook forever and a day just talk-ing about your big ass. 'Girl, I'm not dancing for that club any-more; they scared me. Every time I go there, I pee on myself!'"

Train laughs at Danny's clowning of his little brother. "D, you're burnt!"

Cheddar flips Danny the bird.

Danny points his cellphone in Cheddar's direction as if he's recording. "Don't even think about it, Cheddar. I keep 9-1-1 on speed dial for you bad actors. I'll record your big ass until the police get here. Technology! That's how we handle you bad actors. I have your parole officer's number in here too. I got the technology for your ass, Cheddar."

Cheddar blows Danny off, giving a halfhearted attempt to lunge forward. He says, "Hurry the fuck up and get somewhere with all that simple bullshit."

Danny screams like a girl as he escapes into the strip club. "Somebody call the police. A crazy man is outside bothering people."

As Danny strolls to the cashier's booth, the song "Bad Sexy Muthafucka'" plays during a dancer's performance. Danny talks over the music to get the cashier's attention. "Hey, hey, hey, Danny boy's arrived, and the building is the official place to be. What's happening up in this piece?"

The cashier moves her head to the beat as she watches the dancer's performance. She presents the next admission ticket with a swallow from her shot glass. "It's been a long time, Danny boy. Where you been? We have a lineup of hot girls workin' and poppin' it like it supposed to be done. It's standing room only in Les's Joint. By the way, Danny, I know someone who needs a good credit plug, so leave a few of your business cards on your way out."

Danny smiles. "Crystal, you know how I get down. Danny stays ready, so there's no need to get ready. Unspoken Matters is what I handle. Here you go, ask for the executive package when you're ready; I'll hook you up."

"My business in order, Danny. I'm good! Cherelle needs the plug. You know how young girls don't appreciate their credit status until they have to settle down."

"Yeah, Crystal, I'm feeling all that, but is your sister still fine like you?"

Crystal accepts the card, dismissing Danny. "Boy, don't play with me, and this is business."

Danny plays it off with wit. "Ha hah! Girl, I'm just talking. Have Cherelle give me a call. Should anything come about risqué, consider it an Unspoken Matter between grown folks; you feel me?"

"It's all good, Danny, but it's not me or Cherelle you need to be feeling. It's Cherelle and Big Cheddar who's working on getting their credit repaired; they're the ones buying a house together."

Hearing Cheddar's name mentioned, Danny saves face. "Girl, you know I was just playing; you and Cherelle is like family. Besides, Big Cheddar doesn't have any damn credit anyway. He's been locked up over half his life making mad furniture for two dollars a day! Who would give Cheddar a damn loan to do anything?"

Crystal takes another swallow from the shot glass with her answer, "You'll have to talk to Big Lester about that; Cheddar's working for him now."

Realizing Crystal has the ups signifying, Danny concedes her brilliance. "Girl, bye! I need a few drinks to get my head right is all. Just have that ass here when I'm faded, and we'll see who's funny."

Crystal questions with feigned perplexity. "Who, me?" She's another one up on Danny.

Realizing he can't match her wit, Danny gives up. "Girl,

shut up! I walked through the door with plenty of lap dance money. You're not funny, and I'm not laughing, so I'll be about my business to get my money's worth." Continuing on, Danny pops his fingers to sing along with the song aired in the club. "Workin' that ass, workin' that ass, sexy muthafucka, workin' that ass. That's what I'm talking about!" Approaching the turnstile expectantly, Danny presents his ticket to enter the showcase. He acknowledges, ""Damn it's going on up in here!" He then places the contents of his pockets in the property tray.

Security commences with the protocol with the waving of the metal detector across Danny's body. Danny talks during the process. "Believe me, I understand, a player's been recognized in the establishment. I stand before you, frozen, posing, and waiting to be chosen! A player doesn't pretend; if he's droppin' paper, he intends to win. As a player in the midst, playing my hand and went broke, another player would peel off a knot of big faces, fat enough to make a white mouth mule choke!"

Danny pats the money outline in his pocket reassuringly. "As long as big face currency stays in print, true players will have them creased and stacked like faithful tenants paying rent. That's rain, shine, and every day, player. Whatever a good time costs." Danny wiggles his fingers, indicating the player's dap. He questions, "You recognize boss game sprinkled?"

"That's what I'm talking about. Recognize a player! Big Les and I have been doing this since the sandbox in elementary school, and we're built for everything that comes with it! Should anything foul go down, we'll be in the last booth facing the entrance. That player's pass allows all that, and while I'm handling the bizness, I'll speak on your well-being. I'm definitely feeling your style, so I'll talk to partna to lend you out to me two days a week. I've been looking for a driver and a big body to push the line while a player conducts the bizness; you feelin' me? By the way, player, I'm D-boy." Danny presents his hand with his introduction.

The two men give dap, bumping fists.

"Is that right? I'm Big Kickass! Big Les is around the way; he's in conversation, player."

Danny walks toward the direction motioned. "Good looking out! No doubt he's waiting on D-boy."

Kickass calls for Danny's attention, "D-boy, you're moving way too fast, player. You left your business in the property tray!"

Danny reacts dramatically with a sniffle. He holds his nose as though he left behind player's candy or contraband. With an about-face turn, Danny puts on a hip stroll in his return to collect the tray's contents. He admits, "Under other circumstances, I'd leave the crumbs and chalk it up as gratuity for the working man, but to equate time with money, I'll make an exception this time. I'll hold on to these crumbs to clear my head." Danny clears his nose with a sniffle. "By the way, Kick-ass, I like how you handled that. You and me, we need to connect. Without question a hater would have kept what belongs to a player. When I chop it up with my man, I'll put a few dollars in your pocket for that play. As you know, respect is the player's oath. No true player can be himself without that integrity. You know what I'm saying?"

As Danny comes upon the property tray, in full view is

the box of Big Shot condoms. Quick with wit, he makes an adjustment. "Oh yeah, those was for just in case. The way these choice females are throwing themselves at a player, he has to protect himself at all times. Shee-it, a player never knows when he's subject to be chose."

Kickass chuckles. "Yeah, I'm hearing you on that, D-boy! Don't forget to put in that good word to your player partna. I'd appreciate that, you know what I'm saying, player?"

Continuing on, Danny strolls into the club's interior. He comes across the club owner who happens to be in conversation with a patron. Danny talks over the music to interrupt. "Ha hah, Big Les! What it do, big baby? Long time no see."

Big Les cuts the conversation off with the patron. "Kimble, let me get back with you on that."

Danny and Big Les embrace with pleasantries. "Danny boy, you been hiding or what? Don't tell me you've been broke. Last time you were here, you were calling it like the weather forecast." Big Les twiddles his huge fingers. "On top of the lap dance premium, you made it rain with twenty-dollar bills. You popped bottles like you were drinking bottled water. For two weeks the private rooms were booked in your honor like you were the president. The whole time you had the strippers massaging your 'little head,' you kept them with all the jokes. They were all laughing phony and shit like cheap whores in church. Since then you've been mighty scarce with the business, player, but here you stand glowing like Lazarus, so, Mr. President, what brings you back from the dead? You're here to spend a government check?"

Danny laughs. "Ah that's fucked up. Big dude, you got the funnies. You did that, go ahead and clown then. " The two bump fists, giving dap.

"Danny, a dude better get off first when dealing with your-fast talking ass. If he doesn't, he'll be all discombobulated and fucked up with your bullshit. By the time the lame figured out what you were talking about, he'd wake up mad as a mother-fucker. As we speak, every lame you ever worked is plotting to do something to your slick ass."

Danny pats his pocket to indicate he's holding money. "Big dude? Real talk, the real bizness? I need to hook up with Brenda and Joanie, and I know you can make it happen. I'm doing a lil' something for my boy. You know Paul?"

"Uh huh, he's the credit-repair dude we went to school with. What about him?"

"Big Les, he's feeling it tonight. He's having married-man issues that won't go away. That's why I'm here." Danny exaggerates with hand gestures. "He wants to branch out to the other side to where the players play."

Not impressed, Big Les chuckles. "I heard that! Mr. Credit Repair must be expecting a huge extension on his consultation fees and credit lines. Around here, Brenda and Joanie's worth every bit of what their sweet asses look like, expensive! They keep the doors open, you feel me? Look around the joint. In every chair sits an ass. That's twenty dollars a chair plus the three-drink minimum. In this perfect scenario, Big Les wins every time, and its lovely! They come lined up too. The good citizenry pays willingly to watch expensive ass, which I provide literally. Are you doing the math, player?"

"Damn, Big Les, I know you're not trying to work D-boy!"

Big Les motions his huge hands. "Playboy, hold on, let me finish! The dedicated patrons in this establishment, hear how they're feeling Brenda and Joanie? Faithfully they throw five grand a night to watch Brenda and Joanie shake that ass."

Big Les motions to the stage where Brenda's doing her thing. While performing a split routine, Brenda bounces her ass like a ball when it comes in contact with the stage floor. From the split position, Brenda rolls onto her stomach. She then toots her ass toward the audience. With precise muscle control her ass claps and twerks. The crowd cheers Brenda's performance in appreciative chorus.

Work that, beautiful ass, Work that beautiful ass!
Work, that beautiful ass, Work that beautiful ass!

A voice yells: "One more again for me, baby!"
Brenda continues with the twerking and clapping of her ass.

Work that, beautiful ass, Work that beautiful ass!
Work, that beautiful ass, Work that beautiful ass!

"Just once more again, baby!

Work that, beautiful ass, Work that beautiful ass!
Work, that beautiful ass. Work that beautiful ass!

A voice yells from within the audience, "There's still a lot of my pension check left for a private show, baby. Just you keep workin' that beautiful ass!"

Big Les comments on Brenda's performance. "See how she works the crowd poppin' that ass? The house is making money. At the end of the night the patrons go home faithfully to their loving wives with their Johnsons hard. They'll lie in bed with their eyes closed pretending Joanie and Brenda are sliding down their poles. Isn't that a hell of a way to keep a good marriage intact?"

Danny grimaces. "Hell, yeah, I wanna watch too."

"Danny hold on, don't cream your pants yet. When Brenda's finished doing her thing, Joanie works her jelly throwing that ass for another six or seven songs. When the starting lineup breaks, that's the cue for the second squad to be on deck to entertain. Everybody gets in where they fit in. Brenda and Joanie shower and freshen up with a wardrobe change. Like clockwork they'll do private shows for another six or seven songs. That's seven days a week and twice on Sundays, playboy."

"Damn it! Big Les, I wanna come watch too."

Big Les waves Danny off. "This type of entertainment isn't for you. The same goes for Brenda and Joanie. What you want and what you can afford limits you. Danny, it's too rich for your blood."

"Big Les, I know you're not serious, so don't bullshit me."

"I'm as serious as the collection taken right before the good reverend's benediction."

"Big Les, why go that hard in the paint? Don't put me out there. I don't speak on the church like that."

"Oh, playboy, did I hit a nerve? My bad. I won't mention either the collection plate or the benediction. But since this is real talk, when was the last time you've seen high-end goods on sale? Marinate on that one."

Danny has no answer.

"That's what I'm talking about, playboy. Your mouth's open but you haven't said a damn thing, so I'll answer the question. It's fuck! No! Either you walk with what you want or perpetrate petty larceny and get your poor ass downtown buying knockoffs, so get the fuck out of here being sentimental." Big Les glances at Danny's shoes. "Did you learn anything from the marketing ploy, or you're just another fool wearing an athlete's gear because the merchandise is expensive?"

"What ploy? Now you're screaming on Mike? Mike's papered out the game, Big Les. You're letting your money and girls go to your head. If MJ came in here, you'll personally wave him into V.I.P., don't bullshit. He'll eat free, drink free, get complimentary pictures and everything! Once he's plugged with your girls, it'll be a month of Sundays before MJ's seen, because he'll be in the private rooms farting out the sheets."

Looking into Danny's perplexed expression, Big Les addresses Danny's ignorance of his astute business principles. "If you're finished bumping your gums, here's some understanding to a fool! Everybody walking through the door will pay the fee. Whoever plants an ass in a chair will be buying the three-drink minimum, and whoever wants a private dance will pay

V.I.P. Premium!" Big Les gives an emphatic chuckle. "Hmm-hmm-hmm, the sign out front reads Big Les's Joint, not Simple Simon's. Look around the establishment. You come here like everyone else, knowing Big Les has what you willingly pay for. You feeling me? Now back to the question, player. How much did you pay for the kicks?"

Danny raises his right foot slightly to showcase his shoes. In doing so, he looks around the strip club to see if anyone has noticed his kicks. "Shee-it, Big Les, you already know what they go for, big baby. Four bills, but that's not what the kid paid. I flashed my player's card for the player's ticket. Yes, sir. D-boy stays with the latest and the greatest before the crowd with less the cost. It's no secret either, D-boy's living the beautiful life."

Big Les smiles as he schools Danny. "Hold up, player! The secret is they limit the pairs or throwbacks they put out. It keeps simpletons to where they'll stand in line for a week before they're allowed to spend their money, and believe me, player, when you're allowed to break bread, you sho-nuff do feel dignified doing it, don't you, player?"

The crowd's whistling and cheering of Brenda's performance interrupts the conversation. Big Les addresses the crowd's enthusiasm. "You hear that? That's the sound of success! Buying power of willing patrons spending money, and they do this without there ever being any sales. They come through the door knowing there are no knockoffs, just pure raw energy. Everybody's spending and getting what they came for with no shame." Big Les puts his huge hands on Danny's shoulders. "In other words, like everyone else that's here for Brenda and Joanie's services, you pay to play, and be willing to un-ass plenty of the big-face bills!" Big Les releases Danny to chuckle, "Hmm-hmm-hmm. You feeling all this?"

"Big Les, what the hell are you talking about? I thought we was like that. As kids we made pigeon coops together, and what the fuck have I done to have you go so big on me? Damn!"

"Slow your roll, Danny; you haven't done shit! It's what I won't allow you to do, and that's come up in Big Lester's joint hustling. It was all good until you opened your mouth, then you canceled yourself."

Danny questions the turn to seriousness. "What happened to all the love, big baby? You're treating your boy like a righteous lame? We do it like this now, Big Les?" With his arms outstretched, Danny awaits a response, but Big Les remains unobligated. Danny breaks the silence. "Lester? Big Les! Lester, quit bullshitting! If I owed you money you'd have a lot to say. Big baby? Where's the love for your boy, Lester?"

Big Les cracks a smile. "Look at you! Did I have that ass shook? You didn't know whether to shit or run."

Both bump fists, giving dap.

Danny takes his friend to task good-heartedly. "Yeah, you had me, you went big, but I wasn't scared of your big ass. I'm a player, Big Les. I refuse to do any arguing or fighting; that shit's barbaric, but I will bust a cap in that ass! Know what I'm saying? Homies or not, playing me like that I'm scary, and you already know messing with scary people is very dangerous."

Big Les chuckles. "Hmm-hmm-hmm. I hear you talking. I

smell all that gas you're passing too, but you haven't said nothing yet. Look, man, real talk. The square you work for, the credit dude, your so-called partner? The whole tickets on him, and you already know how I move. When Brenda and Joanie's services are rendered, have that square pass the paper with the quickness."

Danny embraces his friend. "Good looking out. Big Les. That's what I'm talking about. Players will make shit happen. Those other dudes, they're not knowing how to conduct the bizness. Man, I love you for this one."

Big Les removes himself from Danny's embrace pitching the dozens. "Get your comical ass somewhere before somebody thinks we're a couple."

Danny laughs, covering his mouth with his fist. "Ah, that's fucked up, Big Les. You're off the chain for that one. Damn!"

Big Les clutches his huge hands, signifying, "Playboy? You talk like you can afford premium ass, knowing damn well that's not how you're living. Send it so you can spend it. I heard all that weak shit before. Danny, who do you know that's simple enough to give you their money or even embarrass themselves being associated with you? You're even standing in the joint like you're supposed to be important. Well, somebody dropped a dime on your important ass, player. Just knowing you're in here, the Feds went on tactical alert, waiting to bust your narrow ass. The Feds got wind you're selling counterfeit EBT cards. The jig is up, so get somewhere with your bullshit." Big Les waves to Danny playfully. "Hey, player, you must have a lot of important people on hold, just so you can bless them with your presence, right? Remove your ass!"

Danny doubles over laughing, "Ah, that's fucked up. You did that, Big Les. Damn! Ha hah, yeah, man. We got the major plug for the night. I'm stepping outside to call my boy. He needs to know we're on deck with it. Later, big baby!"

Continuing toward the cheering and whistles of Brenda's performance, Danny yells over the crowd in baritone, "BIG LES, BABE-BAY!"

CHAPTER SIXTEEN

*L*ester Brown's strip club is located in the inner city, yet his core clientele lived in the suburbs surrounding the inner city's metropolis. An astute businessman, Lester Brown was both savvy and methodical in establishing his targeted clientele of high rollers. Known in some circles for his fierce reputation, no one stepped out of line with Lester Brown. In the event of a situation, there was a squad of loyal bruisers to handle whatever wasn't conducive to either the strip club's ambience or the safety of the surrounding property. As a reflection of his business acumen, Lester Brown provided the limousines, and the beautiful women accompanying them, which picked up and returned the players to the parking lots he owned. Lester Brown's connections and wealthy clientele prevented the groveling for celebrity validation. Whenever celebrities came through, he didn't go out of his way to serenade any of them with promises or gifts. Celebrities paid upon entrance like everyone else. Any self-proclaimed player would have to prove himself by buying the fifty-thousand-dollar V.I.P. membership before Lester Brown was impressed. Another perk that attracted his wealthy clientele was the public knowledge that whatever happened in Lester Brown's stayed there, without the intensive scrutiny from the local vice squads or undercover operations. Put simply, Lester Brown was both politically connected and protected. He afforded the same cover of protection to his clientele whenever they came to enjoy themselves.

Approaching the club exit, Danny comes across a guy who appears to be from the city's outer suburbs. Uninhibited and dancing off beat, the suburb guy gives an honest attempt to do the cabbage-patch dance. Witnessing the ridiculous demonstration, a waitress chooses finesse over ridicule with a forced cough. "Ahem! Dirty martini on the rocks with one chasing."

The suburb guy acknowledges the arrival of his festive persuasion with slurred speech. "Ooh, baby! I hope you made this one really filthy. I was about ready to chase a fire truck for another drink."

Overlooking the humor, the waitress tactfully removes suburb's hand from her arm. She expresses in good taste, "Here you go, Harley; it's exactly the way you asked for it, filthy and dirty. Lucky for you, I found another jar of olives for this round. I explained to the bartender I'd be a minute with the tab, because you asked me to watch as you did the cabbage-patch dance. And you didn't wait for me to return before you started? Shame on you, Harley! Then go ahead with your bad self and do the damn thing!"

Grabbing the first of the two martinis, in one motion Harley throws his head back to finish the drink with one swallow. With a hiss he slams the glass onto the waitress's tray. "Thank you, Ms. Pretty glass of cognac; that one was really filthy." Returning to his ridiculous dance attempt, Harley makes another request. "Ooh-wee! That's just the way I like them, filthy 'n' dirty. Stack two more, baby! That's what Harley's talking about! Be sure to put a lil' something for yourself on my tab for that one, and you come right back here and flirt with Harley."

Placing the remaining martini at Harley's table, the waitress entertains indulgence to other patrons. "Hey, Al, are you ready for another round?"

"Tina, if you're the one bringing it, then I insist on being the one enjoying it. Two French connections with Courvoisier doubles."

"You got it. Courvoisier doubles for Al. I'll be back shortly."

"Hello, player, glad to see you in the house. What can I set you up with tonight?"

"Tina, you already know. I'm spoiled. Bring four bottles of that grand Patrone and have the kitchen send two of the captain's seafood platters for my guests."

"Coming right up, Dave."

"Thanks, Tina, and when you get a chance, let Big Les know I'm in the house."

As the waitress proceeds to the bar, Danny watches Harley's antics from a few feet away. Under other circumstances, Harley would be an easy mark or opportunity. He'd bring it all on himself by being in this part of town looking goofy in his cabbage-patch dance attempts. To Harley's advantage, he's in Lester Brown's joint. As goofy and vulnerable as he appeared, here Harley was off limits and protected, and no one dared disrespect the club's atmosphere. It wasn't worth the risk of being folded up like an old suitcase for being stupid, Big Train, Cheddar, and the fold-up crew saw to that. Being no exception to the rule, Danny becomes uncomfortable from just entertaining the thought. His conscience reveals his respect for Lester Brown. "Damn, where in the hell is Big Cheddar and them?"

Danny approaches his mark from another angle. As Harley continued to cabbage patch ridiculously, Danny approaches the table to smoothly pick up the martini to sip. He smacks his lips, "Damn! This is one of those names I can't pronounce, and you went and fucked it up? What the hell's wrong with you? This is a half a glass of olives. You had that much more space for more expensive drank."

Coming out of his spin stumbling, Harley's words are slurred. "Hey, bud-bud-buddy, that's that's my drink. Whaaat in the hell are you do-doing?"

Danny interrupts with wit. "Oh, hell no! Now you're fucking up the song too? This is 'Lady Doin' the Cab Driver!' Prentz is the man. How in the hell do you fuck up on a Prentz song? Let me show you how to do this here. When you cabbage patch, you have to remember this is a black dance; that's why you're having problems. This dance wasn't made with white folks in mind. That's why you look so stupid doing it, but I'll give you game." Danny instructs, "Everything's in the hips. You need to be smooth with this here, just like I'm doing. Like this! Relax your back and get that hand-foot coordination going. Okay, you work with it."

Harley fails miserably in his attempt. Danny reinstructs, "Oh, hell no. Stop! You know what the problem is? You're too tight. You're nowhere near loose enough. You're out here cabbage patchin,' stiff, like you're tired and sick! Order two more of those expensive martinis—double shots, and leave them damn olives alone. That's all you need."

Harley nods to the waitress. "Pretty lady, you heard my agent; we're getting it right. Two martinis, doubles, hold the dirt, no olives."

Danny interjects, "Triples! Make that two triples. We're working over here, and I'm getting tired fast. I need a wake-up, so hurry up with my inspiration!"

The next stripper's performance brings forth another song, Michael Jayson's "Chiller." The lights dim just as the werewolf howls. Harley attempts the cabbage-patch dance. "This song's fucken great! Too bad I never got a chance to bid on the jacket he wore in the video!"

Danny interjects, "Oh, hell no! Now you're really out here fucking up! The cabbage patch doesn't flow with Chiller! Choose your moves with the groove. You have to feel this shit. You're dancing like you're at a party in the suburbs. Keep it smooth; you need a repertoire of moves with expression. Close your eyes and move your hips like this."

The waitress returns with the requests. "Two premium vodka martinis, triples."

Harley motions to accept the martinis. Danny's admonishing stops him. "Whoa, Harley, hold on! This round wasn't ordered for your benefit. You have to pay for this game. Just you keep fucking up trying to do the cabbage patch. You have to graduate and be certified before you drink the good shit. Just keep dancing and working your way to getting it together." Danny critiques Harley's cabbage patch-dance attempts. "Now you're feeling it; that's it. You're almost doing it. Okay, I like that. Then pretend you know what the fuck you're doing. Dance! That's it. Then come on with it! Now you're doing the damn thing. Hold the fuck up! What the fuck did you just do? Was that the Michael Jayson? You're holding your dick? You don't hold your dick on the dance floor. People from the suburbs don't look right holding their dicks. Damn, you fucked me up with that one." Danny mimics Harley's diction. "Make mine reee-ly filthy. And what the hell is with you and those big-ass olives? You're out here dancing and looking goofy like you're at your best friend's wedding. Oh hell no! I need a drank."

Danny grabs the first martini. He empties the drink in two swallows before returning it to the tray. Reaching for the second drink, he smoothly spins to dance with the music. As he swallows he maintains his balance. With the liquor's burn traveling down his throat, Danny hisses like a cat to slam the martini glass onto the tray. "That shit was good!"

Witnessing Danny's impropriety, the waitress has an expression that leaves nothing unsaid. Danny defends his actions. "And what the hell is supposed to be wrong with you? You're looking like some shit tastes nasty in your mouth. I've seen you around, and you're off the block, so you already know what it is. The game's to be sold, not told, and game recognizes game. You got the fat tip, and I worked him for a fat drank. Charge it to the game. That shit wasn't easy, either. Look at the lame out here cabbage patching, all off-beat, grabbing and posing with his dick like he's a grown-ass Michael Jayson. Look at him. I'm not mad at you for being paid. I put in work too. Sometimes it's on you, sometimes it's on me. On them, it's all the time, they pay what they weigh." Danny motions to Harley and the other squares that appear out of place. "Shee-it, see what I'm saying? Look at them already lining that ass up. It's always supposed to be on them."

The waitress looks at Danny disbelievingly. "I'm telling Train and Cheddar you're in here hustling Lester's people."

Danny regresses immediately to the simpleton he's accustomed to being. He bats his eyes nervously. "Why put Train and Cheddar in my life like that? They aren't nice, and you already know they have people scared of them. The shit you're doing is illegal. It's a terrorist threat."

CHAPTER SEVENTEEN

*I*t's 10:00 p.m. Within the silence of her bedroom, Kelly drinks wine while watching the cupcake candles diminish to a liquefied glow. During her vigil she's reprocessed the events leading to the misunderstanding. As she reflects, Paul left appearing cool and collected, but Kelly knew better. Paul was cut deep from what appeared in his mindset to be high treason. Having the purest of intentions, Kelly's reasoning behind bringing the letter home was simply to use it as a tool to renew the romantic spontaneity in her marriage. Because of the turn of events, Paul's ego has negated what Kelly envisioned for their evening together. Without a doubt, Kelly knew Paul's mind was running in every direction. He would never understand Kelly's rationale; it was a man thing, and inadequacy was something Paul would never stand for. From Kelly's perspective she's emotional not because Paul left, but rather he chose to react with his ego while knowing in his heart he doesn't believe the circumstance. Kelly would never betray her husband with lies. Egos and men! How did the two ever come together? With another sip of wine, Kelly recalls the name of the letter's intended recipient. "Tiffany Adams. Well, Ms. Tiffany, hopefully Paul will read more into the letter and realize it was written to you. I opened it only because I liked the letter's fragrance. Believe me, girlfriend, it wasn't worth all this."

Kelly sighs, *I did bring it on myself, and I can't stop what's already done. I should've placed that damn letter in the mail for the woman and been done with it. I had no idea I opened a Pandora's Box to be cursed.*"

The phone rings. Kelly's mother has called every fifteen minutes since the initial one-hour conversation discussing her daughter's well-being. Kelly's voice cracks as she holds off her mother's relentless inquisition of Paul's whereabouts.

"Well, honey, is he back yet? Has he even called? Surely someone caring would check to see if you're all right. What sort of man would leave his wife after an argument, especially when the whole fiasco was his fault? It's his fault, you know? Will you trust him after this? Kelly, how could you still love him after what he's done? Look at you; you're gorgeous. He's supposed to be there feeding you grapes or rubbing your feet. Do you know how many men would love to have such a gorgeous wife? Honey, do you remember the show *True Dynasty*? That's the lifestyle I envisioned for you. You're supposed to be J.R. in a woman's perspective. My goodness, why is he still out at this time of night, and why would any decent man be away from his wife at this hour? How many hours has it been since your husband's been gone, Kelly? Do you remember the last thing he said? Were you able to read into his facial expressions? Honey, I can't help if you're not saying anything. Are you listening, Kelly? Let me tell you, before your father died, I told him there was something I didn't like about this guy. I should have known something was with him when he stopped coming with you and me to dinner."

"Mom, that's enough already. When Paul left I wasn't paying attention to the time, and I don't know where he went. He just left with a cold look about him. I can't explain any other details."

"You can't explain? I don't know if I would want you to. He obviously doesn't care enough to call to explain where he is or why he's having another temper tantrum. Kelly, you're making excuses for him. Honey, why? He's nothing like your father! Now that man was something to talk about. He catered to my every whim, no matter what. Your father's the type of man we've should've married you to, but I was so afraid if we didn't allow you to date this jerk you'd run off and elope. Honey, why is he so upset about a letter that belongs to someone else? It's not like you're making love to it. Who does this? How old is the adolescent? My goodness, I imagine he's jealous of Randy too. You did say Randy found the letter? Oh, don't tell me he's accusing the dog! Is this guy ever a piece of work! Honey, maybe after reading that letter your husband's guilty of something that he needs to be doing. Are you asking me what I think, Kelly?"

"No, Mother, I'm not. Randy and I, actually Randy found it, and being nosey, I read it. It was written so well I made the mistake of bringing it home. I couldn't help myself. It was reminiscent of how Paul and I began. It was so sweet it engulfed me." Kelly blows her nose.

"What was that? Are you crying baby? This insensitive man's nowhere to be found, and my precious daughter's crying for him? Honey, please be careful. He may be putting things in your food. I've never known my precious daughter to allow a man to do something like this, and be so willing to take the blame for his wrong doing. He's the one in the wrong, Kelly! I should call the police. Honey, you don't sound right. He may have put a whammy on you. How you found this letter doesn't sound right either, and the way you're acting reminds me of a show I watched on the real-life movie channel. The poor woman's husband was much like that man you married. He was downright despicable. He slowly poisoned his wife to her death, so that he could marry his secretary. Believe me, honey, when they're like that no-good man you married, I can see them coming a mile away. It's obvious you love him and you're not hearing anything I'm telling you, but baby, I'm your mother. Would I tell you anything to steer you wrong? Kelly, I want you to enjoy your marriage like your father and I enjoyed ours. In saying so, I want to clear the air on another thought. Don't pay any attention to those nasty rumors at your father's wake and funeral. Honey, the truth is your father enjoyed working. In order to provide for his family he worked practically every day, sometimes double shifts. It had nothing to do with the foolishness of working himself to death rather than being at home and miserable with me. That's total nonsense! Now back to that man you married. Honey, do you have friends you can talk with that might know what your husband's doing? Have you tried getting tickets to Dr. Feel? From the sound of things it appears you two could use some serious counseling."

"No, Mother, I don't know anyone who knows Dr. Feel personally, nor do I know of anyone who gets tickets to his show."

"Kelly, excuse me for a moment. I need to find my pills. I have really bad gas tonight. Oh, there they are. Woo, my goodness, the bubbling and bloating's terrible! Okay, honey, I'm back. Here's word to the wise, take care of that to-die-for body you have. It doesn't last forever, you know? Look at me; I'm in my late fifties and I'm lactose intolerant. I can't drink milk or eat dairy without running to the bathroom for a twenty-minute stay. Woo, my goodness, its back already! It's a good thing I live alone. What would I do without the air freshener in the bathrooms? Whenever it's extremely bad, I keep the fart fan on with all the windows open. It's so embarrassing to live like this. Oh, it's really bad tonight. Wow! Is it ever going to stop? Oh, boy. Okay, woo! That's a little better. Honey, I was thinking. Knowing which direction you walk Randy, your husband may have planted the letter. I wouldn't doubt he paid someone to introduce himself as the letter's writer, hoping you would flirt. The dirty bastard's probably having people from the *Cheeter's* show follow you around invading your privacy. Honey, just so you know, should there ever be an urge to where you feel emotionally uncontrolled, no worries; I still have your father's guns."

"Mom, that's not necessary."

"I'm just saying, Kelly, if your emotions led you to commit the act, a jury would look at it as a crime of passion. With so many women in this country being abused, believe me, you have nothing to worry about."

Overlooking her mother's warped mindset, Kelly blows her nose. "No, Mom, Paul would never plant anything on my walk route, nor have I noticed anyone filming or following me."

"I'm just saying, honey, pay attention. The people from *Cheeter's* are relentless! People wearing earpieces will film you from vans behind tinted windows. They'll think nothing of it to follow you into the bathroom at restaurants and movies. Kelly, you can't trust anyone. As your mother from time to time, I'd check your father's billfold for his pay stubs just to make sure he was going to work. I did this out of love, to protect our family. You're my precious daughter, Kelly, and I wouldn't want anything to happen to you. Honey, protect yourself. Whenever you leave the house, please look around to see if anyone's tailing you. With that being said, the thought I had earlier was a good one. I'm going to the gun range tomorrow. You wanna come with me? You never know about these things."

Choosing not to respond to her mother's outrageous offer, Kelly takes the high road. "Mom, I love you. Thanks for the advice. I'll pay attention for *Cheeter's* whenever I leave the house as well. Good night."

Ending the call, Kelly reaches to the nightstand for the televisions remote. She turns the television on. Between sips of wine, she browses through the channel guide to notice the real-life movie channel. Kelly rethinks her mother's rationale about the movie she watched. With a shake of her head, she refuses to act on any of her mother's entertaining thoughts. Pressing the remote, she turns the television off. "Mother, this is crazy; you should be doing more with your time." Randy has been posed comfortably on her bedspread the entire time. Kelly rubs the toy dog for comfort between wine sips. "My Wandy knows the truth, doesn't him? Mmm-hmm. Does Wandy wanna sleep with his mommy? Hopefully Daddy will be home soon and we'll all sleep together."

Its 1:30 a.m., Kelly keeps vigil for Paul's return watching the clock. Continuing with the wine and the rubbing of her toy terrier, Kelly sniffles to whine, "Paul, where are you?"

Randy barks as if he were asking the same question. With a slight cock of its head, the toy terrier looks around the room expectantly for Paul to appear.

CHAPTER EIGHTEEN

*J*n luxury suite 1440, the soulful and melodic voice of Melanie Fulani's "Bring It to Me Right" is faintly heard in the corridor of the hotel's fourteenth floor. Coupled in pairs in the suites living room are Joanie, Paul, Brenda, and Danny. As the party dances, Danny holds a handful of Brenda's perfect ass while offering Paul a blunt hit. "Paul, my bad, you wanna hit this?

Paul holds a glass of vodka as he dances with Joanie. Between dancing, he sips his drink to remain motionless to allow Joanie to dance and grind against him. Paul talks over the music. "Danny, I'm good, but we do need to talk. Remember that conversation we had earlier? That shit's been on my mind working like a mad Russian."

Joanie continues to gyrate her ass against Paul's crotch as she sings along with the music. *"That's right girl, make them come correct with it. They need to understand the real thing! Yeah,*

Yeah, Yea-aah. That's how you handle the bizness!"

Paul motions to the bathroom with a request. "Danny, can I get five minutes in the office?" Disinclined to remove himself from Brenda, Danny takes another blunt hit to hold the smoke in his lungs. "P, we didn't come here to talk. Talking wasn't on the agenda for this evening, buddy. We already had that discussion." With another blunt hit, Danny palms Brenda's ass to admit, "Baby's got it good! P, look around; tell me you're not feeling this. A plush suite, the bomb bud, top shelf liquor, and these fine-ass honeys. You're not feeling any of this?" Danny motions to Joanie. "Baby's throwing you that ass, but you stand there like Mr. Belvedere. What more do you need, a serving table and a bib? Paul, loosen up. We came for everything that comes with a good time and everything good that's yet to happen. Believe me, player, we want all this."

Brenda removes the blunt from Danny's lips acknowledging, "I know that's right. We did show up for the big event to please." After a few hits, she returns the blunt assuring, "Here, baby, have some more stress reliever."

Danny takes a hit to hold the smoke in his lungs,

"Player, there it is, you've heard it yourself. You need to get back in your lane and hit that." Danny motions to Joanie, who's holding a blunt while dancing alone. He looks to Paul disapprovingly. "Damn, she's bad, and you're not feeling none of that? You're trippin'! P, I'm not allowing you to fuck my high off because you wanna simp about Kelly. Suffer all by your lonesome, and don't even think about me going anywhere. I'm here for the duration, partna'. Believe me, there's no other place

I want to be, thank you."

Paul raises his hands for silence, motioning to the bathroom. "Danny, come on; don't go there with me. Step in the office. I need to talk to you in private."

With another blunt hit, Danny releases smoke from his lungs blowing smoke rings.

Paul redirects, "Dude! Can I get five ticks of your time?"

As if motioning to a sideline judge in a football game, Danny looks to Brenda, indicating he wants a full thirty-second time out. Danny passes the blunt. "Baby, hold up! The man appears to be having technical difficulties. Let me see what's happening with dude."

Brenda resigns herself to the couch to join her sister Joanie, who's in the midst of preparing another blunt.

Danny in the meantime lowers his voice to go in on Paul. "Dude, smoke a few blunts to loosen up! Look at these honeys! Paul, they're here with us, and they're here to please. What is it, you had a change of heart? It's four in the morning, so now your dick won't get hard either? You miss Kelly? You're homesick? Is that conscience kicking that ass? Dude, believe me, you've fell in love backwards with your self-righteous bullshit this time! I'll tell you what, player; my conscience is nowhere near heavy. I'm getting my helmet massaged and buffed before the sun comes up. That's taking the long route with a little rest in between, know what I mean?"

Danny chuckles in his brilliance. "I didn't put all this together to fuck around. Won't neither of the honeys leave disappointed in Danny boy. You can put them both on my plate."

Paul talks through clenched teeth canceling the chuckling, which brings Danny back to the simpleton he's accustomed to being. "Danny, just shut the fuck up and follow me to the bathroom! Can I talk to your simple ass, and slow your roll with the blunts, you schizophrenic mother fucker? Whenever you smoke that shit you become stupider than what you look like. Get your comical ass in the bathroom. Just because you chopped it up with Big Les, now you're supposed to be the man? Why would that be, Danny? Because you're impressing high-dollar strippers with purple cush? You simple mother fucker you! You work for me; that's what you do, so get in the bathroom and listen to my problems, you dumb bastard!"

Danny explains, "I'm just fucking around with conversation, Paul. Damn! Before you fire me again, remember you'll need help paying for these high-dollar strippers. The next time you wanna do this, we'll be at an economy hotel in the hood."

Paul ignores Danny's conjecture with a shake of his head. Rather than respond verbally, Paul points a finger in the direction of the suite's bathroom. Danny complies giving an explanation. "Ladies, as you can see, my man has digestion problems. His stomach bothers him, and he has these reactions where he can't breathe, so the dude becomes all dysfunctional. It must be his gout acting up. He keeps eating that rich food, and with this vodka and bomb-ass bud on top of everything else, you know he's having problems. Yeah, man! Dude is really hurting."

Paul speaks for the record, pointing to the bathroom. "Danny, who asked you to explain any of how I feel? None of that changes what I need to tell you, so don't make excuses for me. I need only a few minutes to get my point across, so get your simple ass in the bathroom, you stupid mother fucker!"

Danny overlooks Paul's outburst to reassure their guests, "Ladies, believe me, this is nothing, and we will do this. I'll call room service and order some Bismol for his stomach. We'll keep to the master plan like it is, just like that. You honeys feeling what I'm saying? Just like the song, 'All night long,' in a flash Danny boy will return for the other game. To help remove them thongs! Ladies, it's no secret, you're already knowing what it is."

Ignoring Danny's antics, Paul pushes his best friend toward the bathroom. Joanie blows into a party horn in festive protest; its squelching noise brings Joanie and Brenda's high into intense laughter. As Joanie continues with the blunt's preparation, Brenda questions, "Damn, Joanie, you're not done removing that tobacco from the cigar? How long will you have a bitch wait to enjoy a blunt?"

Being forced to the bathroom, Danny rearranges his disheveled attire. "Paul, slow your roll. You straight embarrassed me in front of the females like I stole something."

"Danny, I'm trying to tell you what happened today. Just listen!"

"Listen? Paul, outside of being with these fine honeys, I don't want to entertain anything you have to say. You do the listening for a change. How about listening to the noise I'll be making through the walls with the honeys? I didn't bring them here as a boy scout. I'm not here to bullshit, either. Unknown to you, when I smoke, my dick gets hard, very hard. That being said, I have no business in the bathroom with you, talking about some shit we already talked about. For a dude that has it all together, Paul you're looking real lame right about now."

"I have it together, Danny, it's just uh…"

"It's just Kelly has you all in your feelings; Paul, that's just what it is."

Having no rebuttal, Paul looks to Danny in silence.

Danny breaks the stalemate. "I can see you're really deep in your feelings. Since you already fucked off my high, what is it? No, don't answer; you'll fuck up again. Did you think to bring a blunt with your problems? I have to smoke while I'm dealing with somebody else's problems."

Paul puts his hands in the air to indicate he isn't holding.

Danny clowns. "Damn, you're very, very pitiful! Pitiful, hold on, I'll get one from the honeys. Paul, I'm just going to the other side of the door, so don't kill yourself. Don't cut your wrists or fool with them sleeping pills, either. Fuck around if you want; that's on you. Don't expect me to explain anything to room service or whoever comes to find your pitiful ass. I won't be explaining shit, to anybody, believe that."

Returning to the suite's living room, Danny comes upon the couch to where Joanie and Brenda are enjoying a blunt. Danny goes into character. "Ha-hah, ladies, yes. You two lovelies are not forgotten. We had to step in the bathroom to discuss player's bizness. I'm sure you two honeys can understand. By the way, we'll need that blunt you lovelies are smoking. Feel free to help yourselves to roll another. In between time, there's plenty of the expensive drank. You lovelies feeling me? While in the company of players, you ladies treat yourselves accordingly. We should be away from your presence for only a short time, so there's no need to think about being anywhere else. I'm glad to say yes, ladies, you're in the midst of giants."

Brenda takes a hit, passing the blunt to her sister. "Joanie, you hear player campaigning? I know that's right. He wants us to spend the night and then take us shopping in the morning."

Brenda coyly reassures, "Player, I know you'll step out there suited and booted. While you're blessing us in the Louie store, try not to scare anybody with that player's hand. Between now and then, whenever you're ready to handle the other business, don't worry; we got you. We'll be right here to serve that up."

Joanie takes a hit. Passing the blunt to Danny. "I know that's right. When you 'cum' back from handling your business, don't be stingy with the blunt, player. I like mine proper and thick. I can't wait to take a nice long hit of that big, thick, blunt. I'd like to see what it tastes like before you cum."

Hearing the teasing offer, Danny momentarily loses his player's persona. "No shit! I'll be back. It ain't nothing! Baby girl, be careful of what you ask for. You know Danny stays with the bizness. Hey, uh, seriously though, what you just said? Is that included in what we paid? I mean uh, whatever gratuity Big Les threw in for his player partners?"

To avoid exposing their mockery, each sister looks to the other in hopes for an answer. Brenda, the more direct of the two, whispers seductively, "When you're finished handling your business, just 'cum' back. Player, you won't be disappointed."

Taking a blunt hit, Danny attempts what he thinks is a Cuban accent, "Blanca, you speak me tongue. You know sumting? Listen, and I telling you. A mane has two things, his balls and how he handles them. Lucky for you, Blanca, I got balls, and I do both together, mane."

A yell from the bathroom interrupts Danny's delusional gangster impersonation. "Hey, Scarface! Bring the money-counting machines! I need help counting all this paper. Just hurry the fuck up and get your simple ass back in here!"

Danny points to the bathroom. "I never liked this cockroach! I make a few moves to take care of this bug. When I come back from Miami, me and you; we go on a vacation together. Blanca? I tink maybe you like me."

Danny takes a blunt hit to yell toward the bathroom, "I no more wurking for you, mane. Yesterday, I retire!"

In his return to the bathroom, Danny takes Paul to task. "Slow your roll! I'm pitching the big bang theory out there, and you're screaming through the joint like you're lonely! Since I was so rudely taken away from that fine ass in the living room, hell, you might as well go ahead and simp and whine. You know how everybody has their part to play? Can we just hurry the fuck up and get to mine? My part's the blunt. As soon as the blunt's gone, I'm leaving with it, right back the fuck out there with the honeys. You can believe that! Okay, blunt's burning, so start talking!"

"Danny, I was trying to tell you what happened after you dropped me off."

"Then come on with it, Paul! Just don't fuck with the little high I have left, and keep your pitiful conversation ahead of this blunt. If you can do that, I ain't trippin; let's roll with it."

Paul recaps the events leading to the letter's discovery. "Danny, walking through the front door the gumbo hit me. I didn't see Kelly, but I heard music in the bedroom. Before having dinner, I went to the bathroom with the intentions of washing my ass. Instead I opened the bathroom door to a burning glow of candles everywhere. There was a half-empty wine glass and a bottle of wine next to the Jacuzzi. On the floor was a letter written from some dude to Kelly, and he was going hard at it. You've known Kelly just as long as I have. Danny, when have you ever known her to give anybody any play? Either dude's mack's tight like that, or I'm slipping. Now I've second guessed myself ever since I left the house. Like maybe I don't have what I had. Danny, I think I've lost Kelly."

"Hm-m hm-m! I'm listening, Paul, but you're not making sense. Wasn't your woman at home when you left? Then why would you be looking for her? Hitting this blunt is what you need to do, because you sound just as stupid as you make me out to be. That shit wasn't funny either!" Danny passes the blunt. "Paul, take a hit. You need this good shit. It works wonders! Nobody's ever stressed smoking good shit, know what I'm saying? Take another hit; get real fucked up. Try to relax your mind after you hit it. For this crisis, Paul, I'll tell you like you tell me all the time, thinking and good reasoning isn't for you. Today you're giving me the responsibility to think. Allowing you to think is like calling me stupid. At this point we both know better than that, don't we? Remember, I'm doing the thinking. You just relax and follow my lead. Now go ahead, take another good toke to get your mind right."

Paul takes long pulls to hold the heavy smoke in his lungs. "Damn, Danny. Where'd you find this? It's better than the last stuff. This high's really smooth; no bite. I'm feeling it. I'd like to take some home and smoke with Kelly, but I don't want to seem weak." Paul takes another hit to ask, "What would you do?"

"Paul, two fine-ass women are out there waiting for two players to wax that ass, and you ask what I would do? You're a stupid motherfucker for real. You're not feeling this opportunity, are you? You're deep in your feelings because you found a letter some dude wrote Kelly, but she's not the one that leaves, you do. Kelly can't find you, but you damn sure know where to find her. Damn, and you'll fuck all this off because you and Kelly's bugging?"

"It's not like that, Danny, I'm just kinda—"

Danny interrupts, "Hiding in the bathroom, is just what you're doing. With all the fine ass on the other side of that door, you're hiding in the bathroom? We have the opportunity at premium cuts, the kind of ass everyday Joe mortgages his home for, but to our good fortune, we get the services at half the cost. Why? Because my partna Big Les gave us the play. Dude, I'm smoking blunts thinking about the honeys and my Johnson's hard. I need to be out there with it fucking, not hiding in the bathroom with my best friend. You see anything wrong with this picture, Paul? My dick's hard, but I'm in the bathroom talking. Not to go against the grain, but to think back on our friendship, dude, you've been right all along. I have to be a stupid motherfucker."

"Danny, you know I wouldn't bullshit my best friend. Just thinking about the bullshit and how I've been played has me stuck. Read the letter, Danny; just read it, man. It's deep."

"Paul, how in the hell—where? What's deep, Paul? Deep with it is on the other side of the door smoking big blunts, dancing with the honeys, and getting our socks blown. That's deep! That's the only business we came here for, remember? I don't do anybody's extracurricular, and I'm nobody's damn therapist. Oh hell, no. Now you went to looking pitiful too? Please hurry the fuck up and pass the blunt and give me that damn letter. You've ruined the moment. Hell! I might as well read it. Let me read what's wrong in your life. Look at you, a grown man in here crying and hiding. You ought to be ashamed of yourself. While I smoke and read, don't say shit." Danny takes a hit. "Paul? When I tell people about this shit."

Paul sits on the bathrooms countertop looking pitiful. He offers the letter. "Danny, just read how he's getting at Kelly, and then you'll understand what I'm—"

"Understand what Paul? What I understand just happened with my dick. As soon as I got involved with your problems, my dick went soft. There is no rap for you and me. Damn! Now you go to looking sickly on top of being pitiful? I'll read your problems, Paul, but a brotha needs to smoke in peace. If there's anything to discuss, we'll rap after I get through handling my business with the honeys. Word on that? No, don't answer, just stand there and keep looking pitiful. I'll read it for myself to find out what's going on with you." As he reads the letter, Danny hits the blunt. "Damn, this shit's getting deep. Yeah, no shit. He wants to do what? Damn, player went hard with that line. How'd he say that? That's the bullshit women want to hear!"

The blunt's fire goes out. "Damn it, pass the lighter, Paul. This shit's getting good, uh-uh, light it for me. I didn't know Kelly worked you like this! Dude's going hard with the persuasion, too, so I can understand you being in the bathroom hiding and hurt."

"Danny, that was what I was trying to explain! Let me hit that blunt. I can explain everything."

Danny declines. "Hold up, now you wanna hit the blunt? Shee-it! I'm the one needing a good hit. Reading this good shit has me intrigued! Paul, I admit I was trippin'; this letter's dope. How many blunts are left? I wanna stay comfortable with this here. This shit's getting real good. We should have read this a lot earlier."

Elsewhere in the suite, Brenda and Joanie's buzz has them dancing in the living room. Danny's voice has been heard in the bathroom in the meantime. Brenda motions to Joanie. "Did you hear that? How long have they been in there?" Brenda and Joanie position themselves against the door. As Danny continues, his voice and the blunt's resinous smoke permeates the door and walls of the bathroom.

"Oh, hell no; fuck me. You're really going there with all that? Damn, you're just relentless at that ass!" Danny continues reading the letter:

"*Baby, I miss the massaging of your upper and lower back, while bathing you with the body sponge. I'm definitely looking forward to kissing and biting your feet. The tingling from your touch always drove me crazy, making it that much more painful to be away from you. Every night, I re-live every memory of the eroticism we've shared, whenever I shaved your legs and waxed you down there.*"

Danny hits the blunt to hold the resinous smoke in his lungs. He exhales. "Player, you wasn't fucking around. You worked it how it's supposed to be worked. You're definitely smooth with the persuasion. That's the way it supposed to feel, just like that. You're handling bizness in a major way; no doubt about it."

Danny returns the letter. "Baby boy, believe me, I'm now understanding your pain."

Listening from the other side of the door, Brenda enjoys her blunt with a drink. She throws her head back to allow her throat to receive the vodka shot. "Joanie, I knew something was up with these two. Did you get all that?"

Brenda's sister plays back the recording from her cell phone. "I heard what you heard, and I got it all. Joanie clarifies, "We've smoked what, three blunts, and they've been in there playing house for how long? Who in the hell do they think they are? They just upped and left us out here because somebody's ass is itching? Brenda, they straight dissed us!"

Joanie returns to the couch to rummage through her purse. In doing so she talks toward the bathroom door. "Don't stop playing house now, player, I got the latest ruud boy and a fresh pack of batteries for that deep down itch!"

Brenda compromises. "Girl, who cares if they're in there playing house?

Let them run a round in their panties, or do anything else they want to do. Our times on their tab, place, win, or show. Girl, it's all in the bill."

Joanie offers dap giving a high five. "I know that's right, Brenda! These clowns wanted the wrong show; we don't play in peanut butter. Who in the hell do they think they are with this bullshit? They straight embarrassed Big Lester!"

Brenda and Joanie dressed hurriedly to take what's left of the party goods. With their shoes in hand, the sisters bolt through the hotel corridor toward the elevator. Reaching the elevator first, Joanie hits the button to summon the doors to open.

Brenda meanwhile tweets what transpired:

4 hours at plush suite on Sepulveda Boulevard., nice view! Good time, vodka, (top shelf) had the bomb weed, (purple) the shit, (best weed!). Dancing! Melanie Fulani's "Bring It to Me Right." (That's right girl!) Two studs but no action, we were in the wrong suite waiting to give a show that never happened. The 2 studs turned out to be 2 duds, with a taste for peanut butter. Both of them were 'itching back there' really big! It was deep! Toodles!

Brenda then texted Big Les to inform him of the behavior of the two players he hooked them up with. "Girl, when Lester hears about this! If these punks don't pay him for our time, they'll both need a case of butt lube to pull Cheddar's and Train's boots from that ass." The sisters laugh giving dap with slapping high fives.

Joanie agrees. "Right? Woo, girl! Have we seen it all tonight or what? What the hell? Was that some bizarre shit! The way Lester spoke on them, I was on the please-them-leave-them page. They had me fooled too, and I thought for sure we had two players on our line ready to spend big paper, but girl, you have to admit this one was sweet! Brenda, I hadn't figured it out until we left. They didn't tell Lester everything because they wanted us to watch. Maybe we should have hung around! Brenda, you wanna go back?"

"Girl, you're stupid! Don't even go there with that bullshit."

"DING!" The elevator chime signals with the door opening. Stepping inside, Joanie presses the L button. As the elevator descends, Brenda chuckles. "Oops! Something told me to bring my knife with this move."

"Oh girl, no! Lester returned your text? Don't say he wants us to cut them."

Appearing serious, Brenda retrieves the text message. "Yeah, he did text back. Press the button for floor fourteen."

Joanie questions, disinclined with the request, "Shouldn't Train and Cheddar be doing this? This is their work."

Brenda produces Paul's and Danny's wallets.

Joanie addresses the stunt. "A knife? What the hell, and Brenda, what are you supposed to be doing with those, hitting them in the head?"

Enjoying her wit, Brenda presents her younger sister one of the wallets. "Bitch, what did you think? The knife is for your cut."

Embarrassed over losing her composure, Joanie shakes her head to clear the air. "I'm just saying, Brenda, make it all make sense!" The elevator continues its descent after stopping at a floor with no awaiting passengers.

Taking advantage of the elevator's emptiness, Brenda rearranges the party goods in her handbag. She answers the question her sister asked earlier. "Joanie, you know damn well I'm not going back to that hot-ass bathroom to watch two Gump's Fein on each other. What the hell? With all the cream they're putting in that ass, they should have enough cake batter to make a nut-n-butt cake." The sound of the elevator's chime signals the arrival at the hotel's lobby. Exiting the elevator, Brenda retrieves the valet parking ticket from her handbag. Meanwhile Joanie's anxiety quickens with her every step. "Girl, let's get the fuck out of here before they come looking for us."

Brenda dismisses the thought. "Joanie, listen to you. We're Lester Brown's people. Believe me, if these two were to kick anything off, in a heartbeat Train and Cheddar will be at that ass." Another thought comes to Brenda's mind. "You know what, Joanie? We should let them know we're gone. When have we ever ran from tricks, especially two butt boys?" Brenda notices a hotel employee with a cleaning cart. "Joanie, call her! I'm sending room service to go along with the cake they're baking in that hot-ass bathroom." Brenda motions to a woman cleaning. "Get her attention, Joanie."

Meanwhile the hotel housekeeper methodically goes about her cleaning duties. Joanie's request interrupts her diligence.

"Excuse me. Excuse me, lady. Hello? Excuse me, do you speak English?"

With a feather duster in hand, the housekeeper acknowledges, "Señoritas? You needing sumting for here?"

Brenda replies, "We're sorry to disturb you. We're staying in one of the hotels suites. Guests in our party have been calling room service for at least thirty minutes. No one's answering, and now our party's become exhausted from waiting. We would like to pay you to send our party their room service orders."

"No-no, señoritas! I no wurking for the room serbese! Maybe sum othur purson for the room serbese for helping you."

"We didn't have the time to ask anyone; an emergency forces us to leave. That's why we want to pay you to deliver our party's room service." Brenda instructs her sister. "Joanie, peel some money from that trick's wallet and give it to her. Do you think she understood what the hell I've said?"

Joanie produces a wad of bills. "Damn. This must have been the quiet one's wallet. What was his name?"

"I heard Danny calling him Paul."

"Girl, look at this! Paul was holding. It's a shame his asshole's itching, and he did call for our services to scratch it."

"Joanie! Uh-uh. Brenda don't play with bottle brushes with anybody's ass!"

"Oh, Brenda; girl, you need to quit."

Hearing a familiar name mentioned, the cleaning lady hesitates to question, "You whawning room serbese de-libery for Meester Paul? For my boss?"

Brenda directs, "Oh, you know him? We heard he's

married and has his own business. He has a wifey tucked in a plush house and keeps her riding in the year with nice cars. They even have a maid and a little dog to make them look legit, but what I've mentioned doesn't mean a damn thing. As we speak, he and his boyfriend Danny are upstairs in this hotel playing house. He's sneaking around on wifey. It's a damn shame, mm, mm, mm!"

Joanie passes the cleaning lady a hundred dollar bill. "This is for your inconvenience. What's your name?"

"My name is Maria. Meester Paul cawming for here? Maria taking the de-libery. No problema; heem my boss."

Brenda joins in. "Damn, you work for him? Then you should know the business. His asshole's itching, and keep the change for the embarrassment. Paul's in Suite fourteen oh seven with his boyfriend Danny. They'll both have baked beans with the big fat-ass sausages. What do you call those, Joanie?"

"Knackwurst Brenda."

"Yeah, send a few plates with molasses and pork bacon. Make sure the thick rinds on the bacon. They're real picky about what they eat. Both of them are poking the pork, and they're up there doing the damn thing making bacon. Don't forget the baked beans."

"No, no, no! Meester Paul no eating the baking bean; it too mawch for gibbing heem gas. I making the black bean for Meester Paul and the señora! No baking bean, no good."

Brenda chides, "Uh-uh, is that what he told you? Then he's been fooling both you and his wife. Whatever, I just left him and his boyfriend, and I already know how they get down.

They'll have the long brown buns with the seeds baked on top, and two salads with the extra thick creamy white dressing. Joanie, what's the name of that nasty shit?"

"Creamy bleu cheese, Brenda."

"Yeah, make it thick. With all the meat and toys their putting in that ass, send a few pitchers of a fruity beverage to wash down that bread. Make sure they get these too." Brenda produces Danny's Big Shot condoms; she sticks them inside the wallets. "Maria, they'll need these when they're done with their meal. Before you go up to the suite, add a jar of Vaseline with the order."

Maria looks to Brenda, perplexed. "Oh, my goodneth. Meester Paul nebbur using the Basa-lene! For heem, the señora buy the beeta-meen E; it wurking bettur for heem skin."

Brenda gives Maria another fifty dollars from the wad of bills. "Here, honey, whatever. Believe me, you'd be surprised. He's used more than Vaseline from his wife's medicine cabinet. Just take the money and think nothing of it. His asshole is itching, and you're sending him the relief he wants. Think about it; your time's worth something, Maria. You're providing a good service he needs, so get paid. You know him; he's your friend, and believe me, he'll love you for it."

"Oh, my goodneth! You gib too mawch for the room serbese! Maria no needing the teep. The señora pay this week for Maria cleening." Maria eyes the awaiting tip. "You bery sure Meester Paul cawming for here? Okay? Maria taking room serbese for the de-libery. Ah-huh, Maria taking for heem!" Maria reluctantly accepts the additional fifty-dollar tip. "My goodneth, too mawch mawny for making the de-libery."

Joanie and Brenda laugh at Maria's reluctance. "Hey girl, don't trip; it's the entertainment business. We get weird shit to deal with from time to time too. It's all in their tab, and they've gladly paid for it. You put your conscience out of the way for paying customers. Maria, they're paying, and they'll thank you when you get there."

Joanie marvels at her sister's cleverness as they continue to the valet's parking area. "Brenda?"

Joanie's big sister answers, "Bitch, what?"

"Brenda, I had so much fun tonight, I can't wait to do this shit again. You think Lester has other soft tricks to keep us plugged steady?"

"Joanie, you're expecting miracles. If we asked for anything cornier than these two, we'll be the one's paying for the entertainment."

"Then forget it; I'm not paying for shit."

"Me, either."

"Brenda?"

"Bitch, what?"

"Can you imagine their faces when the room service is delivered? Damn!"

CHAPTER NINETEEN

*I*n the bathroom of suite 1407, Paul sits on the sink's countertop to patiently await Danny's direction. Danny signifies his best friend's demise while seated comfortably on the seat of the toilet. While enjoying the letter's entertainment with a blunt, Danny releases the resinous smoke to surmise, "Paul I share the wealth among friends, so you could've hit the blunt first if you wanted to. I'm just saying, nobody here is being greedy and shit."

Appearing distraught and pitiful, Paul rests his face in his hands for emotional support. He manages a reply. "Danny, I'm good, I just need a little time to think a bit."

Danny takes a blunt hit to hold the heavy smoke in his lungs. He reiterates, "You're welcome to hit the blunt anytime you want. You don't have to wait for me; you do know this, right?"

Paul stares blankly into the tiled floor. "Yeah, I heard you,

Danny, I'm good for right now."

"Now I'm understanding why you're in here stuck. Paul, I'm just saying, you're in here looking real bad and pitiful. When you get a chance to smoke this bubonic, you should be doing it big." Danny exhales to continue, "Now stress weed's a different story. When you have to smoke stress, keep a couple packages of aspirin on your person; it'll help with the headache and crash. Another reason you can't enjoy this good shit is because your mind's already fucked up. When you simp and trip in self-pity, you'll never be able to maintain a good high with your mind tight. That's why you should relax more, Paul. You sure you don't wanna hit this?"

Recognizing Danny's chiding, Paul raises his face from within his hands. "You simple mother fucker you! Every time I talk to you I get dizzy. Explain that! And while you're thinking, explain why I keep paying you to irritate me. Explain for the few moments in your simple existence why you don't feel quite as stupid as you're supposed to? It's a miracle you're not feeling quite as stupid today, Danny. Oh, I forgot, you hit the damn lottery and got lucky. Today you're smoking purple courage and beating your chest. Isn't that right, simple?"

Danny welcomes the camaraderie, "All shit, he's back! Dawg, don't ever scare me like that. You acting simple made me feel like I was running shit. I was trippin' for a minute, but since you did show up, isn't one of the medicinal purposes of weed for minor pains and increased circulation for your dick? I think this purple shit might be too strong for me. Just to let you know, I wasn't trying to be a hero either, Paul. Being brave will get a brotha hurt. All I want to do is smoke in peace and enjoy this good high. Know what I'm saying?"

Paul concedes to his frustration, motioning for the letter. "Danny! Danny, it's okay. Give it to me; I'll finish reading it myself."

Danny admonishes, "Would you hold the fuck up and let me do this? This shit's intriguing, and it goes good with my high. Uh-uh! You've read it already; after this next hit, I continues!" With another blunt hit, Danny blows smoke rings to question, "Where was I? I don't remember any fucking going on, so it'll be hard to find where I stopped. Oh, yeah … here it is … Dude was getting into some real Shakespearean shit. Listen at how he caps at that ass.

"*My beloved, being on another continent stationed so far away, bear with me as I express the pain of not seeing you. As the world rotates on its axis, the moon awaits the sun to set before it appears. As birds cannot take to the sky without wings, man and beast suckle instinctively from the breast to nourish. Needs are a part of everything, whether born or made. I need you to sustain life, just as a body needs its spirit to exist.*"

Finished entertaining himself, Danny returns the letter. "Here you go, player! From my most professional understanding, there's good news with the bad. Kelly didn't leave you yet; that's the good news. You ready for this? Aw, what the hell, I'll lace you anyway. Paul, your girl Kelly's been hanging out. Damn! How long has she worked you like this?" Danny coughs with another blunt hit. "My dude, if Kelly hasn't given up the drawls yet, best believe she's on her way out of both drawl legs.

Man, I bet she's a freak, like a quiet fuse before she explodes. After reading that letter, I'm convinced, when it comes to throwing that ass, Kelly will out throw any pitcher at home plate. Yes sir, consider yourself a lucky man. Kelly turns it on to be as bad as she wants to be. It's been confirmed, player, your wife's a true freak!

Danny slaps his ass as if he were in a saddle. "Kelly worked you with the shy role, didn't she? Believe me, I know the kind! The quiet ones get down like that. I can remember every Tuesday evening at six o'clock sharp, my grandma and I were in church. She went to bible study, and I went to the new converts' class. There was a girl I sat next to every Tuesday, she had to be maybe seventeen. On Sundays she led the youth choir. Man, outside the classroom, she was like Eveira the mistress welcoming you into the dark. You remember that show? She wore all black with those big pretty titties and fine-ass lips."

Danny shakes his head agreeably.

"Don't tell me you never got your fein on with Eveira? In the seventies she was one of the baddest bitches on TV. Anyway, you should have seen how that young honey in the new converts' class handled her bizness. I was about fifteen at the time, and I had to fight her off whenever we were together. She was a straight freak! She had me drinking those milk shakes and taking her father's vitamins. Remember those 'men's booster shots?' I'm telling you Paul, knowing what I know now, hmm, hmm, hmm. I wonder what's she's doing these days. I'd like to get with her for my birthday."

Frustrated with Danny's twisted psychoanalyzing, Paul

raises his gaze from the bathroom floor. "Your birthday? Grandma's bible meetings, the seventies, and Eveira's fine-ass lips. How does any of this fix my problems with Kelly? You backwards down-home mother fucker, you! Don't ever tell anybody you ever worked for me, Danny. Just pass me that blunt so that I can stay sane. Fucking with you, damn." Paul hits the blunt taking long drags.

Danny comments on Paul's blunt etiquette. "Damn, I liked you better when you were down and pitiful. Leave a lil' room for the next man! Hold up, Paul. You're smoking like a broke train! Man! Them was some long-ass hits!" Danny picks up the letter from the sink countertop from where Paul set it down. He hands it to him. "Here, slow your roll and read this incriminating letter. Go back to thinking about how bad you're feeling, and let me smoke this expensive shit as I explain this letter." With the blunt back in his possession, Danny takes a hit. He holds the resinous smoke in his lungs before releasing it with a cough. "Ahem! Like I was saying, real talk, Paul. Wake up and pull your head out, yeah, the big one. That wasn't a compliment, I meant the one on your shoulders. I don't know if you realized it, but you're in a crisis, and your credit score's not what it used to be. Not only can you not buy the house, you don't get the girl, either! Credit repair dude, from the tone of that letter, in the strictest sense of Unspoken Matters, you've been slipping, player, and Kelly's been working on her credit score with someone else."

Reacting from emotion, Paul Frisbees the letter toward Danny's face. Danny escapes, ducking. The letter crashed against the wall with such force, had it been a knife it would have severed Danny's head. Overlooking Paul's frustration, Danny recovers with a blunt hit. "Okay, you've fucked it off! My high's gone, and I'm back out there with the honeys. Paul, do everybody a favor; stay in here with the crying and lying, having your pity party being miserable. I don't need any help removing the ribbons off those two pretty gifts. Fuck you, man!"

Opening the bathroom door, Danny goes into character, popping his fingers just as he enters the living room. "Girls, ladies, my stay was a little extended, but as you can see from the print in my pants, please believe me, we're about to put in serious work. No pun intended; you two lovelies feeling me on this?"

There's no music to talk over. Neither Brenda nor Joanie are in view. Proceeding with wit, Danny voices his intentions. "So, ladies what? Now we're playing hide and go get it? Then let a player get at you. I'm with all that; my Johnson's hard anyway. Wherever Mr. Johnson finds you, you already know what it is. Come on out, honeys. I give up! My circulation's leaving my skull. I'm walking around the joint dizzy! Okay, ladies, don't say I didn't warn you ... See there? I just bumped into the furniture. Y'all done woke up Mr. Johnson ... Come on out, ladies! I give up."

Danny comes upon the suite's door being ajar. Alarmed, he looks to the bar and coffee table to notice the bud sack and liquor missing. Danny then checks the closet for his personal belongings. "Oh shit, say it's not what it is! This isn't happening!"

Danny talks into the hall corridor for Brenda and Joanie's

whereabouts expectantly. "What's happening, ladies? Now we're doing it in the hallway? You honeys took everything to make sure a player came to find you, right? Well, here I am, ladies, me and Mr. Johnson!" The corridor is empty. Danny's voice is heard within the corridor. "Damn, they worked us! They got us, Paul, they're gone! Fuck man, this didn't happen!"

Meanwhile in the suite bathroom, the letter remains where it has lain since crashing to the floor. Clueless to the goings on in the next room, Paul remains at the bathroom sink to immerse his face in water. Overhearing Danny's distressed voice, Paul exits the bathroom with a towel covering his face. Entering the suite's living room, he finds Danny clutching the top of his head.

"Well, you did it, Paul; it's over. Are you satisfied with yourself with that crying and being simple? You got your way. Everything you didn't want to happen has come to pass."

"Hold up, Danny. How am I supposed to react after reading a letter written to my woman? You're the one doing the hollering in the hallway like you lost something. Shouldn't I be the one doing that? You're tripping because you're high. I'm tripping over the revelations of my marriage, and rightfully so. So who's being simple?"

Taken aback by Paul's narrow-minded presence, Danny takes his best friend to task with a reality check. "Have you simply noticed anything? Everything I was enjoying before your pity party in the bathroom is gone! Brenda and Joanie, the weed, the expensive liquor, my hard on! Take a look around, square. Everything's gone! They even took the CD we were listening to." Danny mimics the words to the song. "'Yeah, yeah, yea-aah!' Who's the dumb motherfucker now?"

Paul looks around the room to take inventory of the mentioned items. He jumps over the couch to the bar's countertop to where he last placed his wallet, cell phone, and car keys. "Oh, shit! My wallet and cell phone's gone; they took our stuff."

Danny corrects Paul. "They took our stuff? Square, they took the weed and the vodka. Those are losses you don't report to the police! Think beyond your rectangular box. You'll get another cell phone and credit card in the mail. Come on, we have to find them before they leave the hotel. I didn't pay for that purple weed yet; I got that shit on consignment!"

As they bolt into the hall corridor, Paul slaps Danny upside the head. "You stupid mother fucker, you. Why didn't you listen to me? You tried to think even after I told you what not to do! I told you not to bring those low-bottom hood rat-ass hookers!"

Paul and Danny reach the elevator at the same time. "DING!" Its chime sounds as the door opens. Maria exits the elevator pushing her housekeeping and room-service carts.

"Good mawning, señors." Maria greets the hotel guests. Paul and Danny give way to the cleaning and room service carts before rushing onto the elevator. Continuing into the hall corridor, Maria comes upon suite 1407, finding the door ajar. She steps around the food cart to knock on the door. "Room serbese! … Hello, sumbawdy? Room serbese! Hello, Meester Paul and Dawnee? For you bery nice men, I habing meats and breads! I habing a lot of tick dressing too, bery bery crèmee."

Awaiting a response, Maria gives the elaborate suite a quick visual. She questions, "Hello? Sumbawdy here for the room serbese?" The huge pillows on both sofas appear out of place. Empty fifths of vodka and lipstick-smeared shot glasses are on the marble countertop. On the suite's coffee table, the tobacco removed from the wraps of sweezer sweets are piled in a neat mound. On a plate nearby, what appears to be a bud grinder and finely cut marijuana sits among several uncut buds.

Maria reacts. "Oh, my goodneth, eberybawdy pawdy! Too mawch mota!" [weed.] Maria enters the suite addressing its occupants. "Hello, I looking for the two pursons, Meester Paul and Dawnee ... Sumbawdy home for the room serbese?" On the floor near the kitchen, Maria spots a fifty-dollar bill. She pockets the money. "My goodneth! You leab so mawch teep for the cleening? Ah huh, this room bery nice for the good pursons!"

Looking at the bar, Maria notices the shot glasses and the white powder residue on the marble countertop. Her eyes widen with the discovery of a rolled-up bill. She approaches cautiously. "Hello? Sumbawdy here?" Hoping not to find anyone, she unrolls the greenback to read the bill's denomination. Maria folds the fifty-dollar bill, placing it in her apron pocket.

She reassures herself, "Meester Paul leab nice teep for Maria? No wurry for here. Maria cleen apter pawdy ebery day. Ah huh, I make ebery ting nice for my boss!" Repositioning the sofa pillows in place, Maria comes across a wig and thong. She questions, "Sumbawdy leab sumting for here? No wurry, Meester Paul. I cleen, I throw ebery ting out frum you pawdy!"

Realizing she hadn't yet checked the bathroom, Maria knocks on the door. "Hello? I here for the room serbese! I habing the room serbese, the pursons ordur for Meester Paul and Dawnee ... Hello?" Maria opens the bathroom door, allowing the marijuana's pungent odor to flow into the suite's living room. To dissipate the thick odor, Maria turns on the bathrooms exhaust fan. She quickly steps back into the living room to catch her breath. She says, "No buena, too mawch mota and pawdy for my boss."

While using a towel to physically dissipate the odor, she notices the letter lying on the bathroom floor. She thinks aloud, "Oh my goodneth, Meester Paul leab sumting frum heem bisness!" Retrieving a hair dryer from the cabinet, Maria dries the letter to read it:

"Just as the moon waits for the sun to set before appearing, the birds cannot take to the sky without wings. From the joy I received when touching your feet, I tingled from your lightest touch. Since the time we've been apart, I spend my days looking forward to the eroticism of shaving your beautiful legs, before using my hands to gently wax your warmth down there. From the other side of the world, my sun rises and sets with you."

Not knowing how to grasp what she's read. Maria questions, "Meester Paul? You leabing sumting for you bisness?" Confused with the content of the letter, Maria looks to the food cart to replay the conversation in the lobby with the beautiful girls.

Their names are Paul and Danny! They both want the brown buns that have the seeds in them, and send plenty of baked beans with the big fat-ass sausages! Joanie, what do you call those?"

"Knackwurst Brenda!"

"Yeah, send a big plate of those, and since they're up their having their salads tossed, give them two large, extra-firm cucumbers to play with. Joanie? The salad dressing with the thick white chunks? What's the name of that nasty shit?"

"It's the chunky bleu cheese, Brenda."

"Yeah? Well that shit's nasty!"

"Damn, Brenda, are you going to surprise them with dessert too?"

"What dessert? Joanie, those cake bakers couldn't have been made any sweeter! They're up there doing the damn thing as we speak!" Brenda instructs, "Maria, give them something to make their mouths pucker and their assholes envy! Send two pitchers of a beverage that's both tart and fruity, with a gang of lemons and sugar."

Maria looks at the discovered wig and thong, motioning the sign of the cross. "*Dios mio! (Oh my god!)* I must esplain for the señora!"

Abandoning the suite and food cart, Maria continues to the elevator. She walks the corridor inadvertently talking. "Oh, my goodneth, I tink Meester Paul bery bawd purson! Heem no whawning the señora! Heem whawning Meester Dawnee! Oh, my goodneth! This bery bawd for esplaining!"

"DING!" The chime signals the opening of the elevator's door. Maria descends to the hotel lobby to explain the events to her supervisor. "Hefa! [boss.] I habing bery big esplaining for the señora! I leab to esplain for the bawd trawble!"

"What is it, Maria? Has something happened during you shift?"

"Hefa, I making the room serbese, but the pursons no buena!"

"But Maria, you're with the hotel's maintenance staff. Why would you be doing room service?"

"Ah-huh, hefa, I esplain. The señoritas pay for the de-libery for the room serbese, sausage and bery crèmee salad for Meester Paul and Dawnee."

"You're explaining someone paid for another guest's room service. Why wouldn't the guests do it themselves? Were they splitting the bill?"

"The señoritas leab for the emurguncee! Them esplain, Meester Paul and Dawnee making cake, and they whawning for the drinking, sumting to pucker."

"Maria, it's against hotel policy for maintenance personnel to perform room service transactions. How did they pay for their requests? Did you accept money?"

Maria presents the paid voucher for both the room service and the tip she received.

"Well, the request was nothing out of the way: baked beans, knackwurst sausage, double portions with pumpernickel buns. Two salads with extra thick creamy bleu cheese dressing, and two large pitchers of tutti frutti punch, the Liddle Reechard special. The request totaled sixty-seven dollars and eighty-five cents, you paid with a hundred dollar bill, which left thirty-two dollars and fifteen cents in change."

"Ah huh, hefa, I hab ebery ting." Maria presents her supervisor the change.

"Maria! You were given this as a tip?"

"Si! The señoritas gib more teep!" Maria reveals the fifty-dollar bill.

"That's an eighty-two-dollar tip! Well, what happened? Did you deliver the requests from the kitchen?"

"Si!"

"Were you on time, were the guests happy with the hotel's service?"

"Si, hefa, I making the de-libery, but no pursons cawming for the room. Meester Paul and Dawnee leab teep for the cleening."

Maria reveals the money she recovered from the suite.

"My goodness. An additional hundred dollars to your eighty-two-dollar tip! That's quite an evening! Then why are you so distraught, Maria? Are you upset for accepting the tip?"

"No, Maria cleening the room for the pursons, but nobawdy cawming home. While I cleening, I finding tings!" Maria reveals the wig and thong. "This no buena for the señora! I tink Meester Paul bery bawd purson! Heem make trawble for the señora!" Maria motions the sign of the cross. *Dios mio!* Maria leab now for the esplaining to the señora."

Flabbergasted with surprise, Maria's supervisor tries to connect her employee's mindset with the circumstance. "Maria, of the little effort involved in sending room service, and no one being there to receive it, I somewhat understand why you would feel guilty for accepting the tip. Why beat yourself up?

You accommodated the hotel guests and you did clean the suite in good faith. There's no wrong there, Maria. But I don't understand the connection with Paul and the señora. You mentioned Paul and Danny being in the suite, so wouldn't they be the guests connected to the wig and thong? Hotel guests leave things behind all the time. Why didn't you just throw away what you found? Were you wearing gloves when you touched the items?"

Maria nods her head affirmatively.

"Then what's forcing you to go home? Are you feeling guilty for accepting the money? Maria, you've made an honest hundred and eighty-dollar tip. You have no reason to feel distraught."

"*Si, hefa,* me umbderstand."

"Then what's wrong?"

Maria looks at the floor to answer in shame, "Meester Paul is my othur boss for where I wurking! Heem the señora's husband! This bery bawd for Maria! I must esplain to the señora, I find the bawd tings!"

Realizing what's on Maria's conscience, her supervisor offers, "Maria, until now I hadn't realized what you were saying. You're obviously feeling guilty over what you were asked to deliver, and rightfully so! Large sausages with creamy dressings and what not. When you delivered room service, you discovered your friend's husband wearing women's lingerie and a wig. He's sneaking around in this very hotel with another man. Wow, that could be very shocking! Do you think the thong and wig belong to his wife? My goodness, then I definitely understand why you're so rattled! Good luck with that embarrassment! Maria, if you're not up to it and you need more time to gather yourself, feel free to use a few sick days."

Maria's barrier of fluent English conflicts with her understanding of what her supervisor has rationalized. Maria shrugs her shoulders with pity. "Hefa? I bery ubbset for my othur boss, the señora! Maria finding too mawch trawble."

CHAPTER TWENTY

$\mathcal{B}$ecause of the day's unexpected turn of events, Maria
has left work before her shift ends. During the bus
commute to her residence, she sits between two familiar faces; Hortencia and Flora. The trio has been friends since their
parents paid a coyote [smuggler] to transport them from
Guadalajara Mexico into the States some thirty years ago.
Employed as domestics, the women make their morning com-
mutes to the estates of their wealthy employers.

As each of the trio tells the latest news since they've seen each
other, Maria explained in rapid Spanish what transpired during
her work shift. Hortencia offers advice toward Maria's decision to inform the señora of Paul's infidelity. "No, no, no! This
country's very different from ours. Here, the wealthy people
have parties and share each other's husbands and wives! They'll
look at you differently if you tell what you've seen. From what
you've said, you really didn't see the señoras husband! Could it

have been someone else in that suite, Maria?"

Maria defends her reasoning. "Hortencia, I talked to the beautiful women that were with him! They were disappointed because Mr. Paul and Danny were *hotos!* [gay men] As the women were leaving the hotel, they tipped me to deliver Mr. Paul and Danny's room service. The women ordered baked beans, nutty breads, big sausages, and creamy dressing. I delivered the order, but no one answered. When I went inside the suite, I found these!" Maria opens her bag to reveal the wig and thong. "I'm taking them to show the señora, they're a woman's panties. Look! It's nothing more than a string! My mother would never allow me to wear such a thing!"

Flora joins in. "They're for the young women, Maria! They're the skinny panties … How do you say for English, sexzy? "

"Sexy!" Hortencia clarifies, "It's a G-string! They call it sexy lingerie! My daughter watches the modeling shows in English. Young women all over the world are wearing these, but the wig's a little dated; these days they're wearing the ones you sew into your hair."

Flora continues with her inquiry, "Thank you, Hortencia! Maria, you actually seen the señora's husband and his friend wearing these God-forbidden things?"

"They left before I delivered room service, Flora. I think the señoritas were calling the room to antagonize them. Mr. Paul and Danny knew someone was coming, so they left in a hurry, leaving these nasty things behind."

"Maria, just forget it; it's not worth the trouble. You

shouldn't say anything. What do you think, Hortencia, am I right?"

"Yes, I agree with Flora! Maria, they'll both fire you for telling what you've seen! The truth is too embarrassing for their family's name. Telling what you've seen isn't worth the trouble involved. Maria, be honest. Would you tell the husband if the señora was seen with another man?"

"Flora!" Maria protects her employer. "The señora performs her womanly duty to her husband when he returns from business trips. When her husband's away she goes shopping to occupy her mind. The señora doesn't meet men at hotels, Flora. We talk about everything! I know her. I prepare her meals, and we eat together. She's a good woman!"

"Well, you never know, Maria." Hortencia probes, "who spends the night with her when her husband's away?

"Hortencia! The señoras too classy for any foolishness! Never would she do such a thing. She would never be the one cheating! The señora's a very good person; she's my friend, Hortencia!"

Hortencia twists the knife, questioning Maria's loyalty. "Is her husband a very nice person? Who pays your salary, Maria?"

"The señora pays me."

"Where does the señora get the money to maintain her household?"

"Hortencia, the señora was very rich before she married!"

Flora questions, "Do you know how long they've been married, Maria?"

"They were married two years before I began working for

them, Flora. That was over twenty-five years ago, and the señora still has her own money to do what she chooses."

"Maria, that's our point!" Hortencia reasons, "You've seen many things and every problem with these people, yet they're still married, and neither of them are married to you. Just let it go. Whatever her husband's doing, let the señora find out for herself. She's the one that should be telling you about her husband. It's for the best. Trust us!"

Flora nods her head, agreeing. "Maria, it's true. You can go only so far with someone else's spouse. When it comes to these things, revealing something this embarrassing will only make big trouble for you. Leave it alone and just be thankful for the tip you received."

The automated voice announces the next bus stop. "Jefferson and Slauson approaching." Preparing for her exit, Maria pulls the Stop indicator. As the doors open for the passengers' exit, Maria ends her conversation with her friends. "I'm tired already from all this thinking! Flora and Hortencia, thanks for the advice. We'll talk again next week."

Maria has sat longer than the bus driver allows the exit doors to remain open. Uncomfortable with fluent English, Maria protests to the driver as she maneuvers her way toward the exit. "Oh, my goodneth, I cawming! The door open for me to leab, pleez! I no hearing for leabing the bus. Tank you bery mawch. I cawming!"

Maria exits the bus to wave nervously to Hortencia and Flora. As her childhood friends wave in return, their facial expressions clearly reinforce their sentiments. Maria continues to wave as the bus pulls away. She comments in rapid Spanish under her breath, "I know what you two are thinking. 'Mind your own business, Maria; trust us. It's the right thing to do,' but you guys don't understand! The señora trusts Maria for everything, and this is a big problem. I must tell her everything of what I've seen. Her husband's no good! I'll pray on this to do the right thing."

Maria continues to her residence to walk in thought. She wrestles with the guilt of how to present the bad news to her employer of twenty-five years. Monday through Thursday, Maria takes the scenic bus commute from Culver City through Beverly Hills, around the beautiful rolling curves of Bellagio Road, toward the Benedict Canyon estate of Diana and Paul Levitivitch. On her off days from the Levitivitch estate, Maria Gutiérrez works twelve-hour shifts for the hotel's maintenance section. Sundays are Maria's day of church worship. When morning service is over she returns home to faithfully cook breakfast for her husband, Juan. After having breakfast together, the couple rests for a few hours before their daughters, Soledad and Elizabeth, arrive with the couple's grandchildren, Gabriela and Irma. During the weekly tradition, over the next six hours, Maria listens attentively as her daughters speak of their children's latest awards as students of the month. Soledad beams with pride to praise Gabriela's recent accreditation, determining she's gifted and destined for higher learning curriculums. Bringing to light another topic of weekly discussion, both daughters talk proudly of their husbands' work ethic. Working double shifts, their husbands received promotions with the Bureau of Prisons within ninety days apart. Maria gives praise to her daughters in their native language.

"Our family's truly blessed. I am very fortunate you both are married and have done well finding men that work hard like their father. Our children have given us two healthy grandchildren and they go to fine schools. You both have nice homes for your children to live in, and your husbands have good retirement pensions for their families to live on. Your father and I are proud our children and grandchildren have the things we never had."

On Sunday afternoons, Maria's husband, Juan Gutiérrez, enjoys watching western peliculas and drinking cold beer. Seated comfortably on the couch, Juan gives an occasional smile or nod while listening to his wife and daughters interact. Routinely at 5:30 p.m., Juan breaks from the television to return Maria to church for evening worship. Upon going home, he re-settles into the couch to rejoin the western pelicula with a cold beer. At 7:30 p.m. sharp, Juan returns to evening worship to where his wife of thirty-eight years patiently awaits at the steps of the church. Maria enters the car with a prayer before fastening her seatbelt. The couple then drives in comfortable silence toward the sanctum of their quaint residence. Arriving home, Juan takes his place on the couch to patiently await the evening's meal. When the couple joins at the dining table, they eat in silence over the television's faint dialogue and gunfire. Finishing the evening meal with a heavy stomach, Juan removes his shoes to watch the Spanish news broadcast with a cold beer.

Within several minutes, he's heard snoring with the occasional passing of gas in his sleep. Juan repeats the cycle of passing gas and rubbing his feet together until the odor dissipates. As her husband sleeps at the dining table, Maria works around him to remove the dinner plates and table settings. In a final return to the kitchen, she puts the food away and washes the evening's dishes. With a full day behind her, Maria retires with a long relaxing bath while listening to a Christian ministry.

CHAPTER TWENTY-ONE

*A*rriving at her residence stressed with anxiety, Maria immediately opened her bible to read scripture. As she sought forgiveness through prayer, she slept through the afternoon and into the evening. At 6:00 p.m., Maria awoke to shred chicken breasts for the tamales. In the kitchen's silence, she pondered her dilemma of being a true friend. Should she expose the señora's husband or ignore her discovery and allow him to continue to deceive his wife? As Maria forms the *mata flate*, she speaks in her native tongue. "All this worrying and thinking is too heavy for my conscience. Were I to say nothing, in my silence I am just as guilty as the señora's husband! Reaching to the countertop for a towel, Maria wipes her hands to remove the cordless phone from her apron. The automatic speed dial to the Levitivitch estate is pressed with reluctance. With nervous energy, Maria stops the call before the other party's phone rings. As she adds chicken to the tamale folds, Maria has a change of heart. She admits, "My friends are right. I don't need more problems! From now on, Maria will see everything but say nothing. I'll make tamales for my grandchildren and the Bible study group, and there will be plenty of tamales to take to work for the señora. This way everybody's happy, and Maria has no more problems… Oh my goodness, I didn't cut onions or tomatoes for my tamales!" Maria interrupts her tamale preparation to turn on the kitchen television. The dicing continues. Within several minutes a news segment is aired.

"California's voters cast a unanimous vote for same-sex marriage in the Golden State. Stay tuned for the upcoming news at eight."

Immediately the dicing stops.

Maria expresses, "*Dios mio*! This is a sign; the end is near." She looks to the Virgin of Guadalupe pictured on the adjoining wall of her front door, to quickly motion the sign of the cross. Now ashamed by the day's revelations, she covers her eyes with guilt. Maria reaches for the towel in her apron to wipe her hands. In her nervous energy, she fumbles with the cordless phone to make a phone call. She presses the automatic redial button. The call goes through.

While in the midst of a rowing motion during a Pilates workout, the other party answers wearing an earpiece. "Hello, this is Diana."

Not fluent with English, Maria manages broken dialect with her employer. "For-gib me, señora, we hab to talk today. I must cawm for esplaining ebery ting."

"Hello, Maria. Honey, when I hadn't heard from you today,

I was just about to call. Where has the time gone? It's six-thirty already? I was beginning to believe you weren't coming. Paul's returning later tonight. Have you forgotten, Maria? Honey, you were to prepare the corned beef with the snow peas again. My goodness, that meal was superb! Maria, are you there?"

"Si, señora, Maria umbderstand. I needing to esplain ebery ting! Today I finding too mawch trawble for eberybawdy. A bery big problema I needing to tell."

"Maria, sure honey; just tell me what's wrong. I can send Milford right away! Maria, are you all right?"

Awaiting Maria's response, Diana opens a bottle of imported water to take a light swallow. She asks, "Honey, what's troubling you that has you so disconnected? Do you need to stay here for a few days? Is it Juan, honey? Oh, Maria, it is!"

"No señora! I finding the big meestake sumbawdy leab in the room, while wurking for my othur boss—"

Diana talks over Maria's explanation attempt. "I imagine you're terrified! My god, what has that animal done now? No, tell me everything when I get there! Juan and this foolishness has to stop! Maria, don't worry about anything more. I know the chief detective at the Beverly Hills police station. We're on our way! Oh, what am I thinking? My next hair appointment isn't until Thursday. I'm completely unpresentable. Maria, I'm a total mess. You know I depend on your assistance with everything, but honey, you're not here … Oh, Maria, do forgive me. I'm irritable because I haven't yet seen you. As I think of it, neither have I taken any of my Valium! On another note, were you beaten, honey? Are you injured?"

"No señora, I no habing the problema! Maria must esplain ebery ting! The imp-pormee-shun I hab is bery bawd, so mawch trawble for eberybawdy!" Maria motions the sign of the cross. "*Dios mio!*"

Disregarding Maria's assertions, Diana proceeds to spew venom. "Honey, I'll call the police from the car; we'll meet them at your house. Don't worry, Maria, we're on our way. This all ends now! I knew something was wrong when you didn't phone earlier. That fucking wetback!" Diana catches her slip of the tongue. "Oh, honey, you know I don't feel that way about you? You're different! It's just that, well, you know what I mean. You're different from Juan. Oh, let's forget what I've said. Juan's the root of this frustration. Has he been drinking again? I knew it! Maria, your hesitation says it all. Out of respect for you, I didn't, but honey I could have sent Juan to jail. I've kept his probation officer's card from the last time you know? Has he ever finished his AA meetings?"

"Señora, it's no Juan!" Maria insists, Heem do naw-ting for the trawble. Juan wurking hard! This trawble I find while wurking for me othur job!"

Diana questions, "You're protecting him? Honey, why would you do that? Juan's no earthly good! Why protect him? Maria, are you hearing me? Stop protecting Juan! It's Juan; it always is. He's the problem everywhere he goes." A sigh interrupts Diana's Juan bashing. "Honey, forgive me; I'll lower my voice. Maria, you're the victim here. Juan was born a loser, and you should see to it he goes directly to jail. Oh, forget it. I'm getting nowhere with this!"

In her frustration, Diana presses the intercom button several times to summon her butler and chauffeur, Milford James. Dressed impeccably in English butler attire, Milford sits in the parlor reading a novel. The intercom is answered after the third summons.

"Yes, madam?"

"Milford, hurry, get the car ready. There's a crisis pending. We have to pick up Maria; her life's threatened. Juan's been drinking, obviously, and I believe Maria's been beaten. The poor woman's in shock to the point that she's too frightened to clearly explain herself. What a lowlife! I'll personally see to it Juan does jail time. We have plenty of places in this country to house lowlifes, you know! That Mexican machismo crap doesn't fare here in America. Not in this country; buddy, you're wrong!" Diana terminates the conversation with Milford to redirect her attention to the telephone, "Maria, honey expect us to be there very shortly. Milford's getting the car ready."

"Si, señora, but it's no Juan! The bawd imp-pormee-shun I finding at wurk, no frum here!"

Diana presses on with the defamation of Juan's character. "Maria, there's nothing to worry about! This will be the last time you'll put up with this monster." A frantic Diana disregards her phone conversation to press the intercom repeatedly, "BEEP! BEEP! BEEP!"

"Yes, madam?"

"Milford, if I hadn't already informed you, please hurry! I believe Maria's losing her mind."

"Right away, madam!"

"Oh, Milford, be sure to bring enough of my medications to last for the evening. Maria may very well need some as well…" The conversation is terminated in midsentence. Diana overlooks Maria's awaiting call to concern herself with decision making. "What possibly could I wear to Maria's home? I've surely never been there. I don't believe it would be wise to wear my jewelry in that area at this time of the evening. I'll insist Milford keep the windows rolled up the entire time. There will be the two of us alone; we should be safe behind the glass until the police arrive."

Hearing her employer's rattled reaction, Maria looks to the Virgin of Guadalupe, motioning the sign of the cross. *"Dios mio!* Hello, señora, I tink you leabing the phone. "

Diana and Milford have since embarked on their journey to Maria's residence. Seated in the rear passenger's seat of the luxury Maybach, Diana confirms Maria's demise with the 9-1-1 operator.

"Would you spell your name for the record?"

"D-I-A-N-A L-E-V-I-T-I-V-I-T-C-H."

"Is that Ms. or Mrs.?"

"It's Mrs., thank you."

Mrs. Levitivitch, does your employee's husband have a history of violence, alcohol, or drug abuse? Has he exhibited any threatening behavior?"

"I'm calling you, aren't I? He's everything threatening and violent. He's a repeat offender. He's an alcoholic from Mexico!"

"Is he at the residence as we speak?"

Diana answers disbelievingly, "This isn't the time for dull questioning! I can't believe it, it's totally incomprehensible! I'm telling you a woman's life is threatened, send someone right away!"

"Mrs. Levitivitch, I intend to do so. To prioritize the call, as the questions appear on the screen they have to be answered in the formatted sequence. One last question. Have you seen or heard him physically assaulting his wife?"

"Well, of course he has. He's done everything I've said; he's an animal!"

"Mrs. Levitivitch, A unit has been dispatched to the residence. The information has been entered into the system as you've given it to me. Are there any other questions or concerns in reference to the call?"

"Not really! I just want to make sure he doesn't get away with what he's done!"

"Thank you for dialing 9-1-1."

Ending the call, Diana removes the tops from several prescription pill bottles to indiscriminately swallow a handful.

Noticing his employer's nervous energy, Milford makes an inquiry into the rearview mirror. "Should I assist the madam with anything before our arrival?"

Diana drinks imported water from a crystal glass to swallow her medication. She blinks her eyes calmly with her answer. "Milford, I believe everything's fine here, thank you."

With a confirming nod, Milford continues toward Maria's residence. Ensuring his employer is comfortable, he adjusts the climate control as he explains his reasoning. "Madam, absolutely, it appears the unexpected drive before my evening nap has me out of sorts."

Across town at Maria's residence, she methodically rocks back and forth in her comforting chair. In an attempt to channel her worries, Maria speaks lightheartedly in her native tongue as she crochets a blanket. "I'll make more blankets for my granddaughters in pink and yellow for their Christmas gifts." To keep her mind from racing, she divides her focus between crocheting and listening to a television game show, one of her Spanish favorites.

The game hosts directs to the contestant, "What is referred to as a slender rod used in spinning for twisting, winding, or holding thread?"

Maria answers the question, "What is a spindle? That was simple, and Maria does it every day." Maria laughs. "Oh, my goodness, three hundred points for that question? Maybe I'll visit the show and win lots of money for my retirement."

The show goes into a commercial break with a newsflash. "California to legalize same-sex marriage in the Golden State! Voters voiced the initiative at the polls in today's voter turnout. Stay tuned for the news at eight."

To avoid the news segment, Maria quickly aims the remote to change the channel. She expresses with dissent, *"Dios mio!* People everywhere are going crazy. They have gone against the word of the Most High for such foolishness!" As Maria continues to crochet, her comforting chair resumes to rock in rhythm. She presses the remote's Previous Channel button with hesitation, which returns the television to the game show.

The game host directs another question. "For three hundred dollars, name the Roman god referred to as the patron of beginnings and endings, and honored in the first month of the year that has thirty-one days."

The contestant answers, "who is Aries!' "The Roman god Janus, the first month of the year known as January."

"You are correct! Next question, botany or language for one thousand dollars?"

"Botany!"

"This plant grows in warm regions with fragrant flowers of yellow red or white."

"What is jasmine?"

Maria lets out a yelp, "*Si, mejo!* [yes, son!]"

The program goes into a commercial break with a news flash. "California is one step closer toward legalizing same-sex marriage. Voters' unanimous voice puts the initiative on the November primary. News at eight."

Maria motions the sign of the cross. "*Dios mio,* forgive them! They have gone astray from the light. They don't recognize troubles as gifts from the one cast down."

A knock at the residence door interrupts Maria's reasoning. She questions in her native tongue, "Hello, Juan, where's your house key?"

The question goes unacknowledged with another knock at the residence door. Maria removes herself from her comforting chair. She speaks toward the door, "Juan, have you lost the house key again? I know you're tired, I'm on my way." A beam of light is seen through the curtain, followed by another knock. Maria looks through the door peephole. "*Que onda?*" [Who's there?]

"Police officers!"

Opening her residence door, Maria questions in broken English, "*Policia?* You cawming here for helping sumbawdy?"

Disregarding Maria's question, the officer directs his flashlight toward the home's interior. He asks, "Is there anyone else in the residence?"

Maria hesitates giving her answer. "You habing sumbawdy speaking Spanish for me?"

The officer redirects. "Is there anyone other than yourself inside the residence?"

"Si, señor, I Maria Sanchez Gutierrez. I libbing here with Juan, *mi esposo.* Heem not here, for heem wurking now."

From the distance of the sidewalk, Maria recognizes the woman wearing the white Russian mink and hat ensemble. She gloats within the protection of a police officer, "Be sure to leave nothing out, honey! Tell everything about Juan you can think of to ensure he goes to jail! I've already mentioned the sobriety meetings he never attends. His drinking with the foul language that puts you in constant fear and the roaming around after work until he's sober. They're pros, Maria. They deal with animals like Juan every day. Believe me, he won't avoid jail this time. Do you remember my yoga instructor? She attends my Friday night ladies' forum. She's the one that's always asking for an extra plate of your crab cakes to take home. Maria, she's a chairperson of the International Battered ladies Forum. She's promised they'll appear at every court hearing to ensure Juan goes to prison. Everyone's cheering for you, honey. You'll be so safe with

CHAPTER TWENTY-ONE

Juan in prison for the next five years."

Disconnected from the circumstance, Milford has positioned himself on standby at the driver's door of the Maybach. Noticing the strain on his employer's vocal cords, Milford steps forward with a serving tray, presenting imported bottled water with sliced lemons and cherries. He proffers, "The madam's light refreshment, if necessary."

"Milford, certainly! I believe I've become hoarse from yelling. The sliced lemons are perfect. I find them to be very refreshing. Before the water is poured into the crystal, Milford, be sure to squeeze a few lemons over the ice cubes."

"Madam, absolutely." In his sagacious etiquette, Milford presents a handkerchief, should his employer feel the need to pat the perspiration from her brow.

"My goodness, has my mascara begun to run?"

"Its perfect, madam, not a smudge anywhere."

"Oh, Milford, thank you! In my time of worry what would I do without you?" Diana directs her comments to the police officer nearest her. "As I've already told the 9-1-1 operator, Juan's very dangerous. He's in there as we speak."

Maria assures the officer at her residence porch to the contrary. "No, no, señor. No problemas for here!"

Within the same time, the officer street side directs his flashlight toward the home's exterior. He returns the flashlight beam to the residence porch, informing his partner of his visual via radio. "Street side, all clear with the exterior."

The officer at the residence porch acknowledges, "Roger!" He discloses, "Mrs. Gutierrez? The call was received as a terrorist

threat with intent to cause great bodily harm, along with domestic disturbance, drinking in public, and possible kidnap-
ping. The victim is reported as Maria Gutierrez, attacked and
held hostage by her estranged husband, Juan Gutierrez. Has
there been a situation at your residence that may have escalated
to violence or bodily harm?"

After interpreting the seriousness of the allegations, Maria
answers emphatically, "No, señor! No problema with mi esposo, Juan! The problema's bery bawd, but not for here! I leab
wurk for calling the señora to esplain ebery ting!"

Maria's broken English is questioned. "Is the señora the
one being beaten? Is she working now? When was the last time
she was seen?"

Maria points to Diana, *"Si! mi hefa es ella* [She's my boss].*"

"Oh, I see; she's the señora. Has she been assaulted by Juan?"

Maria shakes her head with denial. "No! No! Juan, heem
wurking hard ebery day! Only for the señora habing the trawble I needing to esplain!"

Diana runs from street side to hug Maria. "Oh, precious,
your frightened. Tell them everything that animal's done!
The police are here to help, honey." Diana maintains her embrace. "Maria, look at you; you're delirious! No one's going to
hurt you anymore. You can move in with me where you'll be
safe, and your beautiful grandchildren can come visit every
weekend."

Attempting to bring clarity to the misunderstanding,
Maria removes herself from Diana's embrace. "No, señora. No
Juan this time for making the trawble!"

Unforgiving of Juan's past, Diana disregards Maria's words as gibberish. "Oh, honey, of course it's Juan. Who other than him would do something so cowardly? Maria, there's no need to be afraid; this is America. Here you aren't arrested for doing the right thing. The authorities in this country protect the victim, honey. They are here for the bad, nasty things that have happened to you. In order for those bad, nasty things to stop happening, you must tell the authorities about that very bad nasty person, the vile monster hiding in back of your mind, Juan. Maria, where is he?"

Maria shakes her head, disagreeing shamefully. "Señora, Maria no whawning to esplain for you the trawble. I finding Meester Paul and Dawnee for where me wurking today. For what I find I bery sawry."

"Why are you sorry about Paul, Maria?"

Maria shakes her head with her answer. "For where I wurking, I see the two bew-tee-ful morenas [beautiful dark women]. Them ordur sumting to Meester Paul and Dawnee for the room serbese."

"Are you saying someone brought Paul food? That's ridiculous! Milford's scheduled to return Paul from the airport later tonight. Maria, Paul's flight doesn't return until ten thirty tonight. Were you hit in the head, Maria? I believe you're delusional."

"No, señora, the senoritas ordur Meester Paul and Dawnee baking bean, and the big meat, for how do you say in English, 'the little cake?'" Maria then forms a circle with her index finger and thumb. She says, "I needing to esplain. What do you say in

English?" Blushing with embarrassment, she finds the word in Spanish, "*Culo* [ass]! You no watching the television, señora? The cakes with crèmee jellies, you drinking with the coffee."

The officer answers excitedly, "Donuts!"

"*Si!*" Maria forms her thumb and index finger into a tight ring. "*The small one.*"

"Donut holes?"

"*Yah, si!* Meester Paul and Dawnee putting meat for the doon-nawt, ah huh, the *culo!*"

The officer's face twists with scenarios as he aligns the pieces of Maria's puzzle. "Meat and bread; they're making sandwiches. Someone brought them sandwiches?"

Maria forms another circle with her thumb and index finger, pinching the circle closed. She advises, "This doon-nawt no for the eating! The senoritas telling Maria, Meester Paul and Dawnee whawning the sausage."

"Oh, I see, they squeezed the meat into the sandwich."

"No, no, no!" Maria becomes more animated. "Meester Paul and Dawnee put meat for inside!"

The officer reasons, "Donut? They put the sausage … inside the donut?"

"Yah, si! Meester Paul and Dawnee make the cake. Ah huh, and them whawning meat for the doon-nawt, the culo!"

The officer's partner solves the riddle with skepticism. "You're saying they put meat in their asses? Is that what this is all about? Well, who is Mr. Paul to this Juan character?"

Maria points to Diana explaining, "No, no, no! Meester Paul, the *esposo* for the señora!"

Beet red with embarrassment, the officer brings closure to the skit. "Okay, we understand. Mr. Paul was in a hotel with Mr. Danny. Someone ordered them room service while they were in the room putting sausage in their ass."

Maria confirms, "*Si, son hotos!* [yes, they're queers]."

"I see, so where does Juan come into the scenario? If he's gay bashing, we can definitely arrest him."

Maria defends, "No, no, no! Juan wurking bery hard! The problema is for the señora, no Juan!"

The officer looks to his partner with a raised eyebrow. He addresses Maria's revelation. "You're informing your employer that you saw her husband at a hotel with another man?"

Maria agrees. "Ah, *si!* I bery sawry for the trawble I making!" She clutches Diana's hands to make amends. "Pleez for-gib Maria. Señora, I no whawning to make trawble for you fambelee. Meester Paul bery good man. Pleez for-gib heem, señora." Maria motions the sign of the cross to present the letter. "*Dios mio!* Si, it is meestake!"

Diana snatches the letter. "Here! I'll end this foolishness! Paul's not in the country! Maria, how dare you speak of my husband? This is absurd! How can you say such a thing? You've obviously misread someone's mindless chatter." Diana mocks, "Oh *my goodneth*! As if English is your first language!" Intending to find error in Maria's accusations, Diana reads the letter with hostile intent. Her expression transitions from confrontational, to dull acknowledgment of what's presented before her. In stunned defeat, Diana blankly blinks her eyes to admit, "This is certainly humbling to say the least! I believe

I may have miscalculated the events as I understood them." Diana looks to the officers, explaining her actions. "There's certainly some truth to what I've said. Juan is definitely a lowlife. From time to time his wife has been frightened to the point of being beaten. Because of Juan's drunkenness, he carouses with other lowlifes until he's sober. There's truth to that! Maria's the victim here. Juan should be arrested immediately for everything that he could be potentially arrested for in the future."

Diana's tirade is dismissed. "Close it, lady; you've gone too far. With no facts to substantiate any of what you've said, you appear foolish. Lady, quit while you're ahead."

Diana questions defiantly, "How dare you talk to me like that? Do you know who my husband is?"

"Frankly, lady, I don't care who your husband is. This is a police matter. Secondly, you should be arrested for filing a false police report and be sued for defamation. If I were you, I'd stop all the talk. It's over."

"I'll … not stop talking! I reported in good faith what was happening at the time! There's no crime in that, you idiot!"

Supportive of his colleague, the officer's partner scrutinizes Diana's actions. "Mrs. Levitivitch? In your erroneous judgment, you've made serious accusations about this woman's husband. Valuable time and resources have been wasted here. In the irony of the senselessness, you mentioned good faith while referring to police officers as idiots! Looking down on idiots, you must feel privileged. Any person that would call an idiot for help is in complete denial, you think?"

Diana seethes. "I don't have to stand here and listen to you! I happen to be wealthy. And having wealth, peasant, my husband has lawyers that will shred you in court unmercifully! You seem to have forgotten the mission statement of your public employment. Officer, remember, you are a public servant. Milford!"

"Yes, madam?"

"Milford, darling, please find something for my nerves; I've become rather bored!"

Milford presents Diana's platinum cigarette case and fashionable cigarette extension holder, "Madam!"

"Milford, how marvelous; it's just what I needed. Thank you!" Diana redirects her attention to the officers. "My heavens, you're still standing here. I hadn't realized what I said until now. Here's consolation for any bruised egos. I'll admit we're all servants in one form or another, aren't we?" Diana exhales cigarette smoke to chuckle. "If I offended either of you with the words public servant, employment, shredding, and of course one of my husband's favorite places, court, hah, hah, hah, forgive me."

The officer questions, "Offended by what, Mrs. Levitivitch? Telling the truth? Wow, your husband's lawyers really frighten us! Speaking of your husband, do you really think he'll break away from the meat patty he's preparing for Danny's donut hole?" The officer directs his comments to his partner. "It was meat she mentioned, wasn't it?"

"I recalled it being big sausages is what I heard, Dave."

"Thanks, Rick! Oh, Mrs. Levitivitch, you're still here?

Forgive us for not giving our undivided attention. According to you, the guy that likes to go to court, your husband, did I get that right, Rick?"

"I believe that's how she put it, Dave!"

"Thanks again, Rick, but then again, it could be we're both mistaken. Her husband couldn't be the guy at the hotel pressing sausage links, because he hasn't yet returned from his business trip. Maria must have mistaken as well. Surely it was someone else's husband in that hotel punching Danny's asshole, because this woman's husband won't be returning until later tonight! Isn't that right, Mrs. Levitivitch?"

Stunned, Diana reacts angrily to save face. "I don't have to listen to you! You're public flunkies! Fifty-thousand-dollar-a-year flunkies! I allot Maria and Milford more earnings! They obviously have more value; they're needed. You both disgust me."

The senior officer brings closure. "Mrs. Levitivitch, it's over. You've said plenty of nasty things during this ordeal. In countering your attacks, as police officers we may have said some things inappropriate and out of line as well. My point is that everyone's out of line here. Let it go."

"My husband's lawyers will have plenty to say about you being out of line, you flunky bastards. You're both sick!"

"Sure, lady; we can't wait to meet them. Here's our names and badge numbers. I've included the incident report number of the false complaint you called in to 9-1-1. Good luck!" The officers return to their squad car. Before pulling away, the passenger yells toward the residence, "Mrs. Levitivitch, us two flunky bastards forgot to ask. Speaking of flunkies." The officer points to Maria and Milford. "How much are you paying them to listen to your bullshit, lady? You can do that when you're wealthy, right? Don't go broke; you'll die a lonely bee-awch!" [bitch.] Laughter's heard within the squad car.

"Wow, Rick, you shut her down with that one. Where'd you pick up the swag?"

"I dunno. This hot chick I'm dating, she's into that old school gangsta rap."

"Since when are you listening to that shit?"

"Hey, it keeps her going out on dates with me. We're going to another concert next weekend!"

"No shit? How old is she?"

"She'll be twenty-eight Saturday."

"Really! That's pretty good, Rick. What about that song 'Screw the Police?' Put that on the playlist during the date. What a way of saying happy birthday!"

"Oh yeah, that'll be a good one. I'm pretty sure she has that one too. It'll definitely be playing the next time she's straddling me!"

"That was pretty good, Dave."

"Yeah, what about that bird back there? Did you hear what she said? She said you disgust her, Rick. You really pissed her off when you mentioned her husband at the hotel punching the other guy in the ass."

"I know; she called us disgusting!"

"Not me, you! You were the one saying it! You would have been better off asking if her husband liked his donut warm."

The police car rolls away, leaving Diana standing on the porch of Maria's residence. Outdone, Diana fidgets at the buttons on her Russian mink. She talks in frustration. "It's obvious they're from around the hood, or whatever they call this piece of shit neighborhood! The system puts idiots like those in place to deal with the likes around here. What civilized person would even consider living in this part of town? Oh, what am I saying? Maria, forgive me. Maria, I would never include you in the bunch. How insensitive of me! I'm so worked up, Maria, I've forgotten this is your home ... Milford!"

"Madam?"

"Milford, I may pass out at any moment, I believe I need settling."

"Yes, madam, right away."

Milford begins with the preparation of the serving tray, complete with imported bottled water and prescription pills.

Diana talks openly as Milford prepares her medications. "My heavens, since the abuse and threats those public servants hurled at me, I've become lightheaded. You both witnessed their unprofessionalism; it's a travesty of public service! This requires my medications. Milford, thank you. We'll all file reports at the police station in the morning. Come now!" Maria and Milford assist their employer to the Maybach. Diana talks in tow. "Maria, my nerves are completely shot. What would I do without you? Honey, would you ride home with me? I don't believe I can make it alone. Maria, you and Milford are the only family I have in California ... Honey, why not be with me at your other home? Who else can I trust but you? Please come stay a few days. Juan will never know you're gone. Please, Maria. He won't be home anytime soon. Juan loves being with the animals he loafs with."

Maria hesitates with her answer. "Si, señora ... Maria taking more clothes for change, and I esplain a note for Juan, *una momenta*."

"Oh thank you, Maria, I'll gladly pay your entire month's salary for next week's stay." Milford and Maria assist their employer into the car's interior. "My goodness, I've become so weak. I believe I'm having a nervous breakdown!"

CHAPTER TWENTY-TWO

*L*eaving Maria's residence, Diana suffered an anxiety attack and lost consciousness. She awakened hot and lightheaded to fan herself in silence just as Milford arrived at her Benedict Canyon estate. Maria exited the vehicle to open the estate door, only to struggle with nervous energy with the alarm code. Milford supported Diana as he guided Maria through the alarm protocol.

"Maria, try the Pound key then the numerical address, followed by the number of years of employment."

A dumbfounded Maria performs with Milford's instructions. "Ah-huh, now I remember the secureety. When I esplain the bawd imp-pormee-shun for the señora, I forget. Milfurb, I bery sawry for taking the room serbese!" Entering the estate, Maria and Milford assist their fragile employer to the couch.

Diana responds after a few moments of gathering herself. "Maria! Oh, Maria, thank God, you came back to take care of me. Honey, what has happened? How long have I been sitting here?"

"You arribing home now, señora. You hab Maria cawm here to help with the mee-dee-cayshun for you bery dizzy!"

Diana stares blankly from the couch. "Milford, my tonic and medications. I need to be settled."

"Yes, Madam, right away. With the madam's medication, would madam prefer Russian vodka or the Mexican tequila?"

"Milford, please mix both with ice."

"Madam, absolutely!"

While awaiting her medications, Diana closed her eyes to move her head in disbelief. "It's all just a very bad dream. I can't believe it! The shame to my family. This is unheard of; my husband's cheating with a man? We were married Catholic!"

Milford presents his employer her tonic and medications. "Madam?"

"Milford. Thank you, I believe my nerves may be getting the best of me."

Maria dismisses the letter's discovery. "Señora, this lettur no buena for you nerbs. Maria take it away from here." Taking the letter, Maria consoles her employer, "Maria making for you especial dinnur! Bery good for you and Meester Paul, for lubbers [lovers]!"

After a brief silence to reminisce about Paul's marriage proposal, Diana becomes insistent about preparing the meal. "No, Maria, I'll make dinner! I haven't forgotten how, you know. Stuffed bell peppers with lamb. How could I forget?" Diana forces a smile. "That was the meal Paul ordered for our engagement dinner. He proposed as we drank wine; it was very romantic. What a rascal he was!" Diana holds the smile to look at photos of periods during and near their marriage of the many places they visited around the world. "Maria, that picture there? It was my twenty-fourth birthday. We were in Thailand on a riverboat, headed to the seaport to have lunch in Bangkok, the capital. It's so busy there and very erotic. The mosquitoes are huge. Being as I'm so fair-skinned, Paul paid for a canopy the entire time, just so I wouldn't be eaten alive. My goodness, the humidity! It's all tropical, you know. Aw, Maria, see the one next to the piano? You would never imagine where we are in a thousand years."

"Ah-huh, señora, bery nice. This pee-shure for you and Meester Paul is Maria's bery fayboreet. Meester Paul and the señora looking bery hansum tugeddur!"

Diana holds her smile. "Yes, Maria, it's very beautiful. We're still in Asia on the Bay of Bengal, for our five-year anniversary. Honey, it was so lovely there."

Feeling it necessary to console her employer, Maria talks openly. "Ah-huh, Maria umbdurstand señora. Ebery pee-shure for you marrege is bery nice. Ah-huh, so bery nice for Meester Paul to gib expensuf baycayshun for the señora. You take bery bew-tee-ful pee-shures eberywhere!"

Yet to face Maria in conversation, Diana has talked into space while remained looking into the far distance. Something catches Diana's eye. "Oh, Maria? Is that something out of place there?

"I don't tink so, señora! I cleen eberywhere!"

"I know you do, honey, it's just that I'm a stickler for the small things. Look at that, do you not see it?"

Maria looks in the direction she thinks her employer is looking. "Yah? No, I see naw-ting! Ebery ting bery cleen, señora!"

Diana gasps. "Maria, how can you not see that? It's a mess! Look, there on the chaise in the sunroom. Is that's Scooter's collar? Honey, how did it get there?"

Maria overlooks her employer's denial, agreeing, "Ah-huh, maybe sumbawdy leab it. [leave] I tink maybe the man cawming for Scootie and Shippie's haircut maybe leab! This no good for the señora's nerbs! No wurry, I take this away now." Maria motions toward the sunroom.

Diana proposes, "Maria, honey? Let's sit in the kitchen and talk; we have to recap what happened at work today. Take your time explaining. I need to know everything. Afterwards, we'll talk about the upcoming holidays. I haven't yet decided how much to allot for your Christmas bonus." Discontinuing her gaze into the far distance, Diana looks Maria in the eyes for clarification. "Honey, let's not rush or leave anything out. This is important. You do understand how important this is?"

"Ah-huh? Maria remembur ebery ting, señora. Maybe the imp-pormee-shun I have, no buena for you and Meester Paul."

"Oh no, Maria, take your time and do tell everything! I have faith in you. Haven't I always? After giving it some thought, it's so lovely to have you working here. I hired you as a complete stranger into my home without any references! Maria, from day one you were given a chance, and since that day you've been working steadily. You're now able to buy things for your grandchildren anytime you want, all because of me! Isn't that wonderful, honey? Let's have tea in the kitchen, shall we? Tea helps with memory, and I've found it to be very therapeutic. Come now, my ears are burning. I'm sure I'll find your story very soothing."

Maria looks to the floor, envisioning Flora and Hortencia's faces. *Maria. Don't get involved,* and *she should be the one telling you about her husband. Wealthy people will fire you for telling the truth and then hire someone else to keep their secrets.* Maria speaks aloud without realizing it. "I bery *estupida*!"

"Maria, what are you saying?"

"For-gib me, señora, I telling sumting in meestake." Maria follows Diana into the kitchen mumbling under her breath, "Oh my goodneth. I bringing so mawch trawble to me!"

Going directly to the kitchen pantry, Diana retrieves a box of tea bags. With teapot in hand, she extends Maria hospitality. "Oh, honey, I've forgotten. How many sugar cubes do you want in your tea?"

"Oh no, señora, no tea for Maria today! Maria bery bizzy for wurking!"

Maria's concerns are dismissed with matter-of-fact omission. "Honey, let's talk about the women at the hotel. You mentioned an unfamiliar word referring to them."

In an attempt to discourage Diana's probing, Maria digs into her nasal cavity. She recalls, "I tink it was two pursons? Morenas maybe. Ah-huh, señora, I tink I forget ebery ting!"

"Yes, that's the word you mentioned. *Morenas.* What does that mean?"

Maria continues with non-recollection. "I tink for the English? Maybe the bew-tee-ful dark ladies."

"Aw, I see! Paul has dark secrets, does he?"

"Ah-huh? Señora, heem hab maybe two ladies for heem room. Ah huh, I tink Meester Paul hab two."

Diana takes a sip of tea with her next question. "You actually saw them in his room?"

"I no see ebery ting, señora! The ladies leab Meester Paul's room bery ubbset!"

"Why, Maria? Why would they be upset with Paul? Were they whores?"

"What is the whore, señora?"

"Cheap women, Maria. Were they cheap?"

"Cheep? Maria no umbdurstanding the cheep ladies!"

"Maria, did the women look like they would have sex with men for money?"

"No, señora! The ladies bery expensuf! One ladies esplain, Meester Paul and Dawnee baking the cake! She esplain Meester Paul and Dawnee whawning meat for the doon-nawt, and baking bean and sausage with tick white crèmee for the kukumbur. One ladies ordur for Meester Paul and Dawnee bery fru-tee with limón, for the culo to pucker!"

Diana gets the gist of what Maria is attempting to recount. "I see, and who paid for this request?"

"Señora, the ladies gib the teep!"

"They tipped you? How much?"

Maria reveals the money. "They gib one hundred for the room serbese! I making change and keeping thurty-two dollar teep. Meester Paul and Dawnee leab one-hundred-dollar teep for cleening the room!"

"How did you get the letter, Maria? Did one of the whores give it to you? You mentioned they were both … I believe you used the word *dark*?"

"*Morenas*, señora! Bery bew-tee-ful ladies!"

"Okay, I understand the meaning. Who gave you the letter?"

"I finding on the floor, señora. Ah-huh, Meester Paul and Dawnee leabing more imp-pormee-shun! I esplain for the señora what I find. Una momenta…"

Diana's eyes widen as she sips her cup of tea. She probes further, "What more did you…"

Maria leaves the kitchen to return hurriedly with her bag. "Señora, I finding clothes for ladies!" Maria brings out both the thong and wig to whisper, "This no buena, señora!"

Diana questions disbelievingly, "You've brought his whore's panties into my home?"

"No, no, no, señora! The ladies no wear theez tings! Meester Paul and Dawnee leab theez!" Maria find when cleening the room!"

As Diana takes a sip of tea, she coughs. She spits tea onto the kitchen table. "What?"

"Si, señora, I finding trawble. You no telling Meester Paul? No bery good for Maria. Apter you esplain to heem, maybe I no wurking for you here."

Diana presses the intercom to summon Milford, "Beep! Beep! Beep! Beep!"

"Yes, madam?"

"Milford, there's a crisis pending; please come to the kitchen."

"Madam right away! Does the madam require more of her medications for settling?"

"Milford, thank goodness you and Maria are here. Please come right away."

Milford arrives with serving tray complete with prescription pills and imported bottled water. "Madam, your Valium and Thorazine for the evening?"

"Milford, no medications. I've become weak; please help me to the couch."

"Madam, absolutely."

"Maria, would you assist us, honey?"

"Si, señora!"

From the sofa, Diana stared throughout the living room transfixed by the many photos of her and Paul.

Meanwhile, Maria attentively strokes her employer's forehead with a wet towel. "Señora? Meester Paul, heem a good man. Maybe heem making the bawd meestake for today only!"

After several moments of standing idle, Milford addresses his employer. "Madam, shall I resume with the silver polishing in the parlor?"

"Milford, as you were, thank you."

Diana reaches for her cigarette holder. She laughs in mockery of her circumstance as if she were Phyllis Diller doing stand-up, "Hah, hah, hah! After twenty-seven years of marital bliss, then comes the big bang! Every woman wants the life I've had, being kept, pampered, and showered with gifts! I've traveled the world eating the best crab and oysters! I've drunk the most expensive cognacs and worn diamonds from all over the world! Well, honey, I've certainly kept my end of the bargain; that's for sure! I've slept with the same man for twenty-seven years! I massaged and sucked his cock faithfully the entire time we've been married. That's certainly putting in the time to keep things going nice and soft, wouldn't you say? How's that for commitment? Talk about sleeping at the wheel! Hah, hah, hah! You know what the biggest bang is yet, Maria?"

"I dunno, señora. You laffing too mawch. Maria bery nerbous!"

"Nervous? No honey, it's pitiful. After twenty-seven years, the wife finds out her husband enjoys having his prostate checked! In the complete opposite of most men, her husband looks forward to his appointments. He insists on having the doctor with the largest hands for the probe! Hah, hah, hah! How's that for excitement?"

Maria nervously wipes Diana's face with a wet towel. "Pleez, señora, it's no good for you talking ubbset. We go back to the kisshin, for Maria make sumting especial for you nerbs."

Maria supports her employer in their walk toward the kitchen. "You know, honey? The entire time we've been married, I've always blamed Paul's diet for his hemorrhoids. Hah, hah, hah!" The exaggerated chuckling abruptly stops. "Maria honey?"

"Si, señora?"

"Please find something to prepare. I'm nearly famished!"

Maria motions the sign of the cross. "*Dios mio*! Señora, you whawning Maria to make the baking bean for Meester Paul only, or for you sumting dipporent?"

"Maria, let's have something more palatable, shall we? Honey, the lamb and bell peppers are fine. There's no telling how he likes his meat these days. Should we trim the fat, or skin the fat back to the lean meat? Hah, hah, hah!"

Seated at the kitchen table in a daze, Diana watched in silence as Maria washed her hands to prepare the entrée requests. Maria's interrupted as she dried her hands with a towel. "Maria, honey!"

"Si, señora."

Diana motions to the kitchen table. "Let's read the letter together again, shall we? Be sure to include everything that happened at work. I haven't really grasped what I've heard. We need to be sure of all this. You mentioned the man with Paul wore the wig and thong, is that what you recalled? Be careful to leave nothing out, honey."

Maria attempts to recant her recollection. "Señora, maybe Maria tired and forget the imp-pormee-shun, its so mawch trawble for rememburing ebery ting!"

Diana ignores Maria's quibbling to press further. "Oh, everything will come back to you, honey. Just take your time. Let's start with the whores and how you described them, the word *morenas*? I'm having trouble understanding this adjective. You described them as beautiful, yet they appeared dark? Surely you meant they were evenly tanned, right, honey?"

Maria probes her nasal cavity nervously. She admits, "Señora, I tink maybe I make a meestake for taking the room serbese!"

Seated at the kitchen table, Maria re-explained the events leading to the discovery of the wig and thong. As Diana listened, she diced bell peppers on the cutting board. She stopped momentarily to reflect, "I can't believe it! Not in a thousand years would I have imagined anything like this! I've never been a jealous woman, nor did I crowd Paul or verify his every movement. From time to time there may have been the inkling of a possibility of another woman … Well, not really another woman, but rather the occasional sex magazine. Lately there's been matchbooks from the strip clubs he visited while on business conferences … Over the past few years, I admit I have been rather uncomfortable with Paul in the bedroom. His requests were so different from our normal way of doing things … This explains why the whores were there, but being with another man? Never!"

Maria goes about working the seasonings into the lamb. Diana interrupts her marriage reflections with a work instruction. "Honey, please be sure to include enough garlic and thyme!"

"Si, señora." Maria taps another pinch of each before covering the meat to marinate.

Diana continues with the dicing of the bell peppers in denial. "Maria, honey, have you ever experienced anything like this?" Disallowing an answer, Diana forces a smile, changing the subject. "Being pampered and having everything you need …

Traveling. Hiring help to maintain your household. Being invited to premiers, or having a wonderful evening of ballroom
dancing. Oh, I didn't mention holding the weekly ladies' forums at your estate." The dicing of the bell peppers abruptly
stops. Diana looks at Maria, answering herself. "Of course not!
You've lived your entire life with Juan. How could you have
ever experienced any of what I've said? Maria, I'm sorry to
bring up bad feelings! Everyone knows you've had your share
of nightmares being married to such a loser, but I do marvel
at your patience … Honey, I don't mean to upset you. It's just
that I'm not accustomed to living a common lifestyle, that's
all. Nothing ever seems to bother you with your lot in life. You
appear so happy with what you're doing; it's a credit to you,
honey. You're much like the salt of the earth. Here you seem
so comfortable with all the cooking and cleaning. I don't know
what I'd do without you."

Maria goes about the kitchen to retrieve a roasting pan
from the lazy Susan cabinet for the oven. "I bery happy wurking here for you and Meester Paul, señora."

Diana continues dicing the peppers. "Honey, I know you
are. Believe it or not, by living such a simple life you're much
better off than most people. I for one couldn't imagine work,
let alone work for other people. I'd go crazy. Pay bills? Having
to deal with car payments? Heaven forbid! How do you do it?
Maria, you use public transportation to come to work! I could
never be the woman you've been. There's a different strength
in you, honey! I couldn't imagine living without the choice
cuts of meat delivered weekly. Of all things, to stand in line at

restaurants or premieres like a commoner … Living without valet parking? Spending Sunday afternoons foraging through the paper for shopping coupons. Using discounts to fly coach? Who would ever want to live that way?"

Diana comes out of her cloud of denial with an abrupt stop of the dicing of the peppers. She looks at Maria, offering an apology. "Oh, honey, forgive me, I've done it again, haven't I? I've compared pearls to marbles. Honey, how could you possibly fathom any of what I've said, when you've lived your entire life with Juan?"

Giving into her emotions, Diana forcefully hammers the vegetable cleaver into the cutting board. She abruptly flees the kitchen in tears. Continuing through the living room, she hurries to the foyer closet to rant, "With everything said and done, he's left nothing to the imagination! No wonder the bastard has more than one briefcase." In her return to the kitchen, Diana inventories the contents of Paul's briefcase: "A tube of anal lube? From what's been gathered today, we can rule out hemorrhoids." She raises the tube to drop it to the floor. "What's this? February's issue of *Ghett* magazine? You did mention his whores were of the darker persuasion. Well, here's Miss February, and she's the beauty of the week!" Diana drops the magazine to the floor. She questions, "A lease receipt in the amount of twenty-four thousand dollars? He's paying his whore's rent?"

Startled by Diana's dysfunctional bipolar behavior, Maria comforts her employer with an embrace. "Señora, no! No good for you to talk ubbset. This no good for Meester Paul to see you ubbset for heem! Pleez, señora, I esplain to Milfurb to dribe to hospeetal for you mee-dee-cayshun for bery dizzy!" Maria motions the sign of the cross. "*Dios mio*! Pleez for-gib me! I making the meestake for taking the room serbese!"

CHAPTER TWENTY-THREE

At 10:30 p.m., after waiting patiently at the L.A.X. international arrival concourse, Milford returns from Baggage Claim with designer suitcases. His employer, Paul Levitivitch, is seated comfortably in the rear of the Maybach. Involved in a cellphone conversation, Paul ends the call hushed, just as Milford approached. "Ah, Milford, you've returned so soon. You've made such short work of a grand task."

"Master Paul, really, there was nothing to it; yours were the first down the chute to appear on the carousel."

"Were all the bags put on the same flight?"

"Absolutely, all seven suitcases are accounted for."

"Thanks, Milford."

"Does Master Paul require any stops before our arrival at the estate?"

"No stops, Milford; home right away, old sport."

"Master Paul, as you wish."

During the one-hour commute to his remote Benedict Canyon estate, Paul Levitivitch confirms his dates of availability for the upcoming month's appointment schedule. Involved and busy is an understatement to describe Milford's employer. Congenial by nature, Paul is methodical with planning. He pays the estate's overhead through his accountant, with a provided slush account for Diana to spend as she pleases.

Relaxing leisurely at home, Diana regulates the estate's household and servants. Having both the flair and the eye for particulars, the estate's lavish décor and landscape concepts are her creative prodigies, down to the minute detail of the linen thread count for the estate's guest rooms.

Equally said, as finance attracts the comforts of beauty, Paul Levitivitch is a stark contrast to his wife Diana. Where Paul is giving and approachable, Diana is one thousand p.s.i. of unyielding suspicion, with zero tolerance for slackers or underachievers. As to Diana's unrelenting scrutiny, she would expectantly await for Paul to over-tip a waitress at one of their favorite restaurants. Insisting Paul was too kind, Diana would reprimand him with indifference.

"People are taking advantage of you. They see you coming every time, Paul. You would have done better having her tip herself." Recalling the bill, Diana would reapportion the tip to the correct gratuity. "This is much more in sync with the bill. She doesn't deserve any more than that. Paul, if you insist on giving away our money so freely, I'll be sure to purchase next year's full line of Bee Bottoms, and I'll award the young salesmen the gratuities you leave here. Don't let me find out you're fucking the help, Paul. Of all people, she's the waitress at our favorite restaurant!"

During the couple's next visit, Diana would arrange to have the waitress stationed at another area, to rule out any possibility of receiving a tip from her husband. Being accommodating, Paul would address his wife's behavior in the privacy of their home. Whenever her condescending antics were questioned, Diana would reply with feigned innocence. "Paul, you know I don't keep track of my medications. It's the Thorazine and Valium, honey; it may be the dosages are too strong. It's not my fault! Look at me; I'm such a little thing. How can I be all that bad? The doctor increased the dosages only because you asked him to, and you blame me for what you've requested? Paul, are you trying to pick a fight, honey? You know I'm sensitive about my medications."

The Maybach rolled smoothly along Benedict Canyon to approach the estate's driveway. With the commute coming to an end, Milford released the trunk latch to gather his employer's luggage. After several trips from the luxury vehicle to the estate's foyer, Milford returned to open the rear passenger door. Respectfully stepping away, Milford affords his employer privacy during his cellphone conversation.

Paul exits the luxury vehicle acknowledging Milford's etiquette. "Thanks, old chum!"

"Master Paul, think nothing of it."

Standing at the rear of the Maybach, Paul resumes the cellphone conversation. "Frank, we'll go back to the table within the next quarter, and hopefully circumstances will be different for the next venture. Looking over the business calendar, have you checked with Jaime for your upcoming quarterly? I anticipate another business summit, and I've requested an open block of availability for the next six months. Mark my words, they'll reconsider our proposal. Honestly, we should have had a point man out front with this one. No, the milk's spilled already, and we can't pour it back. I wouldn't consider them arrogant or uppity either; we just didn't sell our position. Did you expect them to jump at our first proposal? Where was your due diligence? They've been in business for over a hundred years. Evolution! Remember the word for next time. No, I'm not saying it's your fault. Frank, we're a team! I'm assessing our shortcomings so we'll be better prepared for next time. I wouldn't say its Tom Braxton's fault; his presentation was fine. They liked him actually.

"The truth of the matter, they've evolved! For the past fifteen years, they've maintained yields upward of a hundred fifty-five percent. Did anyone see this other than me? Frank, can you blame them? What have we offered? Would it be a chance at opportunity? No, that's not what I'm saying, we're all capable. We're Levitivitch, Meyers, and Rothensberg, a respected reputable, firm. We didn't do our job over there. You're not hearing me. There's no one to blame for our shortcomings, Frank. If you need a reason for why we've been humbled, try approach, along with direction, and maybe just a teeny weeny hint of respect. How's that preposterous? We presented ourselves as the mighty conquerors, there to quell and civilized the indigenous savages under our arrogant authority! Frank, they saw us coming! It's the yellow brick road and the *Wizard of Oz* seventy-six years later! Because we didn't sell, they anticipated where the house would fall. Answer the question? In the Land of Oz, where does the house fall? No, the good witch of the north was the protector of the Munchkins. The house fell on the wicked witch of the east! Okay, and where are we in proximity to Brazil? I've made my point. That's why I anticipate another summit. They used the guys from the East only as leverage, but for sure they'll go with us the next time out. In the meantime, we've been put in check until the next move. Between now and then, you, Rothensberg, and I—hell the whole damn firm—we need to regroup and rethink our position. Vencor Engineering and Mining has to be convinced they will cease to yield their hundred-fifty-five-percent growth per annum unless they have the direction of our firm. Frank, consider this the prospectus for the firm's next meeting. Should Rothensberg have an idea other than what I consider the golden parachute, call me." Ending the call, Paul directs his attention to the dutiful butler and family chauffeur. "Milford, my good man, forgive me for being so long-winded. How have things been with the home team?"

Milford gives no warning to the disarray in the Levitivitch household. "It's been absolute Shangri-La throughout the estate grounds, I'd say."

"Great, Milford! I'd expect nothing less of you during my absence, old sport. As to Chippy and Scooter, have they behaved?"

"I believe Chippy had a stomach virus just two weeks ago.

Feathers were recovered from her stool. It seems she captured a crow that may have been sick. The antibiotics the veterinarian prescribed appear to have revived her quite rapidly then since."

"Ah, she's recovered, has she? Great job, Milford, and Scooter, the handsome devil? Have they had their scheduled maintenance this week?"

"Absolutely! They were bathed with de-flea shampoo, as well as manicured and fragranced, complete with ribbons and colorings."

"Colorings? She's had the groomer changed their color has she?"

"Unequivocally, Master Paul! Madam's chosen popsicle pink for Chippy. For Scooter it's now butterscotch brown and tapioca beige for the sport."

"My god, Milford! Exotic color charts are now being provided with their grooming's?"

"Master Paul, to the contrary. Chippy's coloring came about from a dessert entrée at madam's recent Friday night ladies forum, Italian ice! It seems madam's taken a liking to its color and flavoring. For Saturday morning's brunch, the madam's guest enjoyed French toast with crème brulée. The colors butterscotch brown and tapioca beige came about for Scooter."

"Well, Milford, I'd say there's never been a dull moment in paradise."

Disconnected from the disorder of his employer's estate, Milford answers giving no indication of scandal. "Master Paul, I'd say both animals are quite extraordinary."

"Thank you, Milford, and the madam's behavior during my absence?"

With a graceful sweeping motion toward the estate, Milford extends a hand with his answer. "Indubitably the madam awaits." With a hand placed over his heart, Milford bends at the waist as if finishing a theatrical performance.

"Good show, Milford! You'll teach me to become the perfect Englishman yet." As Paul approaches the residence from the courtyard, Maria opens the estate door from the interior.

"Hello, Meester Paul. I hearing you talking frum inside. So bery good you arribing home. You looking bery hansum today." She asks, "How was your baycayshun? The weddur bery nice for you trabbling to Brasíl?" Maria removes Paul's blazer. "I hab sumting bery especial. Maria make you fayboreet dish, and making the meent tea for drinking." Maria grabs Paul's cheeks playfully. "No more baking bean for you! Today the baking beans too mawch trawble for ebery bawdy."

Clueless, Paul responds, "Great, Maria, baked beans are one of my favorites. Are they included in tonight's entrees?"

"No, no, no!" Maria wags her finger. "The señora telling Maria, no baking bean for you! The señora bery bery ubbset. I esplain ebery ting for when you go to Brasíl. Ah-huh, you whawning you doon-nawt to pucker."

Deciphering words from Maria's broken English, Paul continues the conversation based on what he thinks Maria intended to say. "Oh, Maria, the trip was fantastic. You'd never imagine how Brazil has developed since the last conference. With the trade agreements in place, the high rises over there are now built on rollers to offset the sandy terrain. There's something for both California and New York to set benchmarks to. They are truly amazing! Maria, I had such a lovely time there, and the flight both ways was absolute textbook. I'm telling you, Maria, you would never believe you were in a third-world country. Where's Diana? She's awfully quiet. I'll be forced to tell the story twice."

Maria motions the sign of the cross. "Oh my goodneth! The señora taking her mee-dee-cayshun for bery dizzy. The señora waiting for you." Maria wags her finger at Paul. "She whawning you to esplain what happened for your baycayshun. Ah-huh, and I make the especial dinnur frum the señora's marrege." Maria motions to the intercom. "I telling the señora you arribing!"

"No, instead let's all give Diana a surprise together, shall we?"

Reading into the idea, Maria folds her hands nervously. "Meester Paul? Maybe serprizing no good for the señora. Too mawch serprizing for here today. The señora bery dizzy!"

Oblivious to Maria's concerns, Paul explains his reasoning, continuing up the staircase. "To the contrary, Maria, surprise is good for the soul. It keeps the spice and spontaneous juices alive. Surprise is the epitome of presentation! Washington's crossing the Delaware in the middle of the night was certainly surprise. On your anniversary, your wife finds diamonds on her pillow; is that not the embodiment of surprise? Imagine life without surprise. Would a marriage proposal have the paramount effect without the element of surprise?" Paul stops his rationale to look in the direction of his trusted butler and personal valet. "Milford, if you would please?"

Meanwhile in the second parlor, Milford has commenced with the polishing of the estate's silver. Donned in a white smock, he uses a polishing rag to work the precious metal to a brilliant shine. Milford interrupts his labors to look over his reading glasses to acknowledge his employer. "Master Paul, absolutely! Surprise is the complete opposite of expectation! The antonym of the planned or predictable! The yin and yang, unequivocally, of Chinese philosophy!"

As though Paul were acknowledging royalty, he bends at the waist to bow. "Milford, marvelous; I commend you. Well said. Bravo!"

"Master Paul, think nothing of it. During my time at Cambridge, I had a great uncle who allowed me to read in his study from time to time."

Paul counters with a sheepish grin. "Impressive, Milford, that English swagger! I'm sure you'll show me how to carry it properly one day."

Milford nods. "As Master Paul wishes."

"Great, Milford thank you. Ah, and to the good part? Maria! For the evening's meal, the madam and I will dine in the master suite, where we shall retire for the evening. I recall baked beans mentioned as a dinner entrée. Marvelous! Perhaps a salad with creamy avocado dressing and dinner rolls, I presume?"

Maria probes at her nostrils nervously. "No, no baking bean for here today! The señora no whawning baking bean!"

"Of course she eats baked beans, Maria. You prepare them to where we can eat as much as we want without gas disturbance.

Maria, do you recall the meat delivery coming this week? There's a spicy Louisiana sausage that would be perfect as a jambalaya entrée. Would you include that request with the next delivery? Thanks!"

To avoid giving an answer, Maria hurries toward the kitchen, covering her ears. "Oh, my goodneth! I no putting the timer for dinnur. I needing to check sumting!"

Paul questions the whereabouts of the family pets. "It's awfully quiet, Milford, are both Chippy and Scooter in the main quarters?"

"Master Paul, I didn't mention, madam has hired a personal trainer to create an exercise regimen for the two. Their walks have been increased an additional mile in hopes of preventing obesity. This is their first week with their new regimen, so both have retired to their new bedding in the first parlor."

Caught off guard, Paul raises an eyebrow. "Well, the madam's certainly been quite busy! Marvelous, old chap! Release them both in one hour, which gives me time to digest dinner before the privileged are summoned. Thanks, Milford."

Milford continues polishing the silver flatware. "As the master wishes, in precisely one hour!"

Proceeding up the staircase, Paul whistles as he lightly runs his fingertips over the exquisite railing. "Oh, Milford? Notify the cabinet finisher to re-sand and lacquer the railings. I believe their losing some luster. Thanks, Milford!"

Whistling with his approach, Paul opens the door to a darkened master suite. After a light touch of the light switch, Paul is taken aback with the sight of Diana sprawled in the chaise lounge. Undisturbed in the darkened room, Diana has lain in deliberate silence for Paul's return. Her face covered in facial exfoliating cream, large hair rollers have been placed around her head as if worn as a crown. Perfectly cut cucumber slices rest coolly on top of her eyelids. Diana's designer robe draped her slender body as if tailored. At the knee of the parting robe, smooth slender legs lead to Diana's beautiful feet, a testament to her weekly pedicure and foot spa appointments. Positioned in the chaise cup holder are prescription medications and a fifth of Juan Julio 1600. Scattered about at the floor of the chaise were items from Paul's emptied briefcase: hemorrhoid suppositories, anal lube, airline ticket receipts, several issues of *Ghett* magazine, and what appeared to be several lease agreements. As Paul takes in the unfolding, he looked again to his wife sprawled on the chaise lounge. A black sleep mask now covers the cucumbers positioned over Diana's eyelids. Paul closes the door behind him.

"Hello, honey, what are you doing in the dark? Have I surprised you? Surely you were expecting my return. Today's the twenty-first." Unanswered, Paul re-directs the question. "Have I surprised you, honey? Today's the twenty-first! You weren't at the airport with Milford, which made the ride that much longer without you. I've heard Chippy and Scooter's new fashion statements are sentiments from your Friday night ladies' forum. Their colorings were inspired by crème brulèe and Italian shaved ice. What's next? Mind you, I have no grand expectations of being the topic of discussion among members of your ladies' forum, so I might as well tell you how everything went. The business summit wasn't a total loss. We're working toward our redemption with hopes of another meeting. Are you listening, honey?"

Diana responds with guttural reproach. "You son of a bitch! You bastard! How could you? All this time you've been lying and sneaking around? Throughout our marriage you were pretending to be a man? You disgusting filth, where's your dignity? You're a virus! The nasty germ in a whore's douche is what you are!"

Blindsided by his wife's tone and language, Paul's face contorts with shocked amazement. "Diana, whatever has happened? You're behaving with such sharp language and venom! It's Paul, your husband. Has Dr. Heisenberg changed your medication without consulting me? Maria mentioned you weren't feeling well, but this is a bit much! Should I have Milford bring warm tea to settle you?"

Diana's guttural reproach continued with more contempt. "You're an embarrassing wet spot. A mistake that never should have happened, Paul! Even an animal refuses to shit where it eats. After what you've done, don't ever touch me!"

Paul's forehead wrinkles; he's perplexed. "Diana, what have I done?"

"You're an animal. What haven't you done with your dark whore or your male concubine? Freak! You're nothing more than a conniving man with a little dick! Twenty-seven years, Paul! Twenty-seven years we've slept together as man and wife! In spite of your shortcomings, I've sucked your little dick faithfully, pretending to be satisfied." The guttural reproach transitions into a sinister chuckle. "Hah, hah, hah! You disgusting little worm!"

"Diana, you're hallucinating. You've gone mad!"

"Mad? I'll tell you how mad I've become, maggot! I've been hallucinating so much with prescribed medications, you would never think I'd find the lease agreements you've kept in your safe deposit box for the past seven years. Surprised, Paul. You know Carol Dryfeuss? She attends my ladies forum. Her husband's the bank president, so I had no problem with your safe deposit box being brought to our home. Guess what I discovered. Everything! Look on the floor and see what else I've found … I even Googled the address on the lease agreements. It's rather dark over there, Paul. Whatever would you be doing on that side of town? Is that where you keep your secrets? Does the whore have a name? After you explain your other secret, men, would your whore feel betrayed, Paul?" Diana yells with anger, "You conniving piece of shit! Whose turn was it to wear the panties today, while you ate baked beans and sausages stuffed in brown buns? Let's talk about how you relished the thick creamy dressing after having your salad tossed! The fruity beverage, the Liddle Reechard Special? Please tell me that was the chaser to a screaming orgasm. Hah, hah, hah! I married a man who enjoys having his prostate probed. You've been going out to play with men to feel adequate? Is that what you've been doing with your little thing? That explains who's wearing these." With the sleep mask still in place, Diana blindly tossed the thong and wig from under the chaise lounge. "So who's wearing the panties in this relationship, Paul? Hah, hah, hah!

Since the shit hit the fan, at least come clean to relieve your conscience. You've lived a lie with the woman you married, so at the very least you owe this much. Paul, did you enjoy having your donut greased today?"

"Diana...I—"

"No need embarrassing yourself further, pitiful man. Your breath probably smells like someone's ass. When you kissed him, did you rinse with a mouth wash before kissing your whore? You don't want to be known as a potty mouth. Hah, hah, hah. No wonder your dental premiums keep increasing; it's your breath odor, and it probably smells like the calcified buildup of an uncleansed toilet. What else have you been entertaining with your mouth, freak? I want a divorce!"

Blank-faced and stunned speechless, Paul no longer recognized Diana's dialogue. As the seething performance continued from the chaise lounge, Diana's facial exfoliating cream remained smooth and intact, her large hair rollers were still aligned and rolled tight. Draped in her designer bathrobe, Diana's delicate feet have cotton balls placed between her toes, to allow the toe nail polish to dry. The sleep mask remained positioned, as the insults continued with the demeaning chuckle. "Hah, hah, hah. I'm married to a despicable little worm. What's wrong, Paul? I hope your panties aren't bunched! Hah, hah, hah. Have you anything to say? Now I'll have to explain whose bloomers are in the bathroom, along with that antiquated douche bag hanging on the door. What are you using for enemas these days, Paul? Is warm water and olive oil soothing enough, or do you prefer the thick jism? Hah, hah, hah. You lousy little fucker! I wondered why my cute panties have been disappearing; you've been stealing them to go play! Hah, hah, hah. Paul, are the firm's partners aware you've been sneaking around in hotels with whores, not to mention the breach of trust, you filthy maggot. You've been playing newlywed with men while wearing your wife's panties!"

CHAPTER TWENTY-FOUR

Paul studied the items strewn about the bedroom floor in silence. After a questionable look at the wig and thong, he walked to the bedroom's wet bar to pour a drink. Loosening his tie, he sat on the couch to sip shots of Irish whiskey. Paul closed his eyes to process what just transpired. To face his guilt, his mind drifted to a scenario during his recent business summit in Rio de Janeiro, where Paul is joined with his African American male companion, Donte. As a couple, the two are having dinner with friends, Marcus, an Asian American male, and Ignacio, a male Hispanic.

Donte sipped from a half-empty wineglass as the party conversed. He compliments the waiter's pierced bellybutton. "That is so cute. Look, Paul, it's the neon belly piercing we were talking about. When I get your name tattooed somewhere sacred, and no, I won't dare say where, I'm definitely having my belly button pierced the same day. Look at that, it's so tea, and you're rocking it so well."

The party's waiter is a Caucasian male who wears a spiked dog collar around his neck. Wearing a black cap, he appeared more like a member of the 1970s retro group, The Village and the People. The waiter accepts the compliment blushing with femininity. "Thank you, sister girl, and welcome to the meat grinder. Here you will always have it to your liking; you're guaranteed leaving satisfied. Because we aim to fulfill your every craving, our only requirement is simple. How do you prefer your choice of meat?" The waiter covered his mouth, blushing girlishly. "Forgive me, I meant how you want it prepared?" He nods to Ignacio and Marcus. "Will we be venturing further with Sex on the Beach and another Fuzzy Navel?"

Ignacio declines. "I can't go any further; I'm there already!"

Marcus winked at Ignacio. "Rio's the place, Tarzan! Take me home whenever you're ready."

The waiter licks his lips invitingly. "Careful, the mystifying temptations of Rio are in the air, and it's getting warm!" He then directs his comments to the couple, Paul and Donte. "Whenever you're ready to enjoy another White Russian, would there be a Screaming Orgasm to follow?"

Paul declines with a smile. "No more Russians or chasers; I'm fine, thanks."

Donte bats his eyelashes dramatically with a girlish giggle. "Aw, that was so clever! I never thought I'd ever say this. Pardon the expression, but I've had enough already!" Donte blows Paul a seductive kiss. "Speaking of being full, you shouldn't be so manly, white Russian! I've changed my panty liner already twice this evening."

Laughter erupts within the party.

The waiter speaks over the bliss of the elated couples and makes an announcement. "Compliments to the birthday guest, Rio's world-renowned Dulce Chocolate Inferno. Not only is the decadence delightful, but it's also dark and cavernously delicious!" The restaurant staff presents the complimentary dessert with a round of applause.

Caught by surprise, Donte gives Paul a lighthearted admonishing. "You can't hold anything for long; you're just like an old refrigerator! Paul, did you dare tell my age? A girl without her vanity is like waking up to old Mother Hubbard! Simply boring. Who wants any of that? My vanity happens to bring out the best in me. I for one enjoy walking around in my negligees and silk teddies. I'm serious! I have a pair of Bee bottom pumps just for my lingerie."

As the party's laughter is heard, the restaurant staff positioned themselves to sing the happy birthday chorus. Several women of the assembled staff stand in heavy-soled motorcycle boots. Having close-cropped hair, the proud beneficiaries of male hormone injections lightly brush their beards or adjust the thick suspenders on their dungarees. The males of the assembled staff include themselves in the table's festive bliss with girlish giggles and exaggerated gestures of admiration toward Donte. "Oh, who's the lucky girl? She's beautiful! Girlfriend, I love your eyelashes, and you're working them perfectly!"

"Oh shut up, Lawrence; oops, I meant Lauren, and celebrate our sister! It's her blossoming night, and of course she looks marvelous; she's from California!" At the direction of the table's waiter, the servers commence with the happy birthday chorus.

Relishing the attention, Donte bats his eyes nervously to kiss Paul's cheek. "You're quite the man, and I've always known it. Paul, you're remarkable!"

Paul removes his face from Donte's ear. He instructs, "No, no, don't talk! Close your eyes and wish for something you haven't yet received."

Donte closed his eyes, prepared to extinguish the birthday candle. In precise timing to the last chorus of "Happy birthday to you," Paul set the velvet box on the table. Donte opens his eyes in amazement. "Oh, my god! Paul, you didn't! Does this mean—Paul! Are we—?"

Paul captures the moment gregariously. "Not yet! You haven't blown the candle out. I've asked our friends to come along for your special day, and you have everyone waiting."

Donte extinguishes the candle. "My goodness, Paul, you're being so handsomely persuasive! It must be Rio's mystifying allure, because your direction is so overtaking! Do be forceful whenever you're ready." The box opens. "Oh, my god … look at this!" The restaurant's assembled staff joins the table's party with celebrating cheers and clapping.

Ignacio taps his glass with a spoon. "Bravo, well done! In honor of our friends and their new beginning. To the lovely couple, Donte and Paul!"

Another spoon chimes with Marcus presenting a toast. "Hear hear! May your blissful relationship shine forever. Here's to every morning this beautiful couple awakes. Start your day with a wonderful kiss! Bless you both with fun times, good health, plenty of wine, and whatever happens in the bedroom!"

A burst of applause comes from the party's table. Paul comes out of reflection to pour a shot of scotch. Gulping it down in one swallow, he pours another. Blinking his eyes to focus, Paul reflects another scenario with more guilt. In a taxi parked in the airport's flight arrival concourse, the newly engaged couple argues as to when Paul is going to confront his wife to reveal his miserable conscience.

"Paul, why am I riding alone in a taxi? Shouldn't I be riding home with you? A contingency plan wasn't mentioned with your proposal. Is this a shared union? If you're uncomfortable to be seen with your princess, which would be me, then maybe we should reconsider our paradigm." Donte snaps his fingers. "This girl's definitely too hot to be ignored! Paul, step to the plate when you're ready to make the transition. I'm definitely not one to force a fit. That can be rather uncomfortable, especially when you're not prepared for it. I've never taken you for a hypocrite, but I'm really starting to feel as if we're on the down low or something! Am I just a booty call now? That wasn't my understanding, especially after what happened in Rio. Will we even be together on New Year's Eve? Paul, you never gave a definitive answer! Well, I hope so. What about your partners in the firm, do they know we're an item? Have you mentioned us to any of your friends? Does anyone know about us, Paul?"

Paul rebuts, "Donte, let's not cloud the issue with your emotions. These things take time. As you knew before we committed to this arrangement, I'm legally married to Diana. I'm supposed to be with her on New Year's Eve. The last I understood, you agreed mutually with the arrangement. You went further with the suggestion of living in the apartment alone until the situation worked itself out. After the fact you're making demands I can't meet. Honestly, life doesn't offer enough consolation to deal with your stress and pressures. The when and where of my departure from Diana comes up whenever we're together. I refuse to entertain this now, and I will not exit with huff and puff. Your huffing and puffing doesn't fix the problem. Diana and I have been married twenty-seven years. What should I tell her? Diana, as of the last seven years, Donte has been very inspirational in my decision to replace you as my wife. That's unacceptable after twenty-seven years, you think?"

Paul comes out of the reflective haze massaging his scalp. He pours a shot of whiskey. Swallowing, he pours another to swallow again. Numb with mental confusion, he rests his head in the couch. Paul rubs his brow. With a heavy conscience, he blinks his eyes to go into a blank stare with more reflective guilt. In this scenario, the driver of the rental convertible has his arm around the passenger as the couple drives over the Golden Gate Bridge. The passenger is an African American male with permanent clean-shaved skin and mascara-embedded eyelashes. Wearing a wide-brim straw hat and yellow scarf, the passenger is a throwback to a beautiful model with strong Afrocentric features, Grace Jonnes. The passenger connects his iPod to the car stereo to play Adeele's version of "Love Song."

As the song plays, the passenger twirls his neck scarf to sing along. Becoming more involved with the lyrics, the passenger moves closer to the driver to voice his feelings. He admits, "Oh, I love this song! It reminds me so much of our situation, Paul! This is a girl's anthem! WOO! Don't you love it?" Donte stands to sing into the wind. He holds the straw hat close to his head to prevent the wind's velocity from blowing it away. As the song ends, Donte looks to the back seat, to where several shopping bags surround a huge teddy bear. "Look, Paul; whoever thought my teddy bear would be the witness for our ceremony?" Donte screams into the wind, "SAN FRANCISCO HERE WE COME! IT'S DONTE AND PAUL'S WORLD NOW!" Donte returns to his seat to nudge Paul in the ribs reassuringly. "Oh, don't be in such a rush; we're here already. Slow down, handsome, your delicate dark princess will take care of you like she always does!" Donte flutters his eyelashes invitingly to say, "careful now, melt in my mouth not in my hands. Whoever said that?" Donte looks around suspiciously for passing cars. Having the mindset they wouldn't be noticed, he removes his hat to allow his face to dissolve into Paul's lap. Donte talks while his mouth is full. "Paul? Pull over for a minute, handsome … I need to make sure your head's in the right place before we cross the Golden Gate Bridge … It's San Francisco, you know? I want you relaxed before we get into the city."

Paul returns from his reflective haze. After a series of coughs, he blinks his eyes to gather his thoughts. With a shot of scotch another scenario plays out with Adeele's "Love Song." During Donte and Paul's San Francisco excursion, the couple walks hand in hand on the beach. Being bare chested, Paul wears a sailor's hat-and-pants ensemble. Donte's very visible thong is seen through his sheer sarong. Reacting on a romantic impulse, the couple removes their sandals to run hand in hand into the tide, where Donte jumps into Paul's embrace. Donte wraps his legs around Paul's body as he reveals, "Oh, Paul! As a child I always envisioned a man of bronze coming to my rescue! I had no idea he'd be wealthy and I'd have him for the rest of my life!"

In another scene, while shopping in a women's boutique the couple purchases a designer handbag. Noticing the wind machine used for the display model's hair to be blown into the wind, Donte repositions it to allow the forced air to blow through his designer dress. Posturing in womanly rapture, Donte replicates Marilyn Monroe's famous pose. "Oh, Paul, it's wonderful. Hurry up and take the picture before someone sees my thong!"

Paul abruptly breaks from reflection to blink with guilt. After another sip of scotch, Adeele's "Love Song" continues. In this reflective scenario, Donte and Paul enjoy a horse-and-carriage ride through San Francisco's restaurant row. Handsomely adorned in a white tuxedo with tails, Paul sports white spats covering white shoes. Wearing a white top hat, the proud groom smiles while waving and rotating his cane to the congratulating crowd. Enjoying the fanfare, Donte showcases a very elegant designer wedding dress, complete with a rented diamond-encrusted tiara. Statuesque at six foot three, Donte performs a princess wave to the crowd. With deliberate coyness, he removes a princess glove to cover his mouth, revealing the elegant engagement ring to the gawking audience. Taking full advantage of the dramatics, Donte blinks his eyes erratically, allowing his eyelash extensions to flutter like exotic butterflies. Theatrics come into play as Donte smiles, presenting a perfect row of teeth. "Oh, thank you, San Francisco! Thank you for supporting us! Every woman's entitled to her special day! Oh, I feel so diva international! I'm in women's world."

Paul returns from his haze of reflection with the sound of horse hooves meeting the pavement. Back within the reality of Diana's guttural rebuke, Paul blinks his eyes in bewilderment as he looks to his wife for a reprieve. "Diana, I never meant to hurt—"

"Go straight to hell, you filthy bastard! Kissing whores, you should be gargling with douche powder. What's wrong, Paul? Have you developed a deep itch somewhere? Hah, hah, hah. Come to think of it, it's been years since you've left the toilet seat up in the bathroom! Hah, hah, hah."

Lifeless and dumbfounded, Paul rises from the couch to leave the bedroom.

As though it were possible to see through the cucumbers and eye mask, Diana calls for Paul's attention. "Paul!"

The broken man turns around to subserviently face his wife. "Yes, Diana?"

"Paul, before your arrival, I had the intentions of commemorating our wonderful engagement. I'll never forget the night you proposed; I was so wonderfully happy. I instructed Maria to prepare that very meal; the stuffed bell peppers with lamb.

With all that's transpired, I forgot to mention not to bake the two together. You probably preferred your bell peppers raw and hard. Hah, hah, hah. You mentioned surprises coming up the staircase. How rhetorical! With tonight's dinner, I'm divorcing you with the same meal you proposed with."

Paul closes the bedroom door behind him to stand in the hallway to collect himself. Meanwhile, the demeaning chuckle descends down the staircase.

"Hah, hah, hah! Your noodle loses its starch, so you sneak around with men for something stiff? What a pitiful thing! I'll insist Maria disinfect the house in its entirety. I'll mention to Milford to place all of your laundry in plastic bags and washed at the laundry mat until we're divorced."

Just as Paul reached the staircase landing, the intercom's frantic buzzing is heard in the kitchen. BEEP! BEEP! BEEP! BEEP! BEEP!

"Si, señora?"

"Maria, disregard the lamb and bell peppers request. It seems Paul's craving unusual entrées these days. Instead, prepare soft noodles with the creamy white thick cheese sauce, with lots of pork sausage fried hard!"

"Si, señora. You no whawning the baking bean for Meester Paul?"

"No, honey, no baked beans. At this point, I'd imagine Paul avoiding the discomfort of anymore air in his bowels. Hah, hah, hah. Oh, Maria? I've forgotten dessert! Be sure to include a thick slice of peanut butter cheesecake, sprinkled heavily with salted nuts! Hah, hah, hah."

As Maria scrambles about the kitchen to make the request, she inadvertently comes upon the discovery of Paul at the staircase landing. Maria looks at Milford, embarrassed, who also pretends not to have heard Diana belittling her husband.

Milford breaks the tension. "I almost have them shined perfectly. Just a bit more of the compound with a dry towel should do the trick."

In her guilt of sabotaging her employers' marriage, Maria offered a consoling question. "Meester Paul, maybe you for-gib Maria for making so mawch trawble for here? I esplain for the señora ebery ting! I tell for the two ladies you habing for you room. I telling about you room serbese, the baking bean. The sausage and the tick bery crèmee for you salad, ah-huh. I telling about the fru-tee drink for you and Dawnee, and making the cake with you doon-nawt. I bery sawry for telling ebery ting, Meester Paul. I no whawning to esplain anymore trawble for the señora. Meester Paul, you for-gib Maria?"

Perturbed with Maria's broken English, Paul questions her ramblings. "Maria, what the hell are you talking about, and you've been explaining what to my wife? Sausage, baked beans, fruity drinks, and the two ladies? What do they and room service have to do with me, and who in the hell is Dawnee? I'm trying to understand, Maria!"

More chuckling descends from the master suite into the staircase corridor. "Hah, hah, hah."

Paul looks toward the staircase blankly.

Milford interrupts his dejected employer. "Master Paul, your direction for the matter?

"Yes, Milford?"

"Chippy and Scooter, I believe they've awakened."

In stark contrast to his arrival, Paul's face has become ashen, as though his spirit left his body. He questions, "Milford?"

"Right here, Master Paul."

"Milford, Chippy and Scooter, you mentioned they became sick after capturing a crow?"

Witnessing her employers' diminished sanity, Maria motions the sign of the cross nervously. "*Dios mio*! For-gib me! I making so mawch trawble for here."

CHAPTER TWENTY-FIVE

$\mathcal{T}$he Levitivitch estate, 1:30 a.m., Milford has recently retired to his sleeping quarters. Diana has since chuckled into a deep sleep after repeatedly summoning Milford for her prescribed medications. Maria works around the estate guilt ridden, nervously asking for forgiveness, insisting she should have listened to Hortencia and Flora. Since returning home to disarray and scandal, Paul has neither removed his clothes nor showered. Being relegated to the estate's main parlor, he sits in near darkness to reflect in silence. Drinking scotch whiskey, Paul looks into the serenity of the estate's courtyard and surrounding landscape to the poplar trees and hedges that rival the estate's beautiful rose beds and gardens. Centered between the winding manicured lawn and the intricate landscape lighting is the estate's one-thousand-foot driveway. Paved in river rock in exquisite tones of green, yellow, grey, and blue, the pattern of abstracts lead to the courtyard's cascading fountain. Paul describes the courtyard's presence swallowing a shot of scotch. "It's magnificent from anywhere you look at it. Truly picturesque and astounding!"

From within the parlor darkness, a voice questions, "Paul, are you there?" Paul comes out of reflection to continue his cell phone conversation. "Pardon me, Donte, it's much too late to meet. With everything in disarray, it's important that we deal with this matter being equally grounded. That being said, I'll be the first to admit, my head wasn't in the right direction. I was so overwhelmed that I lost focus and was undeniably self-ish toward everyone around me."

Across town, meanwhile, Donte is in his apartment meticulously polishing his fingernails. Seated comfortably at the vanity mirror in his silk teddy and fluffy house slippers, he listens to Paul's every word through his cell's speakerphone. Reacting from a hot flash, Donte bats his eyes uncontrollably. Abruptly he stops applying the fingernail polish to use both hands to fan his face excitedly. "Oh, baby, believe me, there's no pressure. I'm glad the man I fell in love with has arrived. I can't believe it. You have yet to see the real diva inside me. This is so amazing!" Donte puts his face in his hands for a moment of emotional purging. He expresses relieved, "Finally this butterfly will get the chance to flutter freely."

Paul interjects, "Donte, will you allow me to finish?"

"Oh, Paul, I've been waiting for you to do the right thing. Is there anything you need me to do? I'm here for you, baby." Donte exhales excitedly. "Does she know I'm coming? Scenes are definitely not cosmopolitan, but no worries, I'll represent us both and remain a lady. I refuse to step down to her level.

Believe me, I know how difficult it's going to be for her. She'll play out her emotions and cold scorn followed with the blame game. No doubt she'll mix in the false miscarriage and guilt trap, along with all of her insecurities and everything else that can be so trifling and fishy."

"Whoa! Let's get past the immediate gratification here. Donte, am I not doing what should've been done from the onset? Is this not what you wanted? Maybe I'm making a mistake. Can you look beyond yourself without the gloating and rubbing it in her face? Ha-ha, I've won. There are other issues here besides your ego. Can you just do as I ask without going into your suitcase of drama?"

"A mistake? After we had such a good time in Brazil, I can't believe you're talking like this, Paul! No mistakes here, baby. Was Brazil a good time? Were my breast implants or the corrective surgery to remove the thing between my legs a mistake? It was disgusting to have it attached to me, yet I went under the knife for you. Have I made a mistake, Paul? The engagement ring, the announcement, our celebration on the beach! The head I gave you while crossing the Golden Gate Bridge? Paul, I'm confused. Have the last seven years with you been a mistake? Was it not enough that when we landed at L.A.X I took a cab home, while you were picked up by Milford or whatever his name is? I can't believe you're talking like this. Paul, I'm in love! I'll be the first to say I'm one hundred percent in love with you. Are you willing to say the same and mean it? Or is it just something conveniently said when you're exploring my tight ass, or when I have your dick in my pulsating mouth? Other men can't say that anymore, can they, Paul? For the past seven years, you've been the only man to enjoy the fruit's full ripeness. No one else has been entitled to those exclusive accolades, Paul."

"Donte, there you go again! Isn't Diana's berating and condemning me with guilt enough? Blame and guilt! I'd say there's plenty of it here with you! Frankly there are other things a lot more rewarding I'd rather be doing! I refuse to play the blame game with you tonight. I've been through enough as it is. Should you want to continue this discussion, we'll do it tomorrow at 3:00 p.m. That's a fourteen-hour window from now. Tomorrow's the conclusion of this chapter for everyone."

"Conclusion for everyone, Paul? The word everyone doesn't get past you and me with me! I'm excited, and a lady loves excitement. Haven't I shown you anything during the past seven years? I believe an announcement would be a better word! A new beginning together to live our lives not for others but for us! Congratulations, Paul, you've decided to come out!"

"Donte, listen to yourself! Do you have to be so self-centered and self-serving? I've decided to make the announcement. Is that not enough? You're nowhere near satisfied; it has to be the way you want it to the letter, doesn't it? Self, self, self! That's all I'm hearing. Tonight I'm embracing your selfish philosophy. I'm going to sleep, Donte. There will be no one to argue with there. I'll make the announcement some other time."

"No, Paul! Paul … please don't hang up … Paul? Please answer! I know you love me! Paul?"

"Yes, Donte."

"Paul, I love you. I'll be wearing my ring."

CHAPTER TWENTY-SIX

*A*t approximately 8:30 a.m., Maria awakes Diana as per the instructive message left during the previous evening. "Good mawning, señora! Lass eebening you sister calling, and she leabing a message. You fambelee arribing for here frum Meenisota. You picking up ebery bawdy from the ereport. [airport.] Maria writing the imp-pormee-shun here!"

Feeling the groggy effects of her sleep medication, Diana removes her sleep mask. Maria presents her employer the message. In spite of what transpired during the previous evening, Diana's exfoliating facial cream and hair rollers have remained intact.

"Good morning, Maria, honey, what's the day's date and time?"

"For this mawning it maybe 8:30, the twanty second, señora."

"Oh, heavens! Today's the twenty-second already. With

all that's happened, I'd totally forgotten. They'll be arriving in less than five hours from now. Honey, we have to prepare! Inform Milford we should be leaving for the airport by noon."

"Señora, you whawning Maria to esplain for Meester Paul for cawming to the ereport?"

"No, Maria, that bastard's not coming. Where is he anyway?"

"I beleeb Meester Paul sleeping in heem room from lass eebening. Heem locking the door, and no cawming out for heem braffeest [breakfast]."

Diana continues with the chuckling from the previous evening, "Hah, hah, hah. Let him stay there, Maria. Apparently Paul's not ready to come out from his closet of lies."

"Señora, no cooking the braffeest? No naw-ting for Meester Paul?"

"Absolutely not! You'll prepare nothing for him."

"Si, señora, you whawning for Maria to esplain to Milfurb, you telling no naw-ting for Meester Paul?"

"Where's Milford, Maria?"

"Heem shining the black shoes for Meester Paul for wurking next week, señora."

"Milford's shining Paul's shoes? I think not!" Diana presses the intercom with persistence. Beep! Beep! Beep! Beep!

Milford answers. "Your medications should you need settling, madam? I shall be there momentarily."

"Milford, that won't be necessary. I have another request, or rather instructions. Effective immediately, you will not assist

Mr. Levitivitch in any way. When you're summoned or directed a request, you are to refer Paul to his dark whore. Is that
understood, Milford?"

"Absolutely. What does madam suggest I do with Master
Paul's shoes, I nearly completed the task before the madam's
summons?"

"Milford, you'll simply have to burn them. All of them!
Oh, Milford, by the way, my family's arriving from Minnesota.
We should be at L.A.X. by no later than one o'clock to receive
them. Be sure to stock the car's bar; mother enjoys a little nip
when she travels."

At 2:30 p.m., Milford exits the busy L.A.X. terminal toward
the return to the Levitivitch estate. Seated in the rear passenger
seat, Diana sits between her parents, Mr. and Mrs. Jaworski. As
the luxury vehicle rolls smoothly along, Diana looks into the
distant road with her right designer glove holding her mother's
hand. Within minutes of leaving the airport terminal, Diana
breaks the commute silence. "I'm famished, and thank God
we're getting close." Diana looks to her left to kiss her father's
cheek; her designer glove clenches his hand. "Father you're so
quietly handsome. I've asked Maria to prepare the table just the
way you like, roast duck and stewed potatoes, with plenty of
rosemary and garnish. How lovely of me to remember your favorite dish, right Father?" In his persona of silence, Mr. Jaworski
blinks his eyes into the road ahead. Diana diverts her attention
to the chauffeur. "Milford?"

Acknowledging his employer, Milford speaks into the

rearview mirror. "Madam, absolutely, I'll make the call right away." Milford dials the Levitivitch estate. "Maria, the madam inquires as to the dinner preparations."

"I cooking the dinnur now, Milfurb; ebery bawdy cawming?"

"Unquestionably, Maria. As per the madam's instructions, roast duck and stewed potatoes, with plenty of rosemary and garnish. Expect our arrival with the madam's party shortly."

Diana directs her conversation to the front passenger seat, to her younger sister. "Grace? You haven't said two words since we left L.A.X. How was the flight, honey? Did Father behave during the security protocols?"

While looking into the distant road, Grace offers a detailed account of events. "Diana, you're forever the accommodating big sister. Thank you. During the three-and-a-half-hour travel in first class, I enjoyed two glasses of wine. Mother had four shots of whiskey with her coffee, in addition to the pint in her purse. Father's medication made him drowsy as usual, but no worries, we were fine."

"Grace, darling, it was the least I could do. Your hands are completely full with Father's medical appointments. The constant looking after him and dealing with mother's issues, you needed a break. You know I would be more involved, if only you would move to the West Coast, honey."

Recognizing Diana's passive aggressive chiding, Grace directs her attention from the road to face her sister. "Come on, Diana, the three of us are conveniently in Minnesota, and your husband's accountant pays our bills. Our family vacations, everything's all-inclusive. Meanwhile in sunny California, big sister doesn't have to deal with bathing Father or putting baby powder on his huge balls and garter-snake dick. How's living in California, big sister? Tell me the last time you've changed your father's diaper hoping he wouldn't pee in your face."

Mrs. Jaworski takes a nip from her jeweled flask to rebut, "Grace, don't heckle your big sister! Diana, we're truly appreciative of you and Paul. What little money we had saved after your father retired went so fast with his medical bills. There's no way this family would have made it without your help. Grace, apologize to your sister; there's only the two of you, you know."

"Thank you, Mother, I would feel so much better if you would just only treat me as a step child." Grace whispers insight of why she's miserable and unhappy with the arrangement. "Diana, you have no idea. With Father's dementia and schizophrenia, he pees and shits his pants. I give him five pills a day and another two for his diabetes. Mother's an alcoholic; look at her! From sunup to sundown she nips at that flask. Diana, I'm your younger sister who has no life. No one will ask me out because I'm too busy monitoring my parents." Grace reflects, "Oh, thanks for the generous invitation. I would really love to have a nice evening enjoying myself, only if you're willing to drive me home every two hours, so I can make sure my parents are taking their medications." She scoffs. "When was the last time I went out? Oh, I'm sure of it, it was last week. Mother and I went to Thursday night bingo."

Mrs. Jaworski inspects her jeweled flask for its remaining contents. Satisfied, she throws her head back to enjoy a nip with a belch. "There are a lot of nice boys in church, Grace. Have you forgotten your father and I met in church?"

Forcing a smile, Grace rolls her eyes in disbelief. "Absolutely not, mother! Let's recap the incident with the youth minister whose crotch you groped at least three times. Surely it was an accident, because you groped his crotch every time you thought he asked if you wanted to exchange the gift you won."

Diana joins in with a chuckle. "Hah, hah, hah. Mother, tell me you didn't think he was referring to the roll of quarters in his pocket."

Tipsy, Mrs. Jaworski licks her lips before pursing them to take a nip. "I did no such thing, and I remained a lady the entire time. My carpal tunnel, it flares from time to time, so I really wasn't reaching for anything in his pants. Whenever I become excited, my hands naturally form into a grip position."

Mr. Jaworski speaks for the first time, "Clara's making that clucking sound again. Has anyone fed the bird today?"

Diana kisses her father's forehead. "Oh father you're so clever! Hah, hah, hah."

Meanwhile, in Leimert Park across town. While in the midst of a cell phone conversation, Donte drifts from the call to the mirror to admire his newly weaved hair. His eyelashes flutter in complete awe of his reflection. "Prince Albert, you've definitely outshined yourself with this one! I'm sure to be the belle of the ball; all the hate will be so excruciating!"

A voice projects from the speaker phone. "Are you still there? Donte, what are you doing?"

Unable to contain his excitement, Donte nervously bats his eyes with a confession. "I am so overwhelmed! Rayfee, it's finally here. After seven years of hiding and living in seclusion, you have no idea of the torment I've gone through! Paul's stress of being seen in public was a living hell by itself. As of today, there will be no more meeting in hotels under assumed names or the long drives to the suburbs for the matinee movies. Rayfee, it's all behind me, and it's all over! This butterfly's finally coming out of her cocoon!"

"Donte, you left your cocoon four hours ago going to Prince Albert's. I've heard already; everyone's heard. You got the full weave, and I'm told it's slamming. You now have everyone's attention. So where did you find the sequined dress and rhinestone pumps? Coming out of your cocoon is an understatement; you made an announcement today. You're such a kept queen, I can't stand you! Did the rich guy buy the accessories? I'm starved for the story. When do I get the exclusive, the whole skinny? Coming from you, I'd expect nothing less than the unimaginable. I'm listening."

"Rayfee, I'm trying to get there; allow me to finish already. It felt like I was involved in a criminal conspiracy. Can you imagine holding hands only in the dark? Really? What couple does that? It was terrible! The nightmare's finally over, Rayfee."

"What's over? You left him?"

"Rayfee, I left the pain! I left every bit of it behind. Finally this flower gets a chance to bloom, and it's going to be so wonderful. Paul's ready to make it official!"

"Make what official?"

"Paul's making the transition today, Rayfee. He's coming out!"

"You're serious?"

"I've been asked to his home, Rayfee! I'm guessing he wants to set things straight with fishy. I also have a few issues to speak on; it'll be brutal! Being quite the bitch, there's no doubt she'll make a scene."

"This is special. You've waited what, seven years? Donte, I can't believe it!"

"Yes, Rayfee, it's very special. Paul and I deserve all the joy. We've worked the entire journey through so many misunderstandings, not to mention my bipolar disorder and temper tantrums, on top of the frustration of not knowing when Paul would come out. Rayfee, believe me, I can talk about the strife for hours."

Rejoicing in Donte's honor, Rayfee becomes animated. "Oh, girlfriend, your ratings will go off the charts for this one. How did you get him to address the issue? I need to take notes. I'm with five married men as we speak. Without a doubt, they're all willing to do everything to make sure I'm comfortable, but no one's stepped up to the plate to make it official."

"Rayfee, you're such a Jezebel!"

"No I'm not! Donte, they don't want commitment, so why argue? Instead I've stepped up my game with lots of variety with the expectance of gifts in return. Fair exchange is no robbery, and I'm always up front with them all. Don't hate the queen; hate the game. As you know, the queen is the most powerful piece on the chessboard; she's all over the place! I see myself in the same way. In line for my every beckoning, mind you, is a king, his knights, their bishops, the rooks, and every pawn. Needless to say, after two head sessions with me, every piece in the game, regardless of its stature, is reduced to a pawn. Believe me, Donte, they're enjoying it as much as I am. They all love being subjects beneath the queen, the baddest bitch!

"So there you have it; everyone has their part to play; I'm just more ruthless playing mine! Oh, never mind, Donte, you're not like me. When all is said and done, it's checkmate for sure for fishy; I'll give you that. Oh, you've just ruined her with this one!" Enjoying his wit, Rayfee giggles girlishly to snap his fingers with a neck roll. "Only a true queen can put a real bitch in her place and smile as she's doing it."

"Rayfee, stop acting silly. Where's your respect for the code? You're more excited than I am. Calm down, why don't you? Okay, where was I? There's a special flower that has been chosen to bloom, and we both know which flower has been picked, don't we?"

Rayfee's laughter came through the phone. "WOO! Donte, no you didn't! Oh, shuki, shuki, now, then talk that talk!"

As Rayfee is heard celebrating, Donte admires his weave and the ring's brilliant reflection in the mirror. Donte resumes the conversation. "So yes, Cinderella has been summoned to the castle to meet the awaiting prince."

Rayfee feeds off the drama, performing a curtsey. "Oh, shuki, ducky now; I know that's right! Donte, you need to stop!"

"Rayfee! Rayfee, stop laughing. Rayfee, listen to me, I'm serious! I need support here. Do you think she'll act out or do something stupid like cry or fake a nervous breakdown? No children are involved here, so she can't go there, besides, fishy's beyond her best years. Nothing's coming out of there now but vinegar and pee!

Rayfee's laughter continues. "WOO! I'll definitely have to put two snaps with that one! Stop driving on her; I want to include a few. As you know, Donte, women by nature are vindictive creatures, and they are never to be trusted. Remembering Eve? Do I need say more?" Rayfee gives himself a very feminine round of applause. "Oh I've set this up to be grand!"

Now sitting on his hands, Rayfee continues in girlish rapture. "That's whyyy, in every man, there's the yearning for the comfort of a beautiful boy, dressed as a woman."

Donte flutters his eyelashes with disbelief. "Rayfee, be serious! Eve was definitely the weaker of the two, and she was misled. Besides, is there anything new under the sun? Everything that happened then is happening today as we speak." Donte proceeds to pencil the outline of his lips. "Rayfee, I was thinking. Will you ride with me to Paul's estate? I'm really overwhelmed, and I need someone there to have my back. I don't want to get emotional if she pushes my buttons. I paid Prince Albert four hundred and fifty dollars for my twenty-two-inch virgin Remy and another three hundred dollars to have it weaved. Rayfee, I don't want to sweat it out if she takes me there. I will step out of my three-thousand-dollar pumps and put this size thirteen up her decrepit ass!"

Rayfee fans his face dramatically. "Oh, please don't go there in my presence. I'll be forced to help you, and then she'll have two of us on her decrepit ass. Of course I'll go with you. What time should I be ready?"

"Thanks for being there, Rayfee; we'll stop at the coffee house to celebrate."

"M-m-m, Donte that does sound yummy; hurry up!"

"Rayfee, do you have any pepper spray? I've searched everywhere, and I can't fine mine."

"I think so. I usually keep a few cans in my purse for protection. After all the hormone injections, my ass is so fat I have horny guys deliberately bumping into it out of nowhere. It's embarrassing. I'll definitely check my purse before you get here."

"Rayfee, be sure to bring some. There's a real possibility I'll have to spray a bitch."

Across town at the Levitivitch estate, Maria goes about preparing the meal per Diana's request. She opens the oven to inspect the roast duck and potatoes. "Ah-huh, bery nice. Maybe twanty minutes more for ready."

Proceeding to the range top, Maria uses a potholder to remove the lid from a pot of boiling vegetables. She tests the tenderness of the cabbage. "Ah-huh, almost tendur. Maybe ten minutes more." Within the same time, Chippy and Scooter's barks are heard from the living room. Moving to the cutting board, Maria resumes chopping the garnish and rosemary. She responds to the barking pets, "Ebery ting almost ready for eating! Maria making sumting for her children too. No wurry today I cooking for eberybawdy." The sporadic barking continues.

"Okay, children! Maria hear you; I cawming! You barking bery loud, and you desterbing Meester Paul." Maria reaches to the countertop for a towel to wipe her hands. "You wake Meester Paul frum heem sleep, heem bery angry with Maria's children." Just as Maria proceeds through the swinging door between the kitchen and dining room, both Chippy and Scooter rush through the open door, each with one of Paul's house slippers in his mouth. Maria turns in pursuit. "No, no, no buena! No playing in here! *No es buena!*" To avoid their housekeeper, Chippy and Scooter dart playfully around the kitchen. Unable to corner the mischievous pets, Maria uses a ploy. She opens the pantry to retrieve doggie treats. "Okay, children, Maria hab sumting especial for you!" Immediately Chippy and Scooter release Paul's slippers from their mouths. Both sit on their hindquarters in anticipation of the reward held above their heads.

"No more desterbing Meester Paul for today. You both play outside! Meester Paul no whawning you playing with heem house shoes. *No buena!*" Maria drops the doggie treats to the awaiting audience. "No more for you." Retrieving Paul's slippers from the kitchen floor, Maria continues to the dining room to discover Paul's robe sprawled under the dining room table. "*Diablitos!* [Little devils!] Sheepee and Scootee eberywhere with trawble!" Continuing toward the living room, Maria speaks reassuringly, "Meester Paul, no wurry for you robe and shoes. Maria cawming! Shippie and Scootie bery bawd for today." Entering the living room, Maria screams, "No, no, no, Meester Paul! This no good for me! This no good!"

Maria runs from the living room onto the estate courtyard.

Her hands covering her ears, she pleads for assistance, "Oh, my goodneth, sumbawdy help me for here! Oh, my goodneth, I needing sumbawdy! Meester Paul ... oh my goodneth, Meester Paul! I needing the señora! Sumbawdy. Help me ... I needing sumbawdy cawming for here ... I needing help!"

CHAPTER TWENTY-SEVEN

Approaching the estate driveway, Milford maneuvered the Maybach down the span of a thousand feet onto the courtyard. Appearing out of place, Maria is discovered kneeled in one of the estate rose beds; her hands grip a rosary as if in prayer. A few feet away, Chippy and Scooter run about the lawn to play tag with Paul's house slippers. After losing interest in the slipper, Scooter trots to Paul's bathrobe to playfully drag it across the lawn. Chippy pursues the flowing garment to bite into it and pull in the opposite direction.

Witnessing the scene from the rear of the Maybach, Diana strains her neck toward the lawn to protest. "Chippy and Scooter's grooming appointments are always at 10:30 a.m. I can't believe Maria's allowed them to be groomed directly in the hot sun. Why would he be this late? Is it Thursday already? Milford?"

Milford refers to his watch to acknowledge, "It's fifteen

after three, madam."

"Milford, thank you. Be sure to stop at the fountain. I'd like Father to see the koi pond. I'll have to talk with Maria as well; Chippy and Scooter being in the hot sun is totally unacceptable!"

"As you wish, madam."

Rolling the Maybach to a stop, Milford proceeds with the passengers' exit.

Grace is the first to be assisted. "Milford, thank you."

Milford nods to acknowledge, "Madam."

From the vehicle interior, Diana summons Maria to assist with the family's arrival.

"Maria, we've made it back, honey."

As Diana awaits for Maria's response, Milford extends a hand to assist Mrs. Jaworski. "Ma'am, whenever you're ready."

Full-on tipsy, Mrs. Jaworski exits the vehicle with her jeweled flask in hand. Tossing the flask back, she expects a swallow, but instead her mouth is pursed with disappointment. She licks her lips, placing the empty flask in Milford's hand with a burp. "Excuse me, but I have no use for this anymore; it's completely dry." Mrs. Jaworski questions, "Diana, where's Maria? I need to be refreshed. The long flight to California has left me nearly parched."

Meanwhile, Milford extends a hand to assist his employer's exit. "And finally the madam."

"Milford, thank you." Following through with her exit, Diana smooths her designer pantsuit while directing attention to the kneeled housekeeper. "Maria, honey. We have guests.

Whatever are you doing? Everyone's famished." Embarrassed by Maria's unresponsiveness, Diana looks to her guests wide eyed. She offers the explanation, "They can be so stubborn." Forcing a smile through clenched teeth, Diana addresses her kneeled housekeeper in a melodic tone. "Maria, everyone's watching. Honey, return to the quarters and proceed with the table setting. Come, honey. You know how I feel about scenes." Multitasking, Diana instructs Milford's assistance with Mr. Jaworski's exit. "Milford, do be careful; father's medication makes him tired."

Diana retrieves a moist wipe from her purse to gently pat her father's forehead. "Father? Wouldn't it be nice to sit in the sunroom and play a game of checkers like we used to? Would you like that, Father?"

After assisting the family party in their exit, Milford makes several trips to transport their luggage to the estate's foyer. As the scene unfolds, Chippy and Scooter bark excitedly to run zigzag patterns around the family party. While being attentive to her father, Diana's voice is heard as she directs to the family pets. "Oh Chippy, Scooter, how is it Maria has allowed you to be outside after your grooming appointments? I'll address this as soon as we get father inside." Diana continues to wipe Mr. Jaworski's forehead. "We'll have rhubarb pie and ice cream after dinner. Wouldn't you like that, Father?"

Without any forewarning, Mr. Jaworski grunts to fart loudly. He instructs after the fact, "Pull my finger."

"Oh, my god!" Grace warns the others before covering her nose to prevent inhaling the foul odor.

Full-on tipsy, Mrs. Jaworski provides insight. "Diana, your father can't drink milk; he's lactose intolerant. It gives him diarrhea on top of the gas. It's become a game to him; he thinks he's shooting at only God knows who. Trust me, we found out the hard way. I've been driven to drink whenever I think about it. No one knows how I've suffered at night with his gas. It's so heavy and dense, it just lingers throughout the house. It's embarrassing. When it's really bad, your father shakes the covers to dissipate the fumes. The odor is unlike anything I can describe. I couldn't tell you how many times I've been awakened from a deep snore. Diana, it's awful. Your father's dementia and Alzheimer's compounds the problem by giving him imaginary characters to blame for his gas. It always starts with a whistle. "Wheerp! He'll then lie there momentarily to fan the sheets. Out of nowhere, he'll go into one of his skits.

"'I shot them all! Every last one of them. I'll never talk, not in a hundred years.'"

Grace uncovers her mouth to set the record straight. "We're on vacation. No way! I do enough of it already! I'm not bathing him. Diana, if you want Father to have ice cream so that he can shit his pants, then prepare yourself to change his diaper." Grace takes Mr. Jaworski's arm to continue toward the estate's interior, "Come on, Father; we don't want you to look forward to any trouble."

Shuffling along in tow, abruptly Mr. Jaworski stops. As if he were testifying, he raises his right hand. He whistles. "Wheerp! I've seen this one here before, and he didn't pay. What's that? You're wasting your time; I ain't saying nothing, not in a hundred years!"

Mrs. Jaworski purses her mouth. "As you see, Diana, our hands are completely full with your father's issues. It's been no picnic, you know. Just thinking of what I go through with your father's gas and all, I need a little something for my nerves." Mrs. Jaworski smacks her lips; "I certainly hope there are no dry counties in California. I need to replenish!"

As her family continues toward the residence, Diana redirects her attention to where her housekeeper is kneeled in prayer. "Maria, honey, whatever are you doing? You're ignoring the guests. This doesn't sit well; the guests are family. How am I to explain your behavior? What are you looking for down there? My heavens, honey, you've become so pale!" Diana clutches her designer purse, noticing Paul's bathrobe and slippers scattered on the lawn. She directs to the housekeeper, "Maria, where's Paul?"

Meanwhile, in the interior of the residence, Mrs. Jaworski enters the kitchen in search of alcohol. Methodically she searches the drawers and cabinets in anticipation of a reward. "It's awfully dry around here! They eat rich food; surely there must be at least a cooking wine." In her rummage through the refrigerator, Mrs. Jaworski inquires of the whereabouts of the estate's liquor. "Milford, where does Paul keep refreshment for his honored guests?" As she continues the search, she scrutinizes a medication label. "Ah, finally. Hopefully it's something I can enjoy with a good nip. Codeine and promethazine? What in the world?"

Milford appears in the kitchen to provide insight. "It's the madam's cough syrup. Today's youth uses it for its intoxicating effect. It's referred to as Lean. Madam's physician prescribed it during the madam's spell of bronchitis. I believe it's expired, and obviously Maria has forgotten to discard it. Madam, shall I?"

Milford extends his hand to accept the medication. Full-on tipsy, Mrs. Jaworski smacks her lips. Pursing her mouth, her head shakes slightly from intoxication. "Well, since you've explained it that way, I do feel under the weather myself, and there's no need for good medication going to waste." She gulps several swallows of the cough syrup before blinking her eyes into focus. "Wow! That's quite a kick! I notice a difference already! The warmth going down my throat and chest is refreshing. I believe I'll hold on to this treasure until I find something better." Mrs. Jaworski burps. "Oh my! It's much stronger than I thought! Where'd you say Paul kept refreshment for honored guests?"

"Yes, madam, I've completely forgotten. There's Juan Julio 1600 and scotch whiskey. Continue through the dining room and further beyond the living room, into Master Paul's parlor. Would you rather I retrieve something, madam?"

Pursing her mouth, Mrs. Jaworski licks her lips for another swallow of cough syrup. "Milford, I believe I've found everything I need." She burps. "Oh, listen to me. I'm exhausted! Inform Diana I'll not be coming to dinner, and I've chosen the parlor as my room of choice for the next several days."

Milford nods his head with acknowledgment. "Undoubtedly, madam."

Reacting from the effects of the cough syrup, Mrs. Jaworski

stumbles her way into the dining room. She uses the dining table for support, noticing a half-full whiskey glass. The cough syrup is poured into the glass without hesitation and gulped down in one swallow. Mrs. Jaworski smacks her lips. "It's scotch whiskey. He must have known I was coming." Stumbling into the living room, she comes upon the coffee table with tequila and whiskey. In celebration of her treasure find, she turns up the half gallon of whiskey to chug. Smacking her lips, she reflects with a vintage tune.

> "There ain't nothing I can do,
> Nor nothing I can say,
> That folks don't criticize me;
> Well, I'm going to do just what I want to anyway!"

Unable to contain herself with her newfound wealth, Mrs. Jaworski opens the fifth of tequila to chug and gulp. Topping off the celebration, she takes a nip of cough syrup as a chaser.

> "If I go to church on Sunday,
> And cabaret on Monday,
> Ain't nobody's business if I do!"

"Nineteen forty-nine Billie Holiday, well, she was certainly one to tell it like it is, wasn't she? I'll say she did!" Mrs. Jaworski takes a nip of cough syrup. She licks her lips to ask, "What was it today's youth called this? Well, mother's definitely on tilt. I've never felt so good." Preparing for a swallow of tequila, her eyes blink to focus at something across the room. She questions with slurred diction, "What . . . what is that; what are you doing over there? I asked what . . . what you are doing. Why are you just—just standing there? You must be trying to sneak up on me. Are you spying? For my daughters? Lucky for me, I've found your stash. Geez, a little, little touchy aren't we? I was going to save you some … I wouldn't drink it all, besides … I talked to Mil-Milford … I was told I was more than welcome." Mrs. Jaworski blinks her eyes to focus. "Well, here's to you … the gracious host you always are." She takes another chug of what she thinks is tequila. "Oh, this is the cough syrup? Are you kidding me? You sure you don't want any? This is great stuff." Taking a chug of whiskey, Mrs. Jaworski blinks her eyes to focus. "Ah-h-h! It's just something about the rye in whiskey that keeps me coming back!" Her head slightly shakes from intoxication. "What's that you're wearing, that's a peculiar outfit? It makes you look like you're just standing there … like, like you're … hanging?" With her scream, the tequila whiskey and cough syrup hit the floor to shatter.

Grace responds to the living room in a flash. Upon Paul's discovery, she flees toward the estate's courtyard. Milford's at her heels. Both run toward Diana, who stands vigil for Maria, who remains kneeled in prayer. "Diana, Diana, oh my god! Something terrible has happened!" Grace continues across the estate's courtyard. "Diana, please hurry! Call the paramedics; it's Paul. He's in the living room … Oh, my god! Diana, we have to call the police."

Diana turns her eyes from Maria, who remains kneeled and clutching her rosary, to look to Grace, who races from the estate's interior in a panic. Diana's eyes dart repeatedly from Maria to Grace. Uneasiness begins to register. A sense of urgency is heard with Diana's questioning.

"Maria, what has happened here?" Leaving Maria incoherent, Diana begins to walk toward the living quarters. "Milford? Milford?"

Milford comes to view, comforting Mrs. Jaworski. "Madam, the unthinkable has happened. It's Master Paul."

Diana drops her designer purse to run toward the living quarters. "Milford! No one's telling me anything. What has happened? Where's Paul? Milford, please tell me what has happened. Why isn't anyone saying anything?"

Reacting to Diana's distressed state, Chippy and Scooter's committed barks follow her into the estate's interior. Diana's voice carries to the courtyard as she goes from room to room to search for her husband. "Paul, are you in there? Paul? Mother and Father—everyone's—arrived. Paul, Maria's prepared to set the table. Paul, are you in there? Paul? No-o-o!"

With her sister's scream, Grace sprints from the courtyard to return to the estate's interior. She blasts past Milford in his attempt to support Mrs. Jaworski, as he communicates simultaneously with the 9-1-1 operator. "Please hurry, it's tragic! Mr. Paul Levitivitch has taken his life! It's very grave indeed; it's a tragedy! I'm lost for words. Please hurry! No, I can't perform CPR. He's been found hanged in the estate's living room. I have neither checked for a pulse. We are at the mercy of your response time. Please send someone right away!"

CHAPTER TWENTY- EIGHT

$\mathcal{A}$rriving to the coffee house, Donte and Rayfee await in line to order Frappuccinos.

"M-m-m, look what the wind blew in, Donte and Rayfee. Welcome to the coffee house. As much as you two have been running through my mind, you both should be tired already! So are the rumors true? Are you two the new item, as in together?"

Rayfee answers, "Mysal! You know the answer already, and we won't thank you for being nosey! If you can find a way to get around that thing that's blocking your eyesight, we'd like to order. Thanks, nosey!"

Feeling smarted, Mysal stretches his arms out spread-eagled. With deliberate exaggeration, he rotates his wrists outward to allow his palms to rotate face down. To add flair to his demonstration, Mysal's back is arched. He stands on the ball of his foot to raise his right heel. Signifying the drama to come, Mysal flickers his eyes while covering his mouth to yawn simultaneously. "Well,

Rayfee, inquiring minds are pondering the truth. Everyone's heard. It seems someone had a little visit to Prince Albert's today. Apparently it's true, because queen Donte stands here before everyone glowing diva-lisha-fied!"

"Mysal, can we order please?" To give his customers his undivided attention, Mysal shifts his body weight to his opposite leg. He hesitates before proceeding with the order. "How rude of me! Your orders slipped my mind completely. What is it that the beautiful people want?" Mysal puckers his lips for the "no-brainer." "Could it be two caramel Frappuccinos? No whipped cream for diva-lisha-fied, because this queen's watching her figure. By the way, Donte, I will admit you look gorgeous! Oh, Rayfee, I just love that color on you in skinny jeans. Is that the new fuchsia? You look so ba-a-d." Mysal purses his lips. "M-m-m, Rayfee, I believe its whipped cream with extra caramel, am I correct?" Mysal sucks his tongue with a seductive whisper to include, "Lately I've had a constant craving for man cream, but I can't seem to find anyone. I for one enjoy being at the pump, as long as the reward is coming from big, clean, hairless balls."

Rayfee rolls his eyes with dismissal. "Mysal, you're such a hater! Donte, be careful; there's something in the air that we might not be able to shake." Rayfee extends his palm within close proximity to Mysal's face. "The hater virus."

Donte and Rayfee find a table and await their order. Rayfee continues to go in on Mysal. "Damn, that skank's bold! Can you believe Mysal? Who is he to question your happiness?"

"Just ignore him, Rayfee; Mysal's miserable. He's trying to

cloud the sunshine. Whenever he's not working here, he's ad-venturing on Santa Veronica Boulevard. Believe me, he's mis-ery at its finest; he's always been."

"Donte, how shrewd! Why didn't I think of that?" Rayfee pokes fun at Mysal under his breath. "Damn, if he doesn't get some female hormones from somewhere. His facial stubble's harsh. Who'll trust him enough to be that close to their balls? I'm itching just looking at him. Who's he fooling?" Rayfee waves from across the room. "Heyyyy, Mysal?"

Mysal returns with the requests. "Two caramel Frappuccinos. Enjoy!" Placing the orders, Mysal presents his card. "Oh, Donte, stay in touch. While you're really busy being wifey, the rich guy may have a friend or two to entertain, so don't be shy; you're so secretive about everything. Anyway, I'm definitely available if there's a need."

Rayfee scoffs. "Can you believe the skeezer?"

"Why wouldn't I, Rayfee? He's a hater. Let me handle him." Donte admires his ring's brilliance to ask, "Mysal, if you were asked to define yourself, other than your obvious facial stub-ble and frequent dick tryst on Santa Veronica Boulevard, how would you describe yourself as others see you? Which nouns would be chosen for your character, Mysal? Would the words *class* or *restraint* ever come to mind?"

Rayfee uses his hand as a stop sign to motion to Mysal. "Oops! Donte, no you didn't!"

"Rayfee, let me finish. There are other nouns to describe this skank."

Rayfee nods his head agreeing.

"Ouch!"

"There's trifling!"

Rayfee co-signs. "Oh, how disgusting!"

"Nasty!"

Rayfee puts his hand over his chest to signify, "You're not done?"

Stirring his Frappuccino, Donte flickers his eyelashes. "Mysal? Since you've managed to squeeze those cheap implants into that size fifteen, I'll call it as everyone sees you, Big Nasty!"

Rayfee covers his mouth. "Oh, I thought for sure you'd be slapped for that one."

Donte uses the straw to sample the Frappuccino. "M-m-m. It's perfect! In speaking of, Mysal, have you ever wondered why you'll never have any part in making any of these wonderful specialties? No doubt you're speechless, so I'll save you the embarrassment. I'll help with the riddle. Before anything wonderful or beautiful is created, it has to be within. In the meantime, Mysal, while you await your time to evolve toward something decent, do your job well and keep bringing what's beautiful to beautiful people. Now, Mysal back to your diss-fest! There are other words to include with nouns to make them more descriptive, which brings you closer to seeing yourself as others see you. There's ugly nasty, nasty big ugly, or nasty big ugly nasty trifling. All that's left to do is choose which adjective best describes Mysal."

Rayfee high-fives Donte with a girlish chortle. "No, you didn't just go in on that skank! If she didn't know, now she knows! Woo, I know that's right! Keep that skank in her place!"

Abashed with hatred, Mysal glares at the two as if he wanted to throw something.

Rayfee pumps up the drama under his breath. "Donte, no this bitch didn't just look at us like that!" Rayfee taunts whispering, "Come on, bitch! Let's tear something up!"

Rayfee steps out of his pumps as he tucked his weaved ponytail into a hair bun.

Realizing what's to unfold, Mysal has a change of heart. "You know what? I'm not going there with you two. Instead I'll congratulate queen Donte on her good find. Ha! There's the high road with my good deed for the day. If by chance the rich guy ever ventures to the boulevard, you should hope he doesn't want his dick sucked." Mysal licks his lips seductively. "In all my years of duty, I can't recall any of the high and mighty willfully denying services from a certified head shrink!" Donte and Rayfee are dismissed with a fluttering of fingers. "Bye, bitches!"

Donte high-fives Rayfee. "Whatever! That skank knows what it is, but can you believe the skank had the audacity to speak on Paul? Rayfee, believe me, before the day's end, a lot of people at Prince Albert's will be put in check."

"Oh, Donte, the way you handled that creature! You can be such a beast when you have to be. You turned it on so smoothly with such control. When Mysal took you there, you went in on him big, and you looked good doing it. Donte, you're working that weave, and Prince Albert definitely stepped up his boutique game with that dress. You're killing it! Look at those pumps. Where did you find rhinestone in a size thirteen? You had them made, didn't you? Make sure they're available for when Mr. Right comes into my life. Well, gorgeous, are you nervous? That wasn't a fair question. What girl wouldn't be? Let's get going! Mr. Right shouldn't have to wait forever. Besides, if that fish steps out of her pond, Mysal's drama was just a precursor of how beautifully you'll handle things. You're rockin' it!"

Continuing their journey toward Paul's estate, the pair now rolls along Benedict Canyon. Rayfee has since connected his iPod to the car radio. "Donte we're making good time to get there; slow down. Here's the perfect song. Let's get our celebration on." Rayfee dances in his seat with the tune.

I know you want me, I know you want me.
I know you do, I know you do.
That's why when I come around, you act the way you do.
And I know you like it, I know you like it.
You wanna do me, you wanna do me.
You fight every thought in your mind,
To leave home to live your fantasy.
Won't you leave your girlfriend for a freak like me?
Won't you leave your girlfriend to be wild and free?
Won't you?

"Yes, they're really hot! Paul and I saw them in concert in San Francisco, and they turned it out. Rayfee, we left there so turned up, the next morning Paul went shopping for the outfits they wore in concert. When he returned to the hotel, I had just awakened exhausted from the previous evening. While I was in the shower, it never dawned on me of why Paul kept playing this song. It played for at least forty-five minutes, and I danced the entire time. As I stepped out of the shower, voila! A gift bag with a bow and ribbons were laid on top of my negligée. It wasn't hard putting the two together; I knneeew what he wanted."

"Oh, you naughty girl! How lucky you are to have someone who spends money so freely and is so creative with the kink, so tell me, how was he rewarded for his deed?"

"Rayfee, allow me to get there. Have some patience, already! Okay, being the consummate queen that I am, Paul pampers me with pedicures and Brazilian waxing's, so there's never much to do on maintenance other than my arms. After freshening up, I put on the fishnet stockings and garter to prance into the living room and worked my jelly. All six foot three of my feminine self! For the rest of the evening, I gave Paul a lap dance in every outfit in the gift bag. After a little rest between dances, or should I say the remainder of the night, I was very generous with reciprocity. Rayfee, it was incredible!"

Reacting to a hot flash, Rayfee fans his face for drama. "Donte, you're definitely the bigger freak. You know this, right? You talk about me because I have more than one partner, but you're just as nasty, maybe even more so than me. You do know this."

Donte adjusts the rearview mirror to admire his weave. "Rayfee, come on! You love dick in its entirety with a lot of variety. I, on the other hand, enjoy dick with discretion. I'm very selective, and when committed to a relationship, I entertain only one dick. No, Rayfee, I wasn't referring to the one that was surgically removed." Making his point, Donte gyrates his neck to the catchy tune.

Rayfee looks at Donte. "Well, lucky for you, you have a rich guy with all the money in the world to assist with your procedures. You do know if you weren't my friend, I'd slap that weave right from your head with the quickness."

"Rayfee, if I weren't your friend, who would you rely on to lend you money? Who else would allow you to repay at your convenience without any questions?"

Each looks to the other as they gyrate their necks with the tune. With a raised hand, the friends exchange a slapping high-five. "That's how we roll!" Rayfee increases the radio volume to celebrate.

> Control your emotions, control your emotions
> Set your feelings aside, set your feelings aside,
> In the back of your mind, you wanna be with me,
> Come on enjoy the ride.
> Let's keep it friendly, let's keep it friendly,
> Tread lightly with care, tread lightly with care,
> We both know the rules of the game, when it's hot
> You'll play truth or dare.
> Won't you leave your girlfriend to spend a night with me?
> Won't you pay my bills and sneak around with me,
> Won't you. won't you.

As the two are being festive, blaring sirens drown out the car's music. Donte's car shakes as a rescue ambulance and fire engine company rips past them. Startled by the sudden intrusion, Rayfee flips the intruders the bird. "You're going the wrong way, on the wrong side of the street, assholes!" Rayfee looks at Donte. "Was that a rhetorical statement or what? Where have I heard that?" In girlish chortle, both flip Rayfee's rhetorical statement. "You're going the wrong way? Oops!"

The car ride smooths out as the emergency vehicles continue toward their destination. Donte motions to turn down the radio. "This will be my first time out here. I've brought you along as my passenger to help look for the address, so get serious and pay attention, Rayfee."

"Donte, relax to present yourself; I'm on point. Really, Donte, but not for real? I hate you. What else could go so very right? You have everything. The relationship, the finances to keep everything in perspective."

Donte takes his hand off the steering wheel to display his engagement ring. "I now have the title and the man exclusively!"

"Donte, you did it; congratulations! I hope my special day will come soon."

"Aw, Rayfee, it will; it has to. You've been there for me every time through thick and thin. I couldn't ask for a better friend. We just left the coffee shop, and you had my back without hesitation. Who else does that? When your day comes, you won't have to look for me, believe it. You know what else, Rayfee? It's therapeutic when we get together. If I had to go a week without our Frappuccinos and girl talk, I'd falter!"

"You?"

"Yes, me! Rayfee, you and I understand each other. Who

else has a clue of the emotional roller coaster ride we took before coming out? Revealing our sexuality? That was a huge undertaking! The ignorant for the most part identify gay as being a perverted freak without feelings. They don't understand what we've gone through. Rayfee, this is why I make it a point to call you regularly. It's my release."

"Tell me about it! Everyone has issues, but no one seems to respect ours. It's really a warped mentality, and the so-called straight façade, believe me, they're really fucked up with their double standards and quiet hypocrisy. We're living in a twisted world where we're expected to live as mutes, so that everyone else can be comfortable with their lives.

"Since when is that a rule? Suppress our feelings because we're gay? What the fuck is that? The straight guy isn't considered gay when he gets what he wants and keeps it quiet? It's only problematic when the gay guy becomes emotional because he wants a relationship in public or be seen together when they're around the straight guy's friends, who by the way have passed their phone numbers on the down low."

"Do tell, Rayfee. I'll never go back there to deal with the guilt and lies. It took seven years for Paul to come out and accept his inner self. Believe me, that was a tough nut to crack, but today we're moving forward. It's official!"

Reacting dramatically, Rayfee raises his chin to put his hand over his heart. "Oh, and I didn't wear my dress for the ceremony."

"Rayfee, be serious and pay attention. We should be getting close to the right block. The address should be on your side."

As they come around the bend, flashing emergency lights can be seen farther up the road. "Oh no, what have we run into? I hope they aren't blocking off the street. Are other cars going around them, Rayfee? Look for a house number. Are the numbers getting higher or lower?"

"I'm trying to find one. These homes are huge, and they sit so far back from the street. Oh, there's a curb address. We're on the fourteen-eight-hundred block, and the numbers are getting higher. Wow, it's really nice out here. It's definitely high end. You never mentioned Paul doing it like this. Are you two going to be staying out here? What arrangements has he made with fishy, and what pond will she lie in after this? Anywhere compared to this neighborhood, she becomes a bottom dweller, a scavenger." Rayfee hisses like a cat retracting its claws. "S-s-s-t! Girlfriend, prepare yourself, because the fish isn't leaving unless she's kicking and screaming. If you pull over before we get there, I'll help you put Vaseline on your face. WOO! Let's do the damn thing!"

"Rayfee, stop! We haven't discussed any of that; besides, Paul's fair. I wouldn't want their house anyway. I'm satisfied having Paul whether he's broke or wealthy. If we had to live under the freeway and wrap up in cardboard, I'd be content. Rayfee, don't you get it? Happiness! Being truly happy is when you're willing to give up all material things to be with the person you love."

"Donte, I'm sorry, but I'm not seeing it. I couldn't fathom leaving something like this behind. This is something that everyone, I mean so many people want to obtain this way of living, and you're willing to walk away and leave it to that dried up she creature? Don't expect fishy to up and skedaddle because you're wearing a two-thousand-dollar dress. Donte, I know you didn't intend to fight or make any scenes, but believe me, fishy will have the National Guard on standby to shoot the both of you. After you take her man, what does she have to lose? Everything! She'll never recover from this way of life. Donte, you don't need my pepper spray; you'll need a shotgun."

"Stop being ridiculous, Rayfee! Paul's making his transition, and neither of us wants to walk under any clouds. Everything will be fine. Rayfee, I've brought you along for your support, so maintain yourself accordingly. Remember that when we get there."

"Okay, Donte; say no more. I'm not you, and that's why you get the guy. While everyone's being dreadfully miserable, when this plays out, they'll hate you even more. You're the poster child for doing the right thing. Have you even noticed? I'm the only person that can stand being around you. But sister girl, no worries; I'll never leave. We're bonded! Don't forget, after you break in those rhinestone shoes, I have first dibs."

"Rayfee, okay, enough already. This is the street. I want fourteen nine hundred. The address will be on your side."

"Donte, we're here already. Relax." Rayfee reads off the addresses, "Fourteen eight hundred ninety, ninety-two, ninety-four, ninety-six, ninety-eight. Fourteen nine hundred? That's where all the commotion is. Why so many police cars? Isn't that the rescue ambulance that passed us on Benedict Canyon? Look at all these people!"

CHAPTER TWENTY-NINE

*A*t 4:30 p.m. at the entrance of the Levitivitch estate, Milford stands within a cordoned area of yellow tape being questioned by a homicide detective.

"Please state your name for the record."

"Milford James."

"James is your last name?"

"Yes."

"Your date of birth, Mr. James?"

"October twenty-seventh, nineteen fifty-six."

"Do you live alone?"

"No."

"Where do you currently reside, and who do you live with?"

"One four nine zero zero Benedict Canyon."

"You're residing in the same residence with the victim?"

"Absolutely."

"You've been living here for how long?"

"Since I began my tenure of employment, some twenty-seven years ago."

"Mr. James?"

"Detective, I would prefer simply Milford."

"Can you offer any reasons of why someone would want to harm your employer, Milford?"

"Nothing comes to mind."

"Has anyone to your knowledge come to the residence within the previous seventy-two hours that may have provoked him in any way?"

"To my knowledge, no one has entered the estate grounds."

"What about phone calls within the last seventy-two hours; does anything come to mind that you would consider hostile or confrontational?"

"I'm not privy to any of my employers' calls, detective."

"Can you offer any information that would be helpful to this investigation, Milford?"

"Sorry to say, other than his discovery, I haven't any clues to offer."

"Were you or anyone known to you in any way involved with the death of Mr. Levitivitch?"

"To say the least, you have a penchant for a rather intrusive line of questioning. The answer is absolutely not! I can't think of anyone who would wish something so terrible on my employer. Are we finished here, detective?"

Nearby within the estate grounds, a homicide detective interviews a witness. "Urrph! Excuse me, I'm Diana's mother, Mrs. Jaworski. Urrph! My goodness, I don't mean to burp, but I can't seem to think straight. I believe I may have become dried out."

"Mrs. Jaworski, what led you to the discovery of Mr. Levitivitch?"

"What's that? How I found him, you say?"

"Yes, what were you doing that led you to his discovery?"

Mrs. Jaworski purses her lips. "What was I doing? Well, I need to think a spell." Removing the jeweled flask from her purse, she twists the cap to take a nip. "Ah, it was this, refreshment. It was time to replenish. I searched everywhere, you know. I believe I started in the kitchen … or was it the laundry room? I can't remember; my head was spinning. I recall being awful thirsty. Those peanuts from the flight made my throat dry. Here, I've brought a few back with me."

"I see. Can you recall the exact time when you had to… um-m-m, replenish, Mrs. Jaworski?"

Mrs. Jaworski purses her mouth. Her head slightly shakes with intoxication. "Hold your horses, don't rush me. I need to think a spell. I turned seventy-four last month, and I'm not as spry as I used to be." She throws her head back to swallow a gulp from the jeweled flask, burping. Urrph! "Oh, forgive me; I've done it again. I'd say I was nearly parched. It was sometime before supper. Yes, it had to be. We were to have roast duck with potatoes. I had retired to the parlor for the evening to catch up on my rest, and that's when I found him."

"Mrs. Jaworski, why wouldn't you retire to a bedroom? Why choose the parlor over the comfort and the greater privacy?"

As she looks for an answer, Mrs. Jaworski's head shakes. She looks the detective in the eye. With her reasoning, she smacks her lips. "I'm an honored guest! Paul does a lot of entertaining, and I was told refreshments were kept in the parlor. I thought I'd save myself a few trips from going up and down that staircase. Have you seen it? I didn't want to work that hard to replenish." Mrs. Jaworski takes a nip from her jeweled flask. "I am seventy-four years old, you know."

Elsewhere in the estate courtyard, Maria sits immobile in a rescue ambulance. Recovering from shock, she breathes into an oxygen mask during a detective's interview. "I Maria Sanchez Gutierrez!"

"Mrs. Gutierrez, what were you doing that led you to find Mr. Levitivitch?"

"Maria cooking for the señoras fambelee. I making the roosting ducks and potatoes. I answering the telefone for Milfurb. Heem calling for the señora."

"Milfurb? A man other than her husband called the residence? What's Milfurb's relationship with Mrs. Levitivitch?"

"Heem wurking here too."

"He works here. What does he do? Does he work here when Mr. Levitivitch is at his home, or only when Mr. Levitivitch is away?"

"Heem wurking for here ebery day. Heem taking the señora shopping, taking the señora for the bank, heem fix the drink for señora and gib señora the mee-dee-cayshun for her bery dizzy. Heem taking Meester Paul for the ereport, and dribe for Meester Paul eberywhere."

"Okay, I understand. Milfurb's the chauffeur, the driver;

I got it. Mrs. Gutiérrez, let's get back to what you were doing when you found Mr. Levitivitch. I don't need anything long and drawn out. Just tell me what you were doing."

"Ah-huh. Maria cooking. Sheepee and Scootee barking for bery long time. *Mi niños* [my children], they bringing Meester Paul's shoes for the kisshin. Maria finding Meester Paul's robe for the dining room. Maria esplain, no bery good niños! Meester Paul bery angry for heem shoes and robe. Maria cawm for the libber room esplaining, 'Meester Paul, Maria hab you shoes and robe. Sheepee and Scootee no bery good, they taking eberywhere!' Maria cawming to the libber room to see Meester Paul. I screeming! I bery scared and I running for the outside."

"Mrs. Gutierrez. Let me direct you to another area for recollection. Has anyone come to the house today other than Mrs. Levitivitch's family?"

"No-o-o, nobawdy cawming."

"Has anyone called the house to intimidate Mr. Levitivitch?"

"No-o-o. Nobawdy calling for today."

"What about domestic disturbances or disputes between your employers? Anything out of the ordinary?"

Maria probes her nose nervously. "I tink the señora bery angry to Meester Paul for whawning the whores. The bery bew-tee-ful ladies."

Stopping the notations in his notepad, the detective questions, "He wants whores. How many did he have?"

Maria continues to pick her nose. "I finding maybe two pursons."

"When did Mrs. Levitivitch find out about this? Was it today?"

"No, I esplaining ebery ting for the señora frum yesterday."

"Mrs. Gutierrez, if no one came to the residence, and to the best of your recollection, no one called to threaten or intimidate Mr. Levitivitch, how would you have known or have information to give to his wife?"

Consumed with guilt, Maria looks away from the detective. Ashamed by the turn of events, she finds solace in picking her nostrils. "Oh, my goodneth, Meester Paul, this so bery bawd for Maria to esplain. I wurking, and I finding Meester Paul's lettur to Dawnee, and I coming for here for esplaining ebery ting to the señora."

"Mrs. Gutierrez, you mentioned you were working. What were you doing when you found property that belonged to Mr. Levitivitch?"

"No, no, no!" Maria motions the sign of the cross, whispering. "I finding sumting at othur job where Maria wurking."

"Where's the location of the other job, and what do you do there?"

"I cleening at Seepulveeda and A-bee-a-chun. I wurking for obertime yesturday." Maria holds her head in disbelief. "I finding trawble for the señora. I finding the thong and wig frum Meester Paul's room. Maria esplain for the señora. The ladies ordur the room serbese for Meester Paul and Dawnee, sausage and bery crèmee for the salad. For the drinking," Maria whispers, "the ladies ordur, Leedle Ree-sherd especial with limón, for making sumting to pucker." Consumed with guilt, Maria holds her head to slowly turn it from side to side. "Oh, my goodneth, I esplaining bery bawd imp-pormee-shun for here."

Nearby in a rescue ambulance, Grace comforts Mr. Jaworski by placing her arm around him. As he sits on the gurney clueless, Grace answers the EMT's questions regarding his health.

"What's your father's age?"

"He's seventy-nine."

"Does he suffer from any chronic illness or discomforts?"

"Yes, he has dementia and schizophrenia."

The EMT releases the valve on the blood pressure cuff. "Your father's blood pressure's elevated. What medication has been prescribed for the dementia?"

"Memantine."

"At what prescribed dosage?"

"Fifty milligrams twice daily."

"What's he taking for the schizophrenia, and at what dosage?"

"Thorazine at fifty milligrams twice a day. He's a type II diabetic as well."

"What's been prescribed for the diabetes?"

"He's taking Metaformin."

"Has your dad had any major surgeries?"

"No, he hasn't. What does this have to do with my sister's husband?"

"Ms. Jaworski, as overwhelming as this may be for your family, this incident has been categorized as a homicide. Protocol is to treat the incident as a crime scene. Therefore, prior to a detective's interview, a witness assessment is conducted. If the assessment cannot be determined on location, the interview will be conducted at the police station with a qualified medical examiner present."

Grace becomes agitated with the EMT's explanation. "Never has my father taken blood pressure medication, and I for one make sure he gets all of his medications daily."

Returning the blood pressure cuff to the medical toolbox, the EMT treads lightly. "Ms. Jaworski, I know this ordeal is difficult. Not to compound added stress or to be intrusive, but examining your father brings me to the next question. There appears to be an abnormal bulge in his crotch area. Has he suffered hernias?"

Grace quickly dispels her defensive demeanor. "Oh, no worries there! Father has a weak bladder. We buy supersize diapers, because he's so well endowed."

"I see. I'd like to check your father's pupils and motor skills to determine his responsiveness."

"Geez, father never takes off his glasses. Give me a moment to make him comfortable." Grace holds her father's face to get his attention. "Father, we need to look at your eyes so that you can communicate with the detectives. Tell them what you remember, Father."

Just as Grace removes the dark glasses, the EMT directs, "Mr. Jaworski, please use your eyes to follow the direction of my pen light. Thank you, sir."

Blinking erratically, Mr. Jaworski appears much like the Mr. Magoo character without his glasses. He blindly blurts out, "Who in the hell are you? Tell O'Banion I shot Capone, for all I care. Trust me on it, and stay outta Detroit. It ain't safe. Let it be known, there's only one rooster with the curly comb around here. I never feared O'Banion or his band of floozies. Who said this debutante was Irish Catholic or a gangster?"

Concluding his assessment, the EMT returns the pen light to his shirt pocket. He directs his comments to a nearby detective. "Detective Johnston, I cannot determine Mr. Jaworski's mental fitness for a field interview."

With that being said, Mr. Jaworski's conjecture resumes. His eyes roll in their sockets as if he were a chameleon. "Did you hear what I said? I ain't sitting on the fucking stool. It's just the ninth round. I'll finish him. Just shut up and pay the numbers guy for the hooch. Hey, slim. What's with you? You're not hearing me? Put more sauerkraut on the franks. You fucking stupid or something?"

On the estate's opulent courtyard near the cascading fountain, attention comes to several EMTs, in their attempts to restrain a woman to a gurney. While grappling with her restraints the bewildered woman condemns her husband's fate. "You cheated me, Paul! You cheated me! This wasn't the way to do this. How could you do this to us? How dare you put me through grief! I didn't deserve this. Not this way! I can't live with guilt, Paul!" Abruptly the woman sobs. "I never believed any of it! I loved you. I never believed any of it. I only wanted to upset you. I never believed anything she told me. I never … I would never believe any of it, Paul. I never meant any of those harsh words. Please forgive me; it was my medication talking. Paul, please forgive me."

CHAPTER THIRTY

*A*rriving to the crime scene, a detective exits a sedan with his hands in the pockets of his creased trousers. After several moments of taking in the compound's vast interior, he walks the rolling terrain from Benedict Canyon to the estate's paved courtyard. As he surveys the proximity of neighboring estates, the detective speaks into his voice recorder: "Tuesday. July twenty-second, at approximately sixteen-forty-five, Detective First-Grade Vincent Destry arriving to fourteen nine hundred Benedict Canyon. Upon arrival there's police activity at the entrance of property … Property's cordoned off with squad cars with officers posted … On the compounds interior are several RAs, with police activity, which includes detective questioning … Destry concludes this segment at sixteen fifty-two hours." Now smoking a cigarette, Destry takes in more of the breathtaking compound. His attention drifts to a scene at a rescue ambulance, to where a woman appearing to be the estate's housekeeper breathes into an oxygen mask between detective questioning.

"I Maria. I wurking here for twanty fibe year. No, nebur trawble for any pursons. No, nebur fighting. Ah-huh, Maria cooking for the señora's fambelee frum Meenisota. Yah, si! I hearing Sheepee and Scootee barking for thurty minutes. I cawm to the libber room and finding Meester Paul."

Within close proximity of the rescue ambulance, a man wearing butler attire responds to detective questioning. "No, sir. During the twenty-seven years of my employment, there isn't anyone I would consider remotely hostile toward my employer. He was the consummate gentleman to everyone."

Destry looks upon a scene at another nearby rescue ambulance, to where EMTs check the vital signs of a woman strapped to a gurney. Standing by witnessing are two dogs that have barked continuously after sensing their owner's distress. In a gesture to appease the animal's owner, a police officer holds the well-kept animals nearby on designer leashes. In the meantime, the distraught woman talks into space.

"Mother! Mother, please make them help me. Has anyone seen Maria? My bath needs drawing, and I'll need my robe and slippers. Have you seen any of my facial crèmes? Be sure to leave fresh cucumber slices for my sleep mask. Honey, have you forgotten? We always roll my hair before bed. Maria, where's Milford? Are my medications nearby, should I become rattled and need settling? Milford, why aren't you answering the intercom? Have you explained to them what happened? Oh, my god! Milford, my medications and herbal teas aren't in the pantry. Please fix this." Severely traumatized, the woman moves her head from side to side in denial. She talks into empty space. "Paul! Not this way. This wasn't supposed to happen … Grace. Father? Milford … is anyone there?"

Detective Destry exhales cigarette smoke through his nostrils. Finishing his cigarette, he steps on its butt, speaking into the voice recorder to note: "Seventeen hundred hours … Destry debriefs detective on scene on the property's courtyard." Proceeding toward a yellow-taped area, Destry approaches a detective who happens to be studying notes of witness interviews. "What are we working with, Johnston?"

"One Paul Levitivitch deceased, married white male fifty-eight years old. Apparently a decent guy that paid his estate bills through his accountant. No traffic tickets or previous arrests. Deceased was the primary partner in Levitivitch, Meyers, and Rothensberg, a trade and investment firm. The timing couldn't have been worse for the guy; he had a birthday coming next month."

Destry watches the activity around the estate's courtyard in thought. "Is the timing of fate ever right for anyone? There's a body here, which means something went very wrong with somebody somewhere. Who are the players?"

Johnston motions to a detective's interview. "See the distinguish gentleman in the fancy butler attire? "He's the live-in butler and chauffeur, Milford James. Just a few hours ago, he returned from the airport with Mrs. Levitivitch's family." Johnston points to a high-end vehicle. "The butler never got his chance to put the Maybach back with the rest of the toys. You should see what's parked next to where the Maybach should have been parked." Johnston nods to a rescue ambulance to where a woman breathes into an oxygen mask. "She's Maria Sanchez Gutierrez, the estate's maid. She works at the estate four days a week. When she's not working here, Maria works at that high-dollar hotel on Sepulveda and Aviation. After attending both church services on Sunday, she rests at home with her children."

Destry casually puts a stick of gum into his mouth. "His maid's going to both church services certainly had no effect on Levitivitch. Did you ask if she mentioned her employer in any of her prayer groups? What happened here, Johnston?"

"From what I gather, the deceased was in the living room drinking scotch. After he started feeling good, he stepped onto a chair. He then tied a bed sheet on the staircase balcony and around his neck to step to his death."

Destry continues the gum chewing, absorbing Johnston's rationale. "Johnston, how sure are you about that, detective? Did the deceased himself step off, or was he pushed to his death?"

"There's no reasoning to support that theory, Destry. There were no signs of conflict or struggle on either hand or wrist."

"Okay, so we set aside the rationale of foul play for now. Who was the first to find him?"

Johnston refers to his notes. "The maid stumbled upon him in her midst of preparing the evening meal. She happened to be at the oven when she heard the dogs barking and making a fuss in the living room. One chased the other into the kitchen, both carrying the victim's house slippers in their mouths. Walking into the dining room she discovered the deceased's robe lying on the floor. She entered the living room calling the deceased. "'Mr. Paul, Mr. Paul?' BOOM! The maid's face to face with her employer! The deceased is hanging from the balcony with a sheet tied around his neck. How's that to go along with the family's appetizer?"

"I dunno, Johnston, it may very well be Levitivitch didn't have a liking for what was on the menu. Had someone asked, he may have settled for a family portrait instead. Geez, Johnston, have they bagged him yet?"

"Not quite, Destry. The coroner's awaiting forensics to complete its protocol."

Destry chews gum as he rationalizes. He looks at the rescue ambulance where Maria continues to breathe into an oxygen mask. He questions, "Did the maid do anything spectacular after finding the victim?"

Johnston refers to his notepad. "I figure the maid went into shock sometime near three p.m. The chauffeur returning from the airport with the victim's wife and family confirms the timeline." Johnston points to a rose bed within the compound. "When the family arrived, they found her in that area kneeling with a rosary. Mrs. Levitivitch couldn't make out what the maid was murmuring initially. Shortly thereafter the nine-one-one call went out."

Over the squawking of police radios, Destry continued to watch the activity within the estate compound. He noticed the crowd of spectators gathered at the estate's entrance. "Johnston, looking into that crowd, what do you see?"

"I dunno, Destry, nothing really comes to mind. Concerned neighbors that wanna know what's going on, maybe. What am I not seeing? You see someone out of place?"

"Who's to say, Johnston; that's why we do detective work. Whatever doesn't appear on the surface will definitely be seen in the wash. Canvass a three-block area for the home security surveillance tapes from homeowners. Look for a suspicious face or license plate to stand out from within the last two weeks. If anything shows up more than once, follow up with the whole skinny with a report."

"Sure thing, Destry!"

Destry chews gum, rationalizing, "Johnston, confirm the maid's nine-one-one call to the coroner's time of death. Speaking of the Good Samaritan, is there anything you didn't mention? In this instance, it's the maid, Johnston. Expound on all the details."

Johnston refers to his notepad. "There is nothing out of the ordinary. One Maria Sanchez Gutierrez, fifty-two years old. Her employers have entrusted her with the keys to their estate for over twenty-five years. Maria sets her own hours and sets the alarm code as she comes and goes. She and her husband have resided in Culver City for the past fifteen years. Maria uses the metro to come to work. No previous arrests or warrants." Johnston flips the page. "Married to one Juan Gutierrez, sixty-three years old. Juan puts his tools in the family car to drive to work to a body shop, where he's painted cars for the past twenty-eight years. On his day off, Juan's at home drinking while watching television. He has two misdemeanor convictions, both drinking in public."

"Well, Johnston, there you have it; simplicity's always been the key to longevity. You would think their employers would be willing to trade places for either of these lifestyles."

Destry motioned to where detectives are questioning a trio of women. "Is the victim's wife within that group?"

Johnston nods at a gurney where a woman lies in restraints. "That would be Diana Levitivitch, fifty-two years old. She married into blue blood after her deceased husband discovered her as a finalist in the Miss USA beauty pageant. She and the deceased were married twenty-seven years. She holds weekly ladies' forums here at the estate, where she stays connected with all the right people. She's also the treasurer of her deceased husband's Aspiring Minds Foundation. Needless to say, no previous arrests or warrants."

Destry's eyes light up. "Bingo! Which means somewhere there's an insurance policy in place. Dollars to donuts someone nearby is a beneficiary in the event of Mr. Levitivitch's untimely death, which means whoever they are, they'll be sure to put on a good show until the insurance check's in the mail." Destry pops a breath mint in his mouth. "Okay! Let's confirm the motive. Start with the beneficiaries. The Mr. and Mrs., who are they seeing on the side? Whoever they're seeing, what is it they do that allows them to pay their bills? Be methodical. Whose sitting next to who in church, and what calls are they deleting before coming home? It's all there, Johnston; we just have to put it together."

Detective Johnston nods his head, agreeing. "Not a problem; I'll follow up as the intel develops."

Setting aside his instructive rationale, Destry watches a hummingbird dart from flower to flower. His attempt at a bird whistle sends the minute bird flickering away. Destry's reasoning resumes. "Johnston, put the full-court press on both the maid and butler. Use immigration as your leverage to open up this investigation. Threaten them both with deportation until you get something to work with. They've been around for a while; they'll know everything we haven't asked. Believe me when I tell you, Johnston, they're walking encyclopedias on the privileged." Destry talks into the voice recorder: "Seventeen fifteen ... Destry notes to Detective-Third Grade Johnston to one, check out the immigration status on both the butler and maid at the Levitivitch estate and two, run a make on the beneficiaries or executors of the Aspiring Minds Foundation." Destry redirects his focus to a comical scene, a detective's interview of a woman who holds a jeweled flask.

The woman smacks occasionally to purse her lips. "I didn't say I was going from room to room looking for anything. I said no such thing! I was searching for refreshment. Our flight from Minnesota had taken its toll; I was practically dehydrated, and I needed to replenish." Appearing intoxicated, the woman's head shakes. "I believe I said in California the weather's dry. I was feeling rather parched, so I went to the kitchen for relief. While looking through the refrigerator, I found it in the form of a cough medicine to relieve my headache."

Destry chuckles. "Who is she?"

"Uh, she's the mother."

"She's the mother to who, Johnston, your ugly sister and brother? Who in the hell is she?"

"She's the wife's mother, Mrs. Jaworski. She entered the residence and came upon the deceased after walking into the living room. Once her screams were heard, the others came running."

"Did she give any reason for being separated from her family?"

"Destry, I have yet to get a straight answer. She stays with needing refreshment or she was dry and near parched. She's everywhere between the air conditioner and the thermostat."

Destry questions, laughing, "You don't know? Are you bullshitting me here, Johnston?"

"Really, Destry, I don't know. She talks in riddles."

"Johnston, you're a detective. You're telling me you don't know what gorgeous was doing or how she came to be in the living room to find the deceased?"

Johnston turns his palms upward, perplexed. "Destry, what do you want me to say, I don't know?"

Destry laughs at Johnston's lack of common sense. "Rookie! The fifth of scotch you allege the deceased drank. Was the fifth full or half full when gorgeous got around to it? Get it? It was dry? Where was it dry, Johnston? Was she referring to those big bloomers she wears? Hell, everyone knows she's dry there! She probably sprays plenty of lubricant down there just to pee."

"I-I dunno, Destry."

"Forget it, rookie; they'll never teach such things in the

academy. Look at it as life one on one, people and vices." Destry puts another stick of gum in his mouth. He rolls up the wrapper between his fingers to flick it toward Johnston. "Aren't you from one of those cornfields in Nebraska? Well, not exactly a cornfield, but you're from rural Lincoln, right, Johnston?"

"Uh yes, Destry; how'd you know that?"

"It's not what I know, Johnston, that makes you wonder. It's what you don't know that makes me ask myself why you're not saying hello every time you see the corn in your shit. You wanna know why?"

Johnston raises his palms, clueless. "I don't think I have the answer to that one either, Destry."

"There's a good reason why you don't have an answer, Johnston. Some things weren't meant for human consumption. Corn, for one, is a filler for cattle and other animals for slaughter. Much like the undigested corn in your shit, good thinking and good sense have no place in your brain. You have no use for such useful things, do you?"

Johnston blinks his eyes, bewildered.

Destry chuckles. "Did I see your mind turning, kid?" Destry lights a cigarette, exhaling smoke through his nostrils. "Geez, Johnston what was that look? I'm only kidding. Loosen up!"

Destry continues with his cigarette to look upon a scene at a rescue ambulance. An elderly man wearing dark glasses stands idle, while his hand is held by a much younger woman. She responds to detective questioning. "We were arriving from the airport."

"Are you referring to L.A.X?"

"Yes."

"Can you recall the time your flight arrived?"

"I believe it was one p.m."

"And how did you arrive at this location from the airport?"

"Milford picked us up."

"Who is Milford, and what is his occupation?"

"He's my sister's butler and driver."

Without warning, the elderly man interrupts the questioning with an abrupt whistle. Wherrp! "She told you already. This bird's flying south. I got nothing else to talk about; see you next year, patsy. You got the wrong bird, mister. What am I, a fucking canary? You'll never find a rat in this outfit. I did time in Sing-Sing, and believe me, it was a fucking lullaby. Whenever I walked the yard the crowd got somewhere, so don't kid me with a weak pipe dream. Build a prison anywhere, believe me, I'll be the first in line for a vacation. Do me a big favor, you fucking gum shoe. No true gangster will ever reform."

Intrigued by the entertainment before them, Destry chuckles to exhale cigarette smoke. "Geez, who pissed off the gangster with the dark shades?"

Johnston flips through his notepad. "One Benjamin Jaworksi! He's Mrs. Levitivitch's father. Seventy-nine years old and very delusional. He believes he's from the old guard. Destry, here's the kicker. The old bird's prescribed a hundred milligrams of Thorazine daily to keep him functional. He has both dementia and schizophrenia."

Destry coughs a chuckle. "Functional? You're kidding.

Imagine this bird without a wakeup. Cancel the goofy from any list of possible perps. If his brain were in a bird, it would fly backward until it regressed, defying all evolution, to the empty shell it hatched from. The cartoon channel without the commercials is what he is." Destry takes a moment to study the woman next to the man wearing the dark shades. "Don't tell me she's the old guy's wife. If so, he has more sense than I gave him credit for. Even in his senility, he knows if he increased the coverage on his life insurance policy, he'd unmistakably be the victim of a mysterious accident, leaving the pretty actress to go about her business with the guy at the bagel shop, right from the funeral. She's playing a good act for the old fart. Who is she, Johnston?"

"Grace Jaworski, the younger of the two daughters, forty-two years old, single and the appointed caregiver of both parents."

"You're kidding, and she's loaded too?"

"I don't believe so, sir! Her deceased brother-in-law bankrolled the entire family. Grace lives with her parents in Minnesota. From what I've put together, Mrs. Levitivitch put the responsibility of both parents on her younger sister's plate, since she had both the convenience and leverage of her husband's financing. Here's another feather for the younger sister's cap. When everyone else was in shock? Grace had the butler make the second nine-one-one call."

Destry studies Grace as he smokes. "I'm impressed, Johnston. Is there anything else about the patient beauty that you haven't yet said? And Johnston, I really didn't mean what I said earlier about the cornfields."

Fired up over his atta boy, detective Johnston goes into a recap of events as explained to him by Grace. "Oh, I didn't take any of that to heart, Destry; it was just water cooler talk during a professional investigation." Johnston adjusts the waist of his pants. "All righty, here we go! Per Grace's account, her mother, Mrs. Jaworski, was rummaging about looking for joy juice. That's how she worked her way to the living room to find the victim hanged with a bed sheet." Johnston gives Destry the photo.

"Hmmph! Candy-striped boxers and a T-shirt? God loves me? He's traveling awfully light, which means he had time to think about this. He's guilty of something. Here he's reaching out to someone somewhere, Johnston. Why argue God and love? It's rhetorical!"

"You may have an argument there, Destry. He may have been stressed out over his finances. Look at how this guy lived. Imagine the overhead to maintain this lifestyle!"

"Hmm-Hmm-Hmm!" Destry chuckles. "The wealthy never cancel themselves over having wealth. Does it look like anyone's missed any meals around here? The dead will talk, rookie. Whenever they self-check-out, they'll leave clues toward their guilt. You have to understand their mindset to know what to look for. This guy? Come on. He could have gone on a vacation anywhere and taken himself out, but instead he's conveniently home to do it in his living room."

Stuck in thought with Destry's rationale, Johnston listens in agreement with his mouth open. "Uh, yeah, that makes sense. Yeah, okay, I'll continue here. Because Mr. Jaworski wears those oversized diapers, Grace takes her father into the bathroom to change his underpants. By the way, she did say his pants were down around his ankles, and he's in his long dress socks with garters to hold his socks in place. Because he never left the bathroom, I doubt the old bird saw anything. As Grace doused his crotch, she recalled saying, 'There, Father, let's put plenty of powder on. We don't want you to have another diaper rash.'

"As she peeled back the one-sided tape to secure the diaper, Mr. Jaworski mumbled more gibberish. Grace couldn't make it out completely."

"No doubt he was all over the road. She probably got dizzy watching that road lizard. What did he say? Go ahead with it, Johnston, entertain me."

"It was just more senseless conjecture. 'When I flick my headlights twice you'll know it's me, so leave the motor running. If no one answers by the third knock, I'm going in.'" Johnston scoffs. "I got a headache writing the notes, and it was all gibberish."

Destry lights a cigarette. "Can you believe this? Is this guy the last of the prohibition gangsters? What a fucking throwback! Pick him up for an interview and record it for fun. I'll watch it with some of the guys for a lunch movie. Ask plenty of questions about Sam Gianacana when you question him. I'd like to hear a few of those. Unfucking believable!"

Johnston smirks to refer to his notepad. "Yeah, sure, Destry, just as long as you're the one taking notes. Geez. Where was I? Okay, here it is. Grace recalled hearing Mrs.

Jaworski's screams, followed by the sound of glass crashing. Grace runs out of the bathroom. She follows the screams to come upon Mrs. Jaworski, standing in the middle of the living room with a fifth of scotch, a half-gallon of tequila, and a bottle of prescription cough syrup all shattered on the floor."

Destry exhales cigarette smoke. "She's juiced up; that's the only reason she didn't go into shock. When she dries out, trust me, that old bar fly will faint from the memory of what she saw. Keep going, kid." Destry continues with his cigarette as Johnston recapped the events.

"Following the screams, Milford arrived in the living room within seconds behind Grace. Milford had the presence of mind to pull Mrs. Jaworski out of the living room. Meanwhile Grace runs to the courtyard toward her sister."

Destry reasons, "It's all coming together! The dogs' barking led the maid to the dining room, where she finds the robe. From there, she walked into the living room to find the deceased, and subsequently she went into shock. Johnston, it all makes sense! The maid found Levitivitch first. That explains why she was kneeling with the rosary when the family arrived. Okay, the picture becomes clearer. Keep going."

Johnston refers to his notepad for his stopping point. "I forgot where I left off."

Destry exhales cigarette smoke. "The alcoholic finds the deceased in the living room. Grace is running toward her sister, and Milford rescues the alcoholic. Go from there and mention the whereabouts of the goofy."

Johnston compares his notes to Destry's reasoning. "His

daughter was changing his diaper. His pants were down by his ankles. He was wearing those long white silk socks held up by garters. Oh, yeah! Grace runs out the bathroom, which left Mr. Jaworski standing with his pants around his ankles."

"And you've said that how many times, Johnston? Did the goof ever leave the bathroom?"

Johnston blinks, perplexed, and refers to his notepad. "During our search of the perimeter, he was found standing in the tub talking to himself."

"Did he mention anything about Levitivitch?"

"It was the same gibberish. 'Who ratted me out? They'll never find me here; I'm on the lam.'"

Destry chuckles. "Okay, we're back on track. Grace and the butler are going to the wife. Start from there."

"Upon reaching the living room, Grace finds her sister, Mrs. Levitivitch, unconscious on the floor. Mrs. Levitivitch had one of her arms cradled in the seat of the chair that the deceased stepped from. Grace walked slowly into the living room calling her sister. 'Diana, Diana, nine-one-one has been called. The police and paramedics are on their way.' She checks for her sister's pulse. 'Thank God. Big sister, I've never known you to be helpless. Diana, please wake up!' Grace pats her sister's face. 'Diana, you're always in control of everything; I need you to wake up!' Grace then positioned Mrs. Levitivitch on her back and awaited the paramedics' arrival. She was holding on to this when her sister found her. It's her husband's suicide letter." Johnston hands the letter to Destry. He includes, "The wife and butler both confirmed this to be Levitivitch's handwriting."

Destry scrutinizes the letter.

Diana, as my wife I thank you dearly for the twenty-seven years we were joined. Together forever! That was the theme of our beautiful wedding. For twenty wonderful years of our marriage, I remained faithfully devoted to our vows. I loved you each and every day of those beautiful years. I never looked elsewhere for the unconditional love and support we gave each other. Never in a lifetime would I have ever imagined to find rapture's fire and unharnessed passion in another. Forgive me, my beloved.

Donte, our seven years together were the most intense and spontaneous episodes of my life. I never considered myself to be challenged in expressing my true feelings. You have shown the power of love to the point that I can no longer masquerade as the loving husband I portrayed prior to our relationship. I loathe my guilt. I can no longer fight the pull in both directions. Being superficial, I made excuses and pretended to think and perform outside the box. I will no longer torment my inner self nor deceive the two people who truly love me.

CLOSETS ARE FOR CLOTHES. DON'T LET YOUR SECRETS BE THE DEATH OF YOU.
I LOVE YOU BOTH.

Sincerely,
Paul

Johnston reassures Destry, "I had Grace and the butler do follow-up interviews with another detective. Neither missed a beat. She and the butler were the most coherent of the group. The rest were too traumatized to get all the specifics."

As he assessed the developments, Destry's forehead wrinkled in thought.

Detective Johnston folds the page in his notepad to where his interview with Grace concludes. Johnston looks to the senior detective for further direction. "What? What's that look for? I thought I covered all the bases. Say something, Destry!"

"Say something! Well, this freakin' guy certainly has. A Shakespearean tragedy is what it sounds like. Mr. candy-striped boxers had a guilt complex and canceled himself. Fragility's the word; he didn't wanna live a lie. I can't freakin' believe the words!" Destry looks around the estate's compound in exasperation. "Is that a guest house or the fucking neighbor's estate?"

Johnston offers, "Uh, yeah, I checked it out during protocol. It's a four-thousand-square-foot guest house."

"What are you, the good will ambassador here? Are you living in a house like that?"

"No, Destry."

"Do you know of anyone owning property of this magnitude?"

"No, sir."

"Then let me finish talking here. I'll make a lot of sense. Look at the cars he owns. Do you know anyone personally who drives cars like those? Johnston, don't dare answer that; you'll only upset a lot of people. He had freakin' everything going for him. The big spread, the zip code, investments, stocks and shares, the whole shebang. Geez! He gave it all up over his guilt. Here a guy's been faithful to his wife for twenty years, and one morning out of nowhere, he decides for the next seven years, he wants to have salami sword fights when he's away from home, so he masquerades around like a freakin' musketeer. On guard, my sword's hard! No, I'm not here for the fight, I wanna pack peanut butter." Destry motions his head disbelievingly. "Has anyone made contact with the other butt jockey? The last thing we need is a double homicide because Donte can't get his freakin' sphincter stretched. I can't freakin' believe it! This guy canceled himself because of a lifestyle and his conscience. I would've understood his mindset of the wife running off with his investments with his best friend, but to end it all over guilt? Over a lifestyle he chose and conveniently forgot to tell his wife? What was happening at home during the seven years he lived as the masked man? You'd think the Mrs. would notice her husband relished her French toilet just as much as she did. He probably put up a foot race to be the first to sit on it. What in the hell was she thinking? During the last seven years of their marriage, her husband's only request ever was for the extra-soft toilet paper. Geez, can you believe this guy? Imagine the Mrs. asking for a little action in the bedroom."

"Hunnee? Its Tuesday again, our night? I hope you're feeling up for our night? I don't think I can go another three months of uneventful Tuesdays?" Animated and lacking self-control, Destry becomes winded. Struggling to breathe, he stops the shenanigans to look at Johnston. Destry pants. "What's with the silence? Just jump in whenever you like. Where's your motivation, and you must know this guy or something. You're awful quiet, Johnston."

CHAPTER THIRTY-ONE

The congestion of emergency response vehicles and police activity at the Levitivitch estate has forced Donte to park his car a block away. Donte has since taken off his pumps. He and Rayfee hold hands to stay together to maneuver through the gathered crowd.

Donte's voice is heard as they make their way. "Excuse me, can I get through? I need to get through to talk to someone. Thank you. Excuse me?" Fitted in a dazzling sequined dress, now standing six foot three without his rhinestone pumps, Donte has worked his way to the cordoned-off entrance of the estate. Donte calls for the officer's attention, reading his name tag. "Officer Williams, I need to talk to someone about my family here."

The officer steps forward, acknowledging, "Do you have identification with your current address?"

Before searching his purse, Donte steps back into his

pumps. He presents his ID.

"Thank you, Mr. Beasley, and your relation to the family?"

"I'm the significant other to Paul Levitivitch," Donte answers politely.

The officer questions, "During what period of time have you and Mr. Levitivitch been involved?"

"We've been in a relationship for the past seven years, and as of two months ago, we became engaged."

Donte is questioned disbelievingly. "You're claiming to be the significant other to the owner of this estate?"

"Yes, that's my very contention. I'm engaged to Paul Levitivitch." Donte offers his ID to reveal the brilliant engagement ring. Playing off the ring's leverage, Donte becomes dismissive. "As I presented my identification, you've witnessed the boulder on my hand. I believe you've seen all that's required, officer."

Officer Williams has his mouth agape, dumbfounded. He looks upward to a much taller man wearing a fabulous form-fitting sequined dress with matching four-inch rhinestone pumps.

Rayfee joins the exchange with a verbal thrashing. "Why all the questions? Yes, we're real! HELLO, are you questioning the entire family like this? Is something wrong, officer? Don't be embarrassed. You're standing with your mouth open like you've never seen a beautiful transgender man in a beautiful dress wearing beautiful shoes and bearing a very beautiful engagement ring that a very rich man gave him. Don't you feel very stupid?"

Standing before the two, Officer Williams comes out of his speechless state, directing his comments to Rayfee. "Sir, I'll need proper identification that identifies you. Are you in any way related to the family?"

In no hurry to answer, Rayfee repositions his weave into a hair bun. After retying the knot in his skinny shirt at the belly button, Rayfee reluctantly searches the pockets of his skinny jeans. He comes across his identification after finding it in his bra strap. "Oops! Here it is. I was hoping to find it somewhere." Rayfee presents his ID. "I am he, Raphael Oliver, forty-six eighty-two Garthwaite, Los Angeles, nine zero zero four seven. Satisfied? To answer your question, officer, I'm not related to the family. I'm actually the maid of honor, and I can't wait to show off my beautiful dress for the big day." Rayfee blows a quiet kiss. "Handsome, if you were only a bit taller, I'd ask you to escort me into the ceremony."

Accepting the identification, Officer William's steps away to request a search for outstanding warrants and criminal history reports.

Several minutes later, the dispatcher gives an update via the officer's handheld radio. "Donte Beasley, California driver's license valid, no outstanding warrants, no arrests. Raphael Oliver, California driver's license valid, no outstanding warrants. One arrest eleven six, twenty twelve. Assault, no conviction ... insufficient evidence, disposition five sixteen, twenty thirteen."

"Williams to dispatch, Roger that."

Rayfee rolls his eyes. "No! Ms. Thang didn't just run a make on us."

Donte pulls Rayfee's hand to get his attention. "Rayfee, they're expecting that from us; don't go there."

Rayfee complies reluctantly. "You know what, Donte? I'm giving you your props. You're a much better queen. You have the patience I'll never have, and I refuse to stand here and accept this bullshit." Rayfee directs his words to Officer Williams. "WOO HOO! Since you put us on blast, let me tell you what's really going on. It's no secret, I live a wonderful alternative lifestyle. Does that make me a bad person? Really? Before you answer, you should know you have a coworker who enjoys being the bad guy. There are no repercussions for him, because he wears a badge that seems to empower him to take what he wants. At least that's what he thought when I stopped seeing him. I guess his ego was bruised. He forced himself into my apartment and beat me before he forced his dick in my mouth. The only way to protect myself was to bite into his dick as hard as I could. I crushed all the veins in his dick. To this day he's still working on the police force. How ironic; I'm attacked and then charged with a crime for defending myself. Talk about hypocrisy! The officer's wife and the district attorney were too embarrassed to bring me to trial, so there you have it, the untold exclusive." Rayfee blows another quiet kiss, dismissing Officer Williams. "Smooches!"

Thoroughly embarrassed, Williams radios detectives for further direction. "Williams to detective Destry! Williams to D-one Destry! Williams to D-three Johnston or D-one Destry!"

"Detective-First Grade Destry, go ahead."

"Sir, are you or D-three Johnston interviewing the next of kin?"

"Williams, to the best of my knowledge, detectives interviewed everyone at the estate. Who wasn't included?"

"Sir, you're not going to believe this. I have an African American male at the estate entrance. One Donte Beasley, claiming to be the significant other to the deceased."

There's silence in the communication. Destry whispers under his breath, "What the fuck?" He speaks into his mike. "Roger that, Williams! D-three Johnston's enroute to your location."

Destry looks to Johnston, giving an exaggerated motioning of his hands. "Is this the love connection we've been waiting for or what? He came to claim the name. You've got him, tiger! Fragility! Fragility Johnston, that's your approach. Go handle it."

Detective Johnston makes his way toward the entrance of the Levitivitch estate. He refers to his senior detective mockingly. "Fragility, or you meant to say *delicate*? Sure, Destry, I'll be as gentle and soft as medicated cotton. That'll be the day for you. Because I'm from rural Lincoln, this is a tough assignment? Yeah, right. I got this!"

Approaching the estate entrance, Detective Johnston overhears Officer Williams engaged in conversation. "A detective will be here to interview you shortly, Mr. Beasley."

"Interview me? I don't' need to talk to anyone but Paul. I'm at my man's estate. I'm where I'm supposed to be."

Meanwhile, Rayfee has begun smoking cigarettes to calm his frustration. "HELLO? Would someone tell us what's going on? There are a million ambulances here. Yellow tapes everywhere, and these nosey-ass neighbors are staring at me and my sister like we're out of place. Truth be told, we're not here to meet any of you nosey bitches. We have business with Paul. A queen is before you to handle her business."

Donte's hand is raised to reveal the exotic engagement ring with the announcement, "The queen has arrived to be married."

Rayfee points to Donte and the estate smirking. "Married to Paul, Paul to Donte and Donte to Paul." Rayfee looks into the gathered crowd to address the onlookers. "Since everyone's standing here gawking, then let it be known." Turning to face Officer Williams, Rayfee snaps his fingers to make his point. "Welcome to the wide-opened world. Here's your chance to marvel at what the new dawn brings. You would never have found it in the closet with your designer purses, that's for sure!" Balancing himself on his toes like a ballerina, Rayfee performs a curtsy. "You've guessed it. DIVERSITY!" Rayfee looks to Donte, smirking. "Oh, thanks for inviting me! This was much more rewarding than when I was accepted into the Juilliard School for theater."

Detective Johnston interrupts Rayfee's performance. "Donte Beasley!"

Donte answers politely, "Please tell me what's going on."

"Mr. Beasley, would you step over here?"

Donte steps in the direction mentioned.

In Rayfee's attempt to follow, he's stopped by Officer Williams. "Sir, just the next of kin."

Detective Johnston proceeds. "Mr. Beasley ..."

"It's Donte, detective, thank you."

"To get directly to the point, when was the last time you spoke with Mr. Levitivitch?"

"It's none of your business when I last spoke with him. What's with all the questioning? We're engaged and soon to be married; that answers everything. Since arriving here, my friend and I have been rudely questioned and asked for identification. It's no secret, we're supposed to be here. Detective, we were invited. Didn't you see the show my friend put on? So why am I being questioned? Tell me why you and this crowd are at my fiancés estate."

"Sir, let me finish—"

"It's Donte, detective, thank you."

"Okay, Donte, I spoke too fast. Take it easy. With my deepest regrets, I have to inform you that Paul Levitivitch committed suicide today."

Wide-eyed with shock, Donte is unable to respond.

Detective Johnston proceeds. "Mr. Levitivitch first tied a bed sheet to the living room balcony before tying it around his neck. He then stepped from a chair to his death. He left a note explaining how much he loved both you and his wife. I'm very sorry for your loss." Giving Donte a moment to reflect on the tragic circumstance, Detective Johnston turns to look beyond the estate's cordoned-off entrance.

In nervous silence, Donte takes his princess glove to push aside his wedding veil to catch the flowing tears.

Witnessing the tragic revelation from the other side of the yellow-taped area, Rayfee strains his neck to yell for Donte's attention. "Donte! The neighbors are saying Paul killed himself. Donte! Did you hear what I said?"

Detective Johnston directs his attention from Rayfee to Donte. "According to Mrs. Levitivitch, she and her husband were happily married, and she had no knowledge of any impending separation. Therefore technically you do not qualify as next of kin; however, due to the sensitivity of the circumstance surrounding your relationship, I felt compelled to inform you of the tragedy. That being said, I'll give you a moment to gather yourself. Thereafter, I must ask for your return to the other side of the yellow tape. I'll see to it Officer Williams collects your information, should we need to contact you during the investigation. I can offer bottled water, if you're in need." Johnston directs, "Williams, see to it that Mr. Beasley, after he composes himself—"

"How much time am I allowed, detective?" Donte screams, "He's dead! My Paul's dead! Listen to you! You're allowing me time? Technically I don't qualify because legally Paul was not separated from his wife? You bastard! Should I go to the other side of the yellow tape and cry? How much time am I allowed? Should five minutes be enough? I was with Paul for seven years!" Donte sniffles. "What's wrong, detective? The cat has your tongue? Any more suggestions to make me feel better before I remove myself?"

Feeding off the emotion of anger, Donte struts in his perfectly fitted sequined dress. As he faces the gawking crowd, glimpses of his long shapely legs are seen through its side slits. Standing statuesque at six feet three inches, Donte wears dazzling four-inch rhinestone stiletto heels. Compliments of Prince Albert's hair salon, Donte appears as a diva. His bouffant weave has been styled perfectly. One curl of hair hangs out of place covering an eye, bearing a close resemblance to Diana Rossi when she was with the Esteems. Elegant and dignified, Donte wears white-laced princess gloves. His hands are placed proudly on his hips as he speaks to the on-looking crowd. "Afraid the bruised fruit may ruin it for everyone? Are there any suggestions for this bruised fruit? Go away quietly, maybe, before Paul's name is further embarrassed?" Donte puts a finger to his mouth, "SHH! Quiet!" Facing Detective Johnston and Officer Williams, Donte displays his elegant engagement ring. "So that everyone hears, THIS MEANT SOMETHING! Paul and I had each other, and we didn't need your validations. Should we have stayed hidden away to make you feel comfortable to live the lies you live? Instead we chose to come out and face your world of hypocrisies. Because of your insecurities with us fruits, our happiness is destroyed. Look at you as you stand to look at me! I see in your faces why Paul hesitated to come out. I pressured him. I was selfish to the same degree as you are. What person in their right mind would want to acknowledge or be around us fruits? No worries; stand up, people; you've done your jobs well." With his flow of tears, Donte's foundation makeup smudges into the material of his wedding veil. Donte's voice cracks with emotion. "This delicate flower has lost its chance to bloom. My spring with Paul has been taken away forever." Looking into the astonished crowd, Donte finds comfort in the face of his best friend. His anger quickly dispels to sadness, which forces him to break down to cry. Rayfee breaks past the yellow-taped area to embrace his grief-stricken friend. Overwhelmed with emotion, Donte buries his face into Rayfee's chest. Between muffled sobs, Donte uses his fist to pound into Rayfee's back to grieve.

"Paul! Please forgive me. I could have waited. I would have waited for you. I should have waited for when you were ready."

Over the muffled sobbing, Rayfee buries his face into the top of his best friend's head. "I'm here for you. We're together on this, I told you. I'll never leave you, Donte. I'll never leave."

Donte's sobbing continues. "I'm so sorry, Paul. I'm so sorry. Forgive me."

Detective Destry looks away from the emotional unfolding, deeply touched by Donte's sorrow. He then offers a cigarette to Johnston, who declines. Proceeding to smoke, Detective Destry looks into the vigil of faces during Donte's mourning.

"Paul, I wanted everything so fast. Believe me, I was satisfied with the beautiful ring. Forgive me! Paul, you know I loved you. Everyone knows. I was willing to sacrifice everything for us to be together. Please forgive everything I've said out of spite. You have my attention, Paul. I want to give you my attention. I'm so sorry for being difficult."

Taken aback, Detective Destry exhales cigarette smoke. Under his breath he directs his comments nearby to Detective Johnston. "As I earlier mentioned, fragility. When it comes to death, truth, and betrayal, the common denominator for your disclosure will be fragility. That being said, Johnston, whenever you bring forth any of these revelations, present them as the last thing on earth you would want to do willingly. Fragility! You got that, Johnston? And next time be more compassionate with the other guy's feelings. You crushed the poor guy! For crying out loud, he's lost the love of his life here, Johnston. What were you thinking?"

CHAPTER THIRTY-TWO

*K*abul, Afghanistan. The American embassy's hospital rehabilitation ward. Sergeant Major John Willoughby sits in a wheelchair. He alternately squeezes a pair of therapeutic rubber balls as part of a daily gripping and squeezing exercise. Peering through government-issued bifocals, Sergeant Willoughby intently watches television. The hospital ward is awkwardly silent, as a news correspondent reports live in front of the United States embassy. Consumed with the broadcast, he has yet to notice the physical therapist in his peripheral vision.

"Sergeant? Sergeant Major John Willoughby?" The therapist taps on the arm of the wheelchair to get his attention. "Hello, Sergeant Major?"

Sergeant Willoughby breaks away from the broadcast, removing his earphones. "Earlene! I hadn't noticed you. Whenever a terrorist bombing is reported, I become distant during the details. Forgive me."

Noting her watch, the therapist documents her patient's progression on the clipboard. "Sergeant? You've improved with the rubber grip exercise by thirty seconds. Let's continue with the towel twist regimen." In exchange for the therapeutic rubber balls, Sergeant Willoughby is presented a towel. "Okay, begin! Twist, hold! Twist, hold! Twist, twist, release. Very good, Sergeant Major!" The therapist notes her patient's progress. "Sergeant, try to match your hands with mine." Taking hold of her patient's hands, the therapist inspects and kneads the joints. "Sergeant, what an improvement! Make a ball with your fist. "That's it. Perfect!" The therapist documents the progress. "Your rehabilitation therapy has improved both your range and motion quite well. I understand you've written several letters without any assistance. Your motor skills are coming along faster than expected. Impressive Sergeant Major! Keep to your regimen, and in no time you'll be writing a series of memoirs of your duty."

Sergeant Willoughby winks in acknowledgment, smiling. He produces an envelope from a satchel attached to the wheelchair. "Speaking of which, here's my second letter in nine months to my fiancée, Tiffany. We envisioned a summer wedding with all the bells and whistles. Tiffany and I shopped for all the arrangements together. We even found a travel agent who booked our honeymoon at half cost." Sergeant Willoughby pauses abruptly to look into the hospital's yellow-painted walls. He continues with a gasp, "Hoping for the pure simple things in life, we never looked forward to any interruptions. As we both listened to those voice mail messages, everything we had looked forward to was set aside." Sergeant Willoughby laughs. "Not in a million years would it have worked out like we planned. Not with circumstance. It's the one indiscriminate variable that's always overlooked. Yes, sir, when it comes, wherever circumstance finds you, expect things to change. We had the perfect little church for our pretty picture. Everything was planned. We each had our vows prepared. Everything that should have happened didn't, because of circumstance."

Sergeant Willoughby raises his hands in disgust. "I've been deployed to the other side of the world to fight for other's freedom. We're fighting for people that don't want us in their country. People who kill themselves before they'll allow us to protect them from their government. How's that for motivation? It's self-defeating psychological warfare. How do you fight that twisted mind game?"

Sergeant Willoughby sighs, disillusioned. "On top of all the stress, I'm hit with circumstance yet again. I'm at the wrong place at the right time for a fanatic lying in wait with explosives strapped to him. He climbs onto the officers' transport to blow himself up, right in front of me and Corporal Wilkinson." To control his emotions, Sergeant Willoughby pauses momentarily to look around the room. "So with circumstance, here I sit six months later with tissue and nerve damage. Loss of motor function and lots of rehabilitation. How's that for enthusiasm?" Sergeant Willoughby looks to the television. "Well, here's to circumstance! I won't deny Tiffany our pretty ceremony in that perfect little church, so God help me!" As a tear forms in the corner of his eye, Sergeant Willoughby ends his affirmation with a salute.

The therapist smiles in agreement giving a light clap. "Aw,

chivalry! The most gallant of officers, you are truly impressive."

Sergeant Willoughby presents his letter. "Earlene, would you see this gets to the drop for today's outgoing mail?"

The therapist smiles. "Certainly, Sergeant Major, and with only the best of circumstance."

CHAPTER THIRTY-THREE

Since returning home from her disastrous audition, Tiffany has remained in bed lifeless. Having running thoughts for the past four days, her face and eyes are now heavy from fatigue. Tiffany closes her eyes with a sigh. "What else could go so very wrong?" The telephone rings. It has rung continuously and she has left it unanswered since her return home. As the answering machine goes to record mode, Tiffany anticipates the caller's identity. "It's probably Trisha."

"Tiffany. Why won't you answer the phone? I've been calling for four days now! Yesterday I went to where you work, and I was told you haven't been seen in a week! Call me, please? Hey, kiddo, if I don't hear from you by tomorrow morning, I'm coming by there. You understand? I have good news, and I wanted to tell you face-to-face. You won't believe it! I got a call back from your last audition. Of all people, the director called. Tiff, you were invited back.

They liked your energy. What do you think of that? The director explained that though you didn't read, he was very impressed with the fire in your rehearsal. Hey, kiddo, call me soon. Thanks. I'm worried, Tiff."

Tiffany recognized the caller as Bobby, her agent. Lucky entered the bedroom purring as the answering machine stopped its record mode. As if understanding her frustration, the tabby affectionately rubs its body against Tiffany's. Tiffany picks up the bronze tabby smiling. She kisses it to reason, "You're lucky, Lucky. You can have a bad life and start over again brand new. Is that rhetorical or what? Shame on you. You know just what to do to make me smile, don't you? You're such a rascal!"

The phone rings. Cradling Lucky, Tiffany answers, partly cheered yet somber. "Hello, Trisha! I know you're expecting a grand presentation, but I have to tell you otherwise. After all the energy we had between us in the early morning, my day fizzled into a dud. Trisha, nothing went right for me! The audition was four days ago, and it was a disaster! I'm starting to feel like maybe auditions aren't for me either. Well, Trisha, I got it off my chest. I haven't eaten in four days. I'm so hungry. I can go for one of those double cheeseburgers with the jalapeños and chili cheese fries, and let's not leave out the free refills. Trisha, it's my treat. Here's your chance to watch me eat my way out of the dumps. Are you picking me up or am I meeting you there? By the way, did you ever make it to the park to see Dale? I'm powerwalking in the morning. Just so you have it, I'll make sure to get one of his personal training cards. Trisha, say something!"

There's a moment of silence before a familiar voice questions, "Tiffany, baby, hello? Did you receive my letters?"

Tiffany's eyes blink as she feels the sensation of cautious surprise within her stomach and chest. Before attempting to speak, she pinches herself. Tingling energy flows up and down her spine during the silence. Preparing herself to be awakened from the dream, she hears her heart beat. She exhales slowly to summon words to deliver to her mouth. Tiffany questions, "John?"

EPILOGUE

Seven days after the suicide of her husband, Diana was released from the hospital into the care of her personal physician, Dr. Heisenberg, to attend the wake and memorial service being held at the Levitivitch estate. During Diana's period of incapacitation, her sister Grace made the necessary arrangements for Paul's services. With the stigma of Paul taking his life, Diana decided to forgo a funeral mass. Instead the liturgy and the rite of committal will be performed at graveside. Supporting their chairperson in her time of bereavement, the members of Diana's Friday night ladies' forum were in attendance as a unit of solidarity. Milford played his position with preciseness, being ever so diligent and accommodating at Diana's side. Doing her part, Maria assisted the caterers in both of the estate kitchens to ensure the entrees and placements were adequate. Under her direction, one kitchen was dedicated to the entrées, the other to desserts and cocktails. As the procession of guests entered the estate parlor to view and pay their respects to the departed, Chippy and Scooter were placed in their rooms. When the viewing came to a close, as per Diana's request, her beloved Chippy and Scooter were released to join the memorial with family and friends. Both animals went immediately to Diana and never left her presence. Being on their best behavior, Chippy and Scooter seemed to revel in the attention. Recently bathed and groomed with colored ribbons, they appeared more like honorary trophies than pets. As the memorial moved toward the celebration of Paul's life, the procession was directed toward the grand courtyard, which was covered with an extravagant canopy. Seated at the honorary family's table were Diana, Grace, their parents, and Dr. Heisenberg. Meanwhile, the caterers went about serving appetizers. In the meantime, the partners in Levitivitch, Meyers, and Rothensberg approached the podium to vow their continued allegiance to Diana.

"Ladies and gentlemen, family, and friends. On behalf of L.M.R. investments and trading, we take our hats off with our sincerest condolences to the widow of Paul Levitivitch. It was her husband's seeds that grew and developed into what our firm is today. Paul's vision set the standard and revolutionized how investments and trade formulates not in just our firm, but worldwide. Under Paul's leadership, L.M.R. is currently ranked number twenty of the exclusive top one hundred investment and trade companies in the world. In honor of our senior partner, we're proud to appoint his wife, Diana Levitivitch, as a member of the board of honorary trustees. With Diana bestowed on the board, Paul's voice and direction will continue within the firm. The vision of L.M.R. will stay the course. Here's to you, Diana!"

Amid the hearty applause, Frank and the firm's junior partner Rothensberg approach the family's table to present the honorary plaque. Numb with medication, Diana manages a soft reply. "Why thank you, Frank; how generous!" Diana gives the firm's junior partner a nod of approval. "Mr. Rothensberg, thank you."

"Mrs. Levitivitch? Please call me Theodore; Mr. Rothensberg sounds so distant. With you installed on the board of trustees, we're practically family now."

Mrs. Jaworski purses her lips with a chuckle. "Well, Theodore, personally I've never met you. Allow me to be the first to welcome you into the family. If you can swing another plaque, I'm sure you and I can be kissing cousins."

A bead of sweat forms on Rothensberg's brow. Perplexed with embarrassment, he manages, "Oh, well, I ...?"

Mrs. Jaworski overlooks the firm's partner with a raised glass. "I've finished my cocktail so soon? Milford, honey, alas!"

Milford steps forward with a serving tray of cocktails. "Madam, absolutely, the madam's fifth cocktail within the hour. To accommodate the madam, I shall remain nearby for the requests and beckoning."

"Why Milford, you're being quite frisky today. Instead, why not leave the tray here at our table? There are five of us seated, you know. Should anyone become thirsty, think of it as saving yourself a trip."

Grace shakes her head disapprovingly. "Mother, of all places! We're at Paul's memorial. Please don't stress Diana out with your obnoxiousness. Mother, if I remind you again, I'll lock you in the guest house myself." Grace smooths over her mother's embarrassing demeanor with a handshake. "Frank, Theodore, those were such wonderful words. What a very generous gesture toward my brother-in-law's legacy. On behalf of our family, we thank you both dearly."

Feeling somewhat smarted by Grace's admonishing, Mrs. Jaworski purses her mouth with disappointment. "Fine, now I'm a stranger in my own family? I'll just stay out of the way and drink myself to the grave. Do I have to remind you, Grace? It wasn't you that found him. I could have had a heart attack, you know."

Grace returns the cocktail tray. "Thank you, Milford." She then points her finger toward Mrs. Jaworski warning, "Mother?"

Sitting in silence, Mr. Jaworski becomes antsy after the exchange between his wife and daughter. He looks at the memorial photo of Paul to bat his eyes in bewilderment. His eyes start to roll as he whistles, "Wherrp! That's why I never ate taffy and puddings. The other guy always sizes you up that way. If you ate pudding, taffy, or soft-served ice cream, they figured you for a sweet ass. Believe me, those kinda guys stayed away from me while I was in prison. They could look at me and tell I wasn't nobody's bitch."

Maria is within close proximity to assist Diana if necessary. Maria whispers, "You desterbing the señora, padre. This no good for the señora's nerbs. The señora taking the mee-dee-cayshun for her bery dizzy."

Having not heard a word of Maria's conversation, Mr. Levitivitch clucks his tongue to whistle. "Wherrp! I need to eat. I'll fart my pants and spray this place like machine gun fire. I'll keep the enemy pinned down until chow's served; you got that? I asked for the Idaho potatoes with my soup. What are you, some fucking pansy?"

Maria motions the sign of the cross. "Oh my goodneth, padre. You bery sick. You needing the mee-dee-cay-shun for bery dizzy."

Meanwhile, a member of Diana's ladies forum steps to the podium. "Hello. Everyone, I'm Stephanie. Diana and I have been friends for over thirty-two years. I've known her and Paul before and during the twenty-seven years they were married. I was the maid of honor in their beautiful wedding. I'd like to take a moment to reflect on how I saw Paul here in their wonderful home. As you all know, Paul was very analytical. He would methodically entertain math equations and theories with numbers. I remember when my youngest daughter, Stephia, was taking a calculus class in her senior year in high school. Calculus was very difficult for her, and she needed a tutor to help her through her assignments. One night I mentioned it while at our ladies forum, I'll never forget it. I asked casually, 'Does anyone know where I can find a calculus tutor for Stephia? I'll never be able to answer the problems she's presenting!' Diana looked at me and said, 'Sure, honey; Paul's a math whiz. He's expected back Monday evening. Bring

Stephia by Tuesday after school. Paul will be more than willing to work with her.' Sure enough, Stephia went from a C minus in Calculus I to an A plus in Calculus II. Isn't that amazing? All thanks to Paul and Diana, Stephia's now a chemical engineering major in her fourth year of college. In my gratitude, I wanted to express the specialness my best friend's husband has in my daughter's heart. Because of the emotional attachment toward Paul for his kindness, Stephia couldn't be here. She was unable to handle the revelation of Paul's passing. However, she did say, 'Mom, please convey my deepest regards to Diana.' Thank you, Diana, for your direction to the wonderful man you married, Paul Levitivitch."

A round of applause follows Stephanie's words.

Being especially fond of Stephia and remembering her struggle, Milford's eyes well with tears of emotion. "Well said, Stephanie! Bravo, Stephia!"

Meanwhile, as the main entrée is served at the family's table, the caterers have begun filling the wine glasses. Diana speaks to her sister. "Grace, how wonderful. You're such an angel. You've commemorated the dinner Paul and I enjoyed when he proposed, along with father's favorite, roast duck with cream of spinach and baked potatoes. Grace, darling, thank you."

The next speaker to approach the podium is an extremely beautiful African American woman. Both tall and graceful, she smelled beautiful by just the way she stepped to the podium. Her clothes were draped on her statuesque body in such a way that it was difficult to begin where the beauty of the woman began. She wore stylish Bee Bottom pumps that revealed the symmetry in her beautiful legs. Her chocolate-complexioned skin appeared to be flawless. Her hips and small waistline accented her designer dress as if she had been poured into it. On her dainty wrist she wore an expensive designer watch that highlighted her elegant platinum wedding ring. With her hair full and flowing, it too looked rich and maintained with countless hours of hairdresser appointments. The woman before them was flawless, and she had the courtyard's attention. Members of Diana's ladies forum looked on speechless. Everyone watched and listened while dabbling at their plate of entrées.

Diana's voice is heard giving praise. "Wow, she's a knockout! She has to be the most beautiful catering director I've ever seen. She has such richness about her. Wherever did you find her, Grace?"

Milford admits, "The lady's astonishing!"

The beautiful woman begins her presentation. "Hello, everyone. While I am standing in your midst and witnessing the expressions of appreciation for this departed man, it is truly amazing to hear the sincerest of sentiments expressed and seen in the faces of those seated. We've come collectively to mourn the loss of a husband, a family member, and a friend. He leaves behind loved ones who no longer have their physical connection to such a complete human being. For those that have spoken and shared their reflective memories, you were on point. The many lives that were touched by this wonderful man attest to his innate beauty. Who better can give praise than those who recognize what is truly beautiful? Forgoing my introduction, allow me to share something special for the special person who shared his life openhandedly with everyone in his presence. It's called 'Something Beautiful.'"

Diana says to Grace, "She's good. You didn't mention you hired a motivational speaker. She's so well versed; thank you, Grace."

The presentation continues.

"For the beauty in our lives,
We all hold someone or something special as aspirations
For our jubilations.
What is one to do when what is beautiful is not appreciated?
Is not the virtue of beauty worthy of declaration and celebration?
Beauty in itself,
Should be forever commemorated and indoctrinated.
What is one to say when something beautiful is no longer
Or is misplaced?
Once there was beauty in my life, but I shunned away from its embrace.
Now my life is in disarray, and I'm full of emptiness and space.
Of all, why me,
To have been dealt a hand so cruel?
Everything was perfect and yet
What was beautiful was taken so soon.
I now appreciate what is beautiful.
What must I do to return beautiful to me?
Please allow me to regain what was beautiful,
So what was beautiful and I can start anew.

I'm lost because my beautiful has been taken away.

Without beautiful what am I to do?

My life was special when you and I were together, beautiful.

Every day was brand new.

You were the dawn after the rain.

You were my season of good weather.

Yet, beautiful, you've gone away,

And because you're beautiful, I wanted you forever.

In an afterthought, your beauty's missed,

But being blind, I could never see. The specialness in your beauty,

Is what made the world a better place for me."

Diana bats her eyes in confusion. As her complexion becomes ashen, the facial nerves in her face begin to twitch. The presentation continues. "Hello, everyone, my name is Donte, and I was born a man. For the past seven years, the specialness in Paul was the beauty in my life. As of two months ago, we were engaged to be married. Indeed, it would have been truly beautiful to spend the rest of my life with such a wonderful man."

A thunderous applause comes from a small contingent of guests seated in the outer tables of the courtyard. "That's right, Donte. You deserve to be heard too, girl. You represented you and your man with class. You go! You did the damn thing!" Rayfee is seen standing in the middle of the aisle motioning his handbag around his head like a flag. Wearing Donte's size-thirteen rhinestone pumps, he stops the celebration momentarily to make sure his formfitting dress hasn't torn. Unabashed in his excitement, he looks to the crowd of gawkers. "Hey, you see how I'm throwing this ass? I had to check to make sure the seams are still stitched. Did you see my girl up there? Was she representing or what?" Rayfee speaks back to the podium. "Don't let anybody take anything from you, Donte. You did the damn thing. Woo!"

Ignacio and Marcus are in attendance holding hands. The couple gives Donte its full support. "Absolutely yes! Paul would have wanted us here for this day, so tastefully done. His departure was not in vain. Donte, you've been heard. Bravo!"

Meanwhile Donte leaves the podium. As graceful as ever, he removes his wig to walk back to his support group. Expressions of devastation are plastered on the faces of the audience.

Dr. Heisenberg attends to Diana after she faints.

Mr. Jaworski gets up to whistle. Wherrp! "Where in the hell is my popcorn for the show? It's over already!"

Mrs. Jaworski grabs a bottle of wine from one of the table attendants. "I don't know what's in those cocktails I've been drinking. My vision's leaving me. I thought for sure that was a beautiful woman talking highly of Paul. It's been a man the whole time, and they were involved in a relationship for seven years. No wonder Paul kept us in Minnesota!"

Maria closes her eyes, motioning the sign of the cross. "Oh, my goodneth, Meester Dawnee? You more bery bew-tee-ful than all the ladies."

Milford looks at Grace, who has since buried her face in the family's table. She sighs with a confession, "She told me she was the catering director."

Milford offers consolation. "Madam Grace, I should say after all the planning, no one expected the unexpected. To say the least, truth has revealed tragedy in more ways than one. I take it we'll go as planned with Master Paul's funeral? Considering what's ensued, I should hope there are no more surprises."

Meanwhile Mysal is in attendance in the audience. He's managed to find a dress size that's relatively fashionable. To accommodate the width of his enormous feet, Mysal wears flats with wrapping gladiator laces. As he jumps up in down in celebration, the laces strain at his huge calf muscles. Contrary to his usual appearance, today Mysal has no visible facial stubble. Compliments of Prince Albert's beauty and hair salon, Mysal's hair has been styled in Shirley Temple curls in brunette. He wears eyeliner and mascara, and Mysal's foundation makeup has taken off most of the edge. The makeover has bolstered his confidence so that he appears to be an ugly woman. Mysal celebrates Donte. "What a way to level the playing field! You've made it all the more exciting to be a woman. Oh for this one, Donte, I can't hate you anymore. How graceful you are! Thank you for the Prince Albert hookup; I believe it's paying off. WOO!"

Donte has worked his way back to within the group's fold. "Okay, everyone it's done. I've said my peace for Paul. Let's get back to the limousine before we're arrested for inciting a riot."

Rayfee joins in, "I'm hungry. What in the hell were they thinking about with that oily ass duck? Roasted or not, it's still nasty. Lead the way, Donte; we all follow the queen!"

As the contingent makes its way leaving the estate court-yard, Mysal remains in place. Rayfee notices the straggler. "Mysal? Mysal, come on. We brought you here for the trouble, not for a social hour. Donte's accomplished everything we've came here to do; we're leaving."

Mysal walks toward Rayfee, posturing with his purse. He admits in a hushed tone, "Hey, not to piss on anyone's parade, but Donte had his day in the sun with Mr. Beautiful, and I never knocked him for his prize. That being said, I see my window of opportunity here."

"What opportunity, Mysal? Are you hungry again? That nice restaurant the limo driver mentioned, that's where we're going to celebrate."

"No, Rayfee, see the super hunk over there with the friar's haircut?"

Rayfee looks in the direction where a man waves shyly. "Who, is that Rothensberg?"

Mysal licks his lips seductively. "He's been watching me all afternoon. Short stack's offering delicious man cream. Rayfee, he needs to have my number. I'm staying!"

Tiffany returned to North Hollywood studios to audition for the very role she fled from. Much to the chagrin of casting assistant Vladimir, Tiffany nailed the role on the first take. "How can that be? Just two weeks earlier, she was in a track meet for the exit, yet on every take, she's the cat's meow."

The director went about with the twirling of his cigar. "She's everything the role called for, Vladimir, and everything you failed to see. That's why I sit where I sit and you go where I point. My job is to brighten the stars as they appear. This kid has just the right luster to shine brighter. Are you understanding me, Vladimir?"

"Yes, sir."

"Good! Get used to cueing her takes."

As Tiffany's agent promised, her big break came with the world premiere of *The Lady and the Gentlemen*. With the director's direction, Tiffany became an A-list actress. "Did I call it, Tiff? Believe me, as your agent they'll stand in line to offer roles nonstop. It's been nine months since the world discovered you, and they're still coming to the theaters. I'm telling you, kid, our rainbow has arrived. We'll hire a staff of interns, just so your publicist has a break."

As Tiffany stayed busy with scripts and celebrity appearances, John returned from Afghanistan nine months from the date of his last letter. Upon his return, he convalesced in a military rehabilitation program. Twelve months later, he received an honorable discharge with the medal of valor for saving the life of Corporal Wilkinson. On a picturesque day in Los Angeles, Tiffany and Lucky await John's arrival at L.A.X. Their wedding plans resumed the moment John walked off the airplane. "John? Oh, baby, it's so good to see you! Oh my god, look at you!"

"Ump! Tiff, careful; my arm isn't as strong as it was, but your Johnny's made it back in one piece, and have I been hearing things. Tiff, you're a movie star? Look at you, Lil' Ms. Tease a

Lot. You stop running from scripts when? Tiff, I'm impressed."

"John, it's just one movie."

"One movie? Tiff, you're on the cover of a magazine. They're referring to you as the next A-list sensation. I've read two articles about you on the plane. Is it not enough the guys on base have my fiancée's pictures taped in their lockers?"

"Stop it, John."

"Really, Tiff, you wouldn't believe it. The reason the army gave me an honorable discharge was to stop the NCOs from sneaking off base to watch your movie."

Tiffany punches her fiancé in the chest. "Fun-nee!"

"I'm telling you, Tiff, the whole base is deserted. When they round those guys up, there won't be any room left in the stockade. They'll sure be glad when that movie goes to Blu-ray."

"John, stop being silly." Continuing from the arrival gate, Tiffany positions John's arm around her shoulders. "I'm so silly in love with you, John, and I didn't know what to expect while you were away. I'm so glad you're home." "Tiff, I'm back and we're silly for each other. Isn't that the way it should be?"

"I know. Give me a kiss, handsome."

"Tiffany, no way! Not in public. Kissing you is too much work. You'll just faint on me. Besides, I can't pick my lil' pumpkin up and hold her in the air like before. My back's bothering me, and I don't have the strength in my hands like I used to."

Tiffany elbows him in the ribs. "What are you saying?"

"See, there you go, Tiff; I'm speaking of the nerve damage. Remember I've been medically discharged."

"You better not mean I am heavy, John."

"No way, baby, not you! Johnny's glad to be in your arms again, and you're looking so good to me."

Tiffany grabs his ass. "It's still Johnny, huh? The last time I grabbed Johnny's ass was because he was being bad. Johnny wanted to be a rapper. You're washing the dishes when we get home, bad boy. You got out of it when I returned you to the airport, remember? I haven't forgotten."

"Sure. Tiff, after I wash the dishes, I'll get a pedicure to keep my hands nice and pretty for you." John chuckles. How's Lucky doing?"

"He's in the limousine, John, and he can't wait to see you."

"Limousine?"

"Yes, John, I didn't have anyone to spoil while you were away. Lucky and I go everywhere in the limousine. I even dedicated a shelf for his finicky mignon. Wait until you see the kitchen pantry."

"Tiff, we should be taking the elevator down to Baggage Claim. You're leading us to the escalator."

"John, I know where I'm taking you. I'll have the limo driver retrieve the luggage. Relax."

John pinches Tiffany's ear playfully. "How would I ever have known? I'm still trying to find my bearings. My fiancée picks me up from the airport in a limousine! The driver's retrieving my luggage, and Lucky has his own shelf of finicky mignon in the pantry? Geez, Tiff, the way you have my head spinning, I have to close my eyes to keep from being dizzy. Did you leave any room in the pantry for my bottled water?"

Tiffany turns to embrace John. "Quit being silly. What was

the last thing we did after seeing Mr. McKinney?"

John thinks for a moment. "Tiff, that's not a fair question. You're asking about an afternoon that was over nineteen months ago."

Tiffany motions her head like a rooster. "John?"

"I dunno, Tiff…"

She struts and exaggerates more head movement. "John?"

"Tiff, I dunno. We made a payment toward our wedding rings was one of the things I remember."

Tiffany puts her thumbs inside her belt buckle to mimic comically, "I say, I say, I say now, boy!"

"Was that supposed to be Guntther, Tiff?"

"That's right, and what was the last thing we did when we went down an escalator?" Tiffany gazes into his eyes.

John looks into hers. "We did this!" The couple entwines to kiss.

The flashing of cameras interrupt the moment. "Ms. Adams!"

"Ms. Adams!"

"For *The Lady and the Gentlemen* premier, you were on the red carpet alone. Is this the gentlemen that should have been with you? Have you anything to say to your fans, Ms. Adams?"

John covers Tiffany protectively. "Who in the hell are they?"

Tiffany's voice comes from against John's chest. "I didn't get a chance to tell you about the paparazzi, honey." She kisses John, addressing the cameras. "Yes, it is he, the very gentlemen. He was in Afghanistan protecting the world!"

Camera flashes follow Tiffany and John as they continue

toward the limousine.

John cracks playfully, "So now we'll need security whenever we're in public. Sure thing, Tiff. With that overhead, we'll go through my army pension in no time. Did I tell you, I planned to put just a little aside for a wheelchair? I had one of those motorized deals in mind. I figured I wouldn't have to use my hands so much."

Tiffany grabs John's ass. "Fun-nee! Do you remember our last night in the shower, Sergeant Willoughby?" Tiffany uses both hands to grab his crotch and ass simultaneously. "Gotcha!"

"Tiffany, they're following us taking pictures!"

"Who cares, John? I'm grabbing what belongs to me. In an hour or so the whole world will read about us being in the airport anyway. We should give them something to talk about."

The flashing of cameras continues.

Tiffany slaps John's ass. "Get used to it, handsome! Oh, you haven't given me a chance to tell you, we live in Calabasas now. Do you remember my girlfriend Trisha? I've asked her to be my maid of honor. She's coming over tomorrow night to introduce Dale, her fiancé. He was the personal trainer I used with my power walk regimen. I gave Trisha one of Dale's business cards, and they hooked up. Can you believe it?"

"I somewhat remember you mentioning Trisha and Dale in one of our phone conversations. When did you move to Calabasas, Tiff? I don't recall any of that."

"Honey, I'll explain everything in the limousine. Let me finish telling you about my best friend."

A montage plays out with Trisha and her personal trainer.

"Okay, Trisha, to familiarize you with the deep squat bends, keep in mind your back remains straight. I'll be positioned to your rear with my hands at your waist to spot you. Remember to exhale as you thrust upward, inhale as you bend your knees going into the squat position. Maintain your balance. Keep your arms positioned forward as you bend and return into the standing position. Okay, on the count of three. One, two, three, squat!" Trisha collapsed purposely into Dale's lap. "Ooh? Mr. chocolatey sprinkles? Oops, I meant Dale? With you positioned behind me like that, my mind went somewhere else. I don't mean to seem like I'm enjoying myself. Believe me, I'm not that kind of girl at all. Just give me a moment, Dale. I'm not moving around purposely on your crotch, I'm really trying to get the feeling back into my legs. Oh, that's it. That's it, oh yes, I can feel something growing against me. Dale? Are you all right? I don't want you to get the wrong idea about me. Oh, it's throbbing! Maybe I should move around on it until the feeling comes back to my legs. We both need to be comfortable with this moment, and I don't mean to cut your circulation off with all this ham. Oh, my legs are weak. That's it, oh yes. It's that raining outside good heat! Oh, now I really have to move around on it; I have to get all these thoughts out of my head. Don't take me for being lonely, Dale, and I'm not a girl that keeps much company. I'm busy working all the time, and I really don't get the opportunity to sit down to enjoy myself like I want to." The montage ends.

Tiffany continues, "I've never seen Trisha so dedicated. I bet she's lost at least fifty pounds. I'm so proud of her, and since she's my best friend, I've asked her to be my maid of honor. John, we'll have so much fun together. Oh, and I haven't forgotten our Claude and Martha. They'll be there too."

"Of course, Tiff. We had to invite Claude and his wife. What about the guy with the clothing store? I promised him I'd return after our big day to buy a suit. Is he still there?"

"I don't know, John; I never went back."

"Tiff, you haven't mentioned Marla. With all the ice cream and candy she's given us, if she's not invited, another war would be upon us for sure."

"Relax, John. She's one of the caterers. She's bringing the chocolate fountain."

"Ooh wee! I can't wait."

"M-m-m-hmm. John, remember your chicken alfredo and shrimp scampi jokes?"

"I do; it was something about you boiling the plastic bags. What about it, Tiff?"

"Well, Johnny, I've hired a cook. You now have your own officer's dining room at home. So feel free to mosey on around back to the mess hall to ask for any fixing's you'd like."

"Really, Tiff? O.D.R. at home? Wow! Did you get a new DVR to record our shows?"

"Yes, I did, John, and you can watch anything imaginable in our theater room."

"Really? Wow, is your new movie in the library for tonight?"

CPSIA information can be obtained
at www.ICGtesting.com
Printed in the USA
BVOW11s1411200516
448898BV00026B/514/P